MW00461357

IMPERIAL DREAMS
HARSH REALITIES

Tsarist Russian Foreign Policy, 1815–1917

IMPERIAL DREAMS
HARSH REALITIES

Tsarist Russian Foreign Policy, 1815–1917

David MacKenzie
University of North Carolina
at Greensboro

Harcourt Brace College Publishers

Fort Worth   Philadelphia   San Diego   New York   Orlando   Austin
San Antonio   Toronto   Montreal   London   Sydney   Tokyo

Editor-in-chief   Ted Buchholz
Acquisitions editor   Drake Bush
Developmental editor   Kristie Kelly
Project editor   Steve Norder
Production manager   J. Montgomery Shaw
Art directors   Pat Bracken/Serena Manning
Photo editor   Lili Weiner
Cover designer   Sok James Hwang
Maps   Academy ArtWorks

Illustration credits: p. 13, Culver Pictures; p. 17, TASS/Sovfoto; p. 39, The Bettmann Archive; p. 43, Itar-TASS/Sovfoto; p. 55, The Bettmann Archive; p. 59, Culver Pictures; p. 61, Ria-Novosti/Sovfoto; p. 84, Culver Pictures; p. 111, The Bettmann Archive; p. 113, The Bettmann Archive; p. 115, Culver Pictures; p. 129, Library of Congress; p. 159, TASS/Sovfoto; p. 163, UPI/Bettmann; p. 178, The Bettmann Archive

Library of Congress Catalog Card Number: 93-77106

Copyright © 1994 by Harcourt Brace Jovanovich, Inc.
All rights reserved. No part of this publication may be reproduced or transmitted in any form or by any means, electronic or mechanical, including photocopy, recording, or any information storage and retrieval system, without permission in writing from the publisher.
Requests for permission to make copies of any part of the work should be mailed to: Permissions Department, Harcourt Brace & Company, 8th Floor, Orlando, Florida 32887

Address for Editorial Correspondence: Harcourt Brace College Publishers, 301 Commerce Street, Suite 3700, Fort Worth, TX 76102.

Address for Orders: Harcourt Brace & Company, 6277 Sea Harbor Drive, Orlando, FL 32887. 1-800-782-4479, or 1-800-433-0001 (in Florida).

ISBN: 0-15-500934-6

Printed in the United States of America

3 4 5 6 7 8 9 0 1 2   039   9 8 7 6 5 4 3 2 1

Dedication

To my long suffering UNC-Greensboro students

ACKNOWLEDGMENTS

I wish to thank my colleague at UNC-Greensboro, Dr. Ann P. Saab, who read the entire manuscript and provided suggestions for its improvement. My warmest thanks go to Dr. Alfred J. Rieber, the designated reader for this manuscript, who supplied very useful recommendations for revisions. Finally, I remain in the debt of my graduate assistant, Ms. Sarah C. Dierlam, who did much of the work on the index for this book.

PREFACE

This volume first took shape during the summer of 1991 while the author sought appropriate materials for an advanced university course on Russian and Soviet foreign policy. Finding no suitable up-to-date survey of imperial Russian foreign policy and having taught courses on tsarist and Soviet policy for many years, I resolved to prepare a volume surveying the late tsarist period. After a respected colleague, Dr. Ann Saab of the University of North Carolina at Greensboro, critiqued the initial draft, I decided to compose an expanded and improved version for publication.

My purpose is to provide a general treatment of the formation and expansion of the Russian Empire down to 1815 and a more detailed survey of the final century of imperial Russian foreign policy. During the century following the Congress of Vienna (1814–1815), the St. Petersburg government sought to protect the territorial gains and dominance in eastern Europe which that congress had confirmed for Russia. In the following one hundred years Russian statesmen and military leaders had repeated grandiose dreams of imperial glory that proved eventually beyond Russia's military and financial strength to realize. Instead, Russian tsars and their diplomats repeatedly encountered the harsh realities of international politics and finance. These imperial dreams and the Russian Empire itself finally dissolved in the conflagrations of World War I and the revolutions of 1917.

David MacKenzie

Greensboro, N.C. 1993

CONTENTS

CHAPTER 1   Building an Empire   1

CHAPTER 2   Muscovite and Russian Diplomacy to 1815   27

CHAPTER 3   Era of Satiation and the Crimean War, 1815–1856   38

CHAPTER 4   Russia and Europe in an Age of Reform, 1855–1881   54

CHAPTER 5   Russia and the Balkans, 1855–1881   68

CHAPTER 6   Conquest of the Caucasus and Turkestan, 1855–1881   88

CHAPTER 7   Russia in Asia and America to 1881   100

CHAPTER 8   The Reactionary Empire Faces Europe, 1881–1904   110

CHAPTER 9   Russia in the Near and Middle East, 1881–1904   124

CHAPTER 10   Expansion in the Far East, 1881–1904   135

CHAPTER 11   The Russo-Japanese War, Revolution, and Reform   147

CHAPTER 12   Russia and the Road to World War I, 1905–1914   155

CHAPTER 13   Russia in World War I, 1914–1917   172

ILLUSTRATIONS

Peter I, "the Great," rules 1682–1725   13

Catherine II, "the Great," ruled 1762–1796   17

Alexander I, ruled 1801–1825   39

Nicholas I, "the Iron Tsar," ruled 1825–1855   43

Alexander II, "the Tsar-Liberator," ruled 1855–1881   55

A.M. Gorchakov, foreign minister, 1856–1882   59

Count N.P. Ignatiev, ambassador to Turkey, 1864–1877   61

The Congress of Berlin, June–July 1878   84

Alexander III and family; he ruled 1881–1894   111

Count S. Iu. Witte, minister of finance, 1892–1903; premier, 1905–1906   113

N.K. Giers, foreign minister, 1882–1895   115

M.G. Cherniaev, governor-general of Turkestan, 1882–1884   129

A.P. Izvolskii, foreign minister, 1906–1910; ambassador to France, 1910–1917   159

S.D. Sazonov, foreign minister, 1910–1916   163

Nicholas II, his wife Alexandra, and their children; he ruled 1894–1917   178

MAPS

1-1	Rise of Moscow to 1533	6
1-2	Expansion of Russia, 1462–1815	8
1-3	Russia's eastward expansion, 1598–1762	10
1-4	Russian expansion in Europe, 1618–1689	11
1-5	Russian expansion under Peter the Great, 1695–1725	15
1-6	Partitions of Poland, 1772–1795	20
1-7	Napoleonic Wars and Russia, 1805–1814	23
3-1	The Crimean War, 1853–1856	51
5-1	Russia and the Balkans, 1876–1885	74
5-2	Growth of Serbia, 1856–1913	77
6-1	Central Asia: "Closing the Lines," 1864	94
7-1	Russia in the Far East to 1914	103
12-1	Anglo-Russian agreement on Persia of 1907	160
12-2	Russia and the Balkans, 1912–1914	165
13-1	War aims of the Entente, 1914–1917	174

BUILDING AN EMPIRE

After the demise of the Soviet Union in December 1991, historical
curiosity might lead us to ask how its predecessor, the tsarist Russian
Empire, was built, and on what principles. How and why did the Russians,
expanding in all directions from the Moscow region, gain control over the
many nationalities that eventually would comprise a vast Eurasian empire?
Did their subjugation ultimately produce irresistible centrifugal pressures
that in 1917 caused the Russian Empire's sudden collapse? Which external
policies did the tsarist empire adopt during its lifetime and why? Did tsarist
foreign policy focus primarily on Europe, or were the Balkans and Asia at
times its chief areas of concern? What were the overall objectives of Russian
imperial foreign policy after the Congress of Vienna in 1815? Were they
defensive or expansionist?

The foreign policy of any country reflects its geographical position, size,
climate, historical experience, and, perhaps somewhat less, the regime in
power and the ideology of its rulers. This volume will survey the world
role and policies of tsarist Russia from the time it attained its full extent
in Europe—1815—until its demise in 1917. Domestic Russian developments
will be summarized because no country's foreign policy is determined in
a vacuum but reflects necessarily trends and events at home.

It would be unwise to begin this story of tsarist foreign policy abruptly
in 1815. To understand nineteenth-century Russian foreign policy one needs
some grasp of Russia's expansion and development as a power during earlier
centuries and its changing relationships with the external world. Unlike the
United States of America with only slightly over two centuries of independent existence, often largely isolated and insulated from European events,
Russia—and its predecessor, Rus*—has existed as an organized entity for
more than eleven hundred years. Over most of that great span Russia was
involved directly in the wars and crises of the Eurasian land mass. In its
early history, first Rus, then Russia, suffered repeated invasions from east

---

*Until about 1300 Rus consisted of the territory that would later become Western Russia
and Ukraine. After 1300 the process of unification began that would lead to the creation
of the Russian state under the aegis of Moscow.

and west and was exposed to a wide variety of external political and cultural influences, including Varangian (or Viking), Byzantine, Asiatic (Mongol), and European. These influences had an important though disputed impact on the country's development, institutions, and outlook.

Ancient or prehistoric Rus prior to the mid-ninth century remains rather obscure and unknown. However, since the 1920s Soviet archeological excavations have unearthed many artifacts that give us some appreciation of that turbulent era of conflict between emerging Slav agrarian tribes and nomadic invaders from the Eurasian steppes. Gradually, from the third to ninth centuries A.D. Slavic and other agricultural peoples in the area north of the Black Sea established tribal federations and advanced towards statehood. Boris Rybakov, a leading Soviet scholar, asserted that one of these tribal leagues in the Dnieper River valley—the Rus—became the nucleus for unifying the eastern Slavs into what became Kievan Rus.

KIEVAN RUS, C. 860–1240

Controversy persists between Russian, émigré, and Western scholars over the formation and initial location of the first Rus state. According to the Norman theory first propounded in the eighteenth century by German and Scandinavian scholars, Kievan Rus was founded by Varangians (Vikings) from Scandinavia responding to appeals from primitive warring Slavic tribes in the Novgorod region to come and rule over them. Rejecting that theory, Soviet scholars argued instead that Kievan Rus was a native Slav product of agricultural tribes inhabiting the region of Kiev. In any case, the result was the emergence in the late ninth century of a federation of ten to fifteen principalities linked by a common dynasty often traced to the semi-mythical Viking prince Riurik and centering first in Novgorod, then in Kiev. In many of these states power was shared among a prince, a council of nobles (initially military retainers of the prince), and a town assembly. Kievan Rus was marked by diversity, limited princely power, and relative prosperity based largely on foreign trade with the Byzantine Empire. The Varangian invaders were soon absorbed by the Slavic majority, most of whom engaged in agriculture as free or semi-free peasants.

Kievan Rus played a significant role in medieval international relations, essentially as an offshoot of Byzantine civilization. Until the twelfth century its chief commercial dealings were with the Byzantine Empire, from which the Rus received the Cyrillic alphabet, the Greek Orthodox faith, the art of iconography, law, and many other basic institutions. Some Western and Byzantine scholars, therefore, regard Kievan Rus as a Byzantine satellite. Vehemently denying this, patriotic Soviet scholars claimed equality for Kievan Rus, arguing that its institutions developed organically from its Slav nucleus. A series of Varangian–Rus attacks on Constantinople during the tenth century forced Byzantium to accord to Kievan Rus regular and equal commercial relations. Dynastic intermarriages between Byzantium and Kievan Rus were frequent. The conversion of Prince Vladimir I of Kiev to Greek orthodoxy and his marriage to the sister of the Byzantine emperor in the late tenth century reinforced these powerful links.

Nomadic pressure from the east and south periodically imperilled Kievan Rus, which by the late tenth century extended from the Baltic to the Black Sea and eastward to the Volga River. The greatest threat came from the pagan Polovtsy (Polovtsians) who controlled the south Russian steppes until the Mongol invasion. By fostering interprincely cooperation to repel their incursions the Polovtsy may have delayed Kievan Rus's disintegration. Kievan Rus also developed significant ties with the Latin West, which then was fragmenting into feudal kingdoms following the disintegration of Charlemagne's empire. The eclipse of Byzantium, confirmed by the Latin crusaders' sack of Constantinople (1204), and attacks by the Polovtsy shifted much Rus commerce westward into European markets. Kievan Rus also had important dealings with the southern Slavs (Serbs, Bulgars) of the Balkans with whom they shared a common Orthodox faith and similar Slavic languages. Externally, therefore, Kievan Rus at first dealt primarily with Byzantium, but its contacts and links with the Latin West and the Balkans grew increasingly important prior to the Mongol invasion.

Free and productive Kievan civilization succumbed in 1237–1242 to Mongol invaders from Asia for internal and external reasons. The political disunity of Kievan Rus after 1132 resembled that of the Greek city-states before their conquest by Rome. Fratricidal wars and interprincely disputes revealed the failure of Rus to create effective central institutions. Kiev's leadership had stemmed partly from its location on the great water route "from the Varangians to the Greeks" (from the Baltic to the Black seas). Never secure from the steppe nomads, Kievan Rus lacked stable frontiers on the east. Rus–Polovtsian wars exhausted both sides and facilitated Mongol victory. Neither Kievan Rus nor other settled peoples could withstand the tremendous Mongol drive of the early thirteenth century.

THE MONGOL ERA AND THE RISE OF MOSCOW, 1240–1462

The Mongol invasion of 1237–1242 shattered Kievan Rus civilization and left it fragmented. Before attacking Rus, the Mongols had conquered China and much of central Asia, causing great destruction and killing all who opposed them. The invasion of 1237 was led by Batu (a grandson of the great Chingis-khan, founder of the Mongol Empire), who overcame swiftly the divided princes of Rus and destroyed many leading towns. Following the conquest of most of Kievan Rus, Batu set up the Khanate of Kipchak, popularly known as the Golden Horde, as the semi-independent western portion of the vast Eurasian Mongol Empire. From its capital, Sarai, a city of tents on the lower Volga River, the Mongols ruled over the divided principalities of Rus and collected tribute and army recruits. In order to rule their territories, Rus princes had to proceed to Sarai, or to Karakorum, the imperial capital in Mongolia, bow down to the khan, and receive from him a patent of authority *(iarlyk)*. Mongol administrative control in most Rus lands lasted at least a century, and in the northeast far longer. However, as early as 1280 the Golden Horde began to fragment into a number of rival khanates; this enabled the Russians eventually to throw off its control.

The effects of Mongol rule upon Rus, and Asiatic influences generally, are still debated by scholars, although they agree that the invasion of 1240 was terribly destructive. Soviet scholars generally attributed later Russian backwardness to the Mongol conquest whereas émigré historians of the Eurasian school viewed Russia's unification under Moscow and subsequent imperial expansion as the direct outgrowth of Mongol rule. The many-sided, far-reaching Mongol influence on Rus, affirms George Vernadsky, a Russian émigré historian, can be measured by contrasting the institutions and values of Kievan Rus with those of Muscovy. In east Rus, the region most exposed to Mongol influences, monarchical power became highly developed. Under Mongol overlordship political life in Rus was deformed and its traditional balance upset. Furthermore, claims Vernadsky, "it was on the basis of Mongol patterns that the grand ducal system of taxation and army organization was developed" in Moscovy.[1] Mongol rule helped subordinate *boyars* (noblemen) to the ruler and prepared the way for enserfment of the peasantry; it laid the bases for a new service-bound society in Muscovy.

While the Golden Horde ruled Rus from Sarai, the obscure principality of Moscow rose to power and prominence. During the late fourteenth century Moscow emerged as the successor to the grand principality of Vladimir, which had been predominant in the northeast. Winning a difficult competition with Tver, another new principality, Moscow became the focus of religious, political, and economic life in northeastern Rus. The unexpected victory of Moscow's Prince Dmitrii "Donskoi" (of the Don) over Khan Mamai's Mongol army in 1380 shattered the myth of Tatar invincibility and confirmed Moscow's leadership among Russian principalities. Factors in Moscow's rise include its central location on a network of rivers, its astute and long-lived princes, and its special relationship and subservience to the Golden Horde. From a central core Moscow expanded in all directions much as did the French monarchy from the region around Paris. The great early twentieth-century Russian historian V. O. Kliuchevskii argued that during the fourteenth century the northern Russian population came to regard the grand prince of Moscow as a model ruler, the creator of order and civil peace, and their leader in the struggle against external enemies. However, Moscow's rise—an ebb and flow process—was very difficult, bloody, and interrupted by serious setbacks.

Meanwhile the formerly vast and relatively unified Kievan Rus had fragmented into several rapidly differentiating segments that were not destined to be reunited until the late eighteenth century. In the southwest, Galicia and Volhynia escaped Mongol rule initially but during the fourteenth century were incorporated into Poland and Lithuania. In western Rus the two leading states were Novgorod and Lithuania. Novgorod, escaping direct Mongol control, became one of medieval Europe's largest city-states and developed an extensive empire to the north and east. As Russia's gateway to the west, Novgorod developed a flourishing trade with the Baltic German

---

[1]George Vernadsky, *The Mongols and Russia* (New Haven, CT, 1953), p. 358.

cities of the Hanseatic League and continued the Kievan traditions of freedom and diversity. Meanwhile Lithuania became a major force in western Rus as a federation of princes and nobles controlling all of Belorussia (White Russia), and under Vitovt (ruled 1392–1430) threatened Moscow itself.

The reign of Vasili II, grand prince of Moscow (1425–1462), proved crucial for the destiny of Muscovy. Civil wars and struggles for the throne were followed by internal consolidation and gradual extension of Moscow's influence over neighboring states. In 1452 Moscow ceased paying regular tribute to the disintegrating Golden Horde. The following year Constantinople fell to the invading Turks, leaving the Russian Orthodox Church with its chief seat in Moscow largely independent. A successful campaign against Novgorod in 1456 prepared the way for its subsequent incorporation into Muscovy.

THE MUSCOVITE ERA, 1462–1700

Vasili's son and successor, Ivan III, "the Great" (ruled 1462–1505) and his successor, Vasili III (ruled 1505–1533) achieved the unification of Great Russia* around Moscow. Like his west European contemporaries Henry VII of England and Louis XI of France, Ivan III subordinated other princes to his rule and expanded the power of the crown. The lands of Novgorod, Tver, and Viatka were all added to the expanding Muscovite domains by this so-called "gatherer of the Russian lands." Preferring diplomacy and intrigue to war, this awe-inspiring Machiavellian grand prince achieved ambitious goals with a minimum of bloodshed. In 1472 Ivan married Zoe Paleologus, niece of the last Byzantine emperor. Brought up as a Catholic, she converted to Orthodoxy and took the name Sofia. As Ivan sought full independence as ruler of a greatly enlarged Muscovy, Moscow became the heir of Byzantine traditions. In 1480 the last attempt of the Mongols to reassert their former authority was defeated. Great Russia's unification and independence enabled Ivan III to inaugurate regular diplomatic relations with a variety of foreign powers, including the Holy Roman Empire, Poland, and Sweden. In 1486 when the envoy of the Holy Roman Empire hinted that the German emperor might deign to grant Ivan a royal title, Ivan rejected the offer haughtily:

> By God's grace We have been sovereign in our land since the beginning; . . . and as beforehand We did not desire to be appointed by anyone, so now too We do not desire it.[2]

Subsequently, Ivan set as the ambitious goal for Muscovy's external policy recovering and reuniting all lands that had ever been part of a Russian state. Inevitably, this placed Muscovy on a collision course with its neighbors in

---

*One of the three segments and linguistic groups of the eastern Slavs, the others being Ukraine ("Little Russia") and Belorussia ("White Russia").

[2]Cited in J. L. Fennell, *Ivan the Great of Moscow* (London, 1961), p. 121.

MAP 1-1   **Rise of Moscow to 1533**

a drive for imperial glory and began the largely expansionist foreign policy of the next three centuries. Lithuania, directly to the west, was Ivan's principal opponent, and by 1494 Ivan's armies had scored considerable gains. Demanding all Lithuanian territory to the Berezina River, Ivan claimed all lands that had belonged to Kievan Rus and entitled himself sovereign of all Russia. Vasili III continued most of his father's policies successfully at home and abroad.

The lengthy and disputed reign of Ivan IV, "the Terrible" (ruled 1533–1584) was crucial to the development of both an autocratic, centralized Russian monarchy and a multinational Russian empire. Soviet scholars under Stalin depicted Ivan IV as a farsighted, progressive statesman who crushed selfish opposition by reactionary princes and boyars, whereas Western historians and recent Russian scholars view him as a bloody tyrant and Oriental despot. In Muscovy during Ivan's youth prevailed feudal disorder and boyar intrigue that threatened to destroy its nascent central institutions and resembled the Wars of the Roses in England. In neither country was the central bureaucracy developed enough to govern effectively without a strong ruler.

Consequently the formal coronation of the seventeen-year-old Ivan IV as the first tsar (Caesar) of Muscovy under the auspices of the Orthodox Church marked a crucial turning point in Russian history. For the first thirteen years of his reign as tsar, Ivan IV governed with the advice of a Chosen Council of boyars and churchmen who aided him in building a powerful centralized monarchy. In foreign affairs Ivan IV had a mixed record with a major success in the east counterbalanced by disastrous failures in his policies toward European powers. In 1552 Ivan and his advisers decided to attack the Khanate of Kazan, one of the successor states of the Golden Horde. The Orthodox Church represented the Kazan campaign as a crusade against the Muslim world. The conquest of Kazan, and subsequently of Astrakhan khanate to the south, led to the annexation of the entire Volga River valley to the Caspian Sea along with its significant Tatar population: the first major non-Russian people to be incorporated into Muscovy. In 1583 Cossack troops under Ermak Timofeevich conquered the western Siberian domain of Khan Kuchum, taking the Russians across the Ural Mountains. That region had to be reconquered later, but Ivan IV helped lay a basis for a Eurasian Russian empire and for the conquest of vast Siberia. To the north, direct relations between Russia and England were established accidentally when an English expedition under Captain Richard Chancellor landed on the shores of the White Sea. Ivan welcomed Chancellor warmly to Moscow and granted the English Muscovy Company a monopoly of duty-free trade with Russia. Anglo–Russian trade led to the development of the port of Arkhangelsk (Archangel) as Muscovy's only direct sea link with western Europe.

However, Ivan IV failed in his major effort to break a western blockade and establish Muscovy as a major Baltic Sea power. Inaugurating the Livonian War (1558–1581) in an attempt to expand Ivan III's modest Baltic foothold, Ivan IV was drawn instead into a lengthy war of attrition with Sweden, Lithuania, and Poland, which overstrained Muscovy's resources and ended in defeat. Early in that war Ivan broke with his moderate advisers of the Chosen Council to launch a reign of terror associated with the *Oprichnina* ("separate domain"), which created chaos in large parts of Russia. Nor could Ivan IV break the hold of the Crimean Khanate, another of the successor states of the Golden Horde, over the northern shores of the Black Sea. At Ivan IV's unlamented death Russia remained mostly isolated from western Europe, relatively backward, and severely weakened. Then followed

Map 1-2   Expansion of Russia, 1462–1815

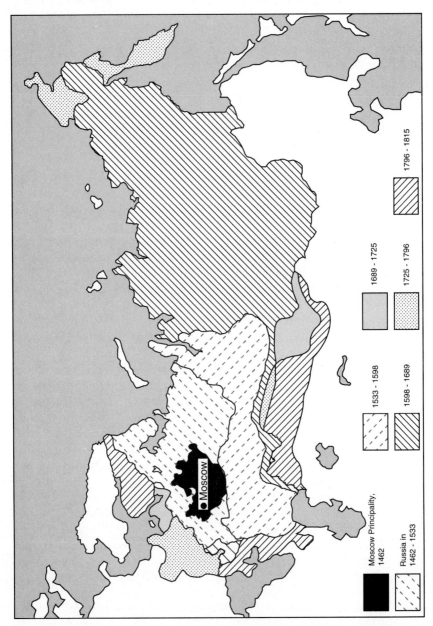

1796 - 1815

1689 - 1725

1725 - 1796

1533 - 1598

1598 - 1689

Moscow Principality, 1462

Russia in 1462 - 1533

Moscow

the so-called "Time of Troubles" (1598–1613) involving a political power struggle to establish a new dynasty, civil war between the Moscow center and the southern borderlands and between the nobility and a peasantry falling into serfdom. Exploiting Russia's numerous troubles, Sweden and Poland invaded the country, and for several years the Poles controlled Moscow.

In 1613 the "Time of Troubles" finally ended with the expulsion of the Poles by a patriotic movement inspired by the Orthodox Church. An assembly of the lands *(zemskii sobor)* elected the new Romanov dynasty that would rule Russia for more than 300 years. Under undistinguished early Romanov rulers (1613–1689) Russia gradually recovered from the "Time of Troubles" and resumed its expansion in the east and west. Between 1580 and 1650 Russian fur trappers and Cossacks, supported by Moscow, advanced from one river course to the next to move swiftly across vast Siberia to the Pacific Ocean. First they established log forts, then permanent fortifications, and eventually towns. In the process Russian rule was established over the numerous small native tribes of Siberia. Few Russian settlers entered the region freely until the nineteenth century. Reaching the Pacific shores at the frigid Sea of Okhotsk in 1638, the Russians moved southward until in the 1670s they clashed with the Chinese. By the Treaty of Nerchinsk (1689) a regular frontier was demarcated, leaving the strategic Amur River valley to China and establishing diplomatic relations with the Chinese Empire. Thus in the seventeenth century all of Siberia, with millions of square miles but few people, was added to Muscovy. Until the nineteenth century Siberia remained an undeveloped tsarist penal colony, but its acquisition represented a vital step in transforming Muscovy into a huge multinational empire.

In the west, Russia's foreign relations during the seventeenth century revolved around disputed Ukraine *(ukraina* or borderland). Originally there were several *ukrainy* along Muscovy's exposed southern borders, including Riazan, Tula, and Kursk. Later, the large region south of those territories and intersected by the Dnieper River became known as Ukraine, developing eventually into a separate nation. The dominant element there were Cossacks, a diverse and restless group of runaway serfs and freebooters who settled along the Don, Volga, and Dnieper rivers and formed communities of independent farmers and warriors. In the years after 1580 a Cossack army with elected leaders developed in the Zaporozhe rapids region of the Dnieper valley on wooded islands. Neighboring Poland sought to convert these Ukrainian Cossacks into a frontier militia and subject them to Polish rule and the Catholic faith. However, in 1648 an Orthodox Cossack leader, Bogdan Khmelnitsky, led a revolt against Polish rule, won the support of the Ukrainian peasantry, and, allied with the Crimean Tatars, defeated the Poles. Khmelnitsky dreamed of becoming king of a united and independent Ukraine, but when the Crimean Tatars abandoned him, his forces were defeated by Poland. Khmelnitsky in desperation turned to Moscow, and after lengthy negotiations the Union

Map 1-3 Russia's eastward expansion, 1598–1762

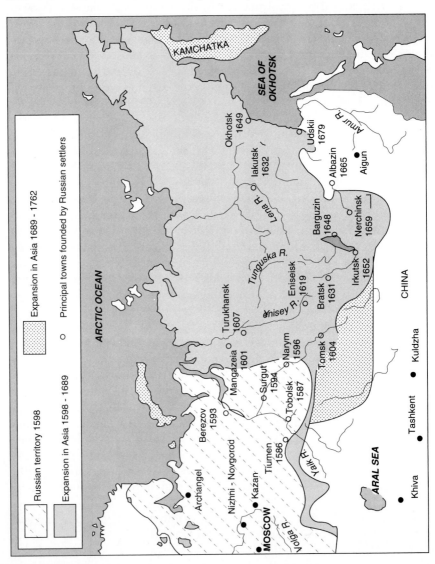

of Pereiaslavl (1654) was created. By this treaty the Cossacks and people of the eastern Ukraine swore allegiance to the tsar of Muscovy, although their autonomy was supposedly guaranteed. Ever since scholars have debated whether Pereiaslavl constituted a voluntary act of submission by Ukraine to Moscow or Russia's forced incorporation of Ukraine. Initially, Ukraine was partitioned, with the east becoming a Moscow vassal and the region west of the Dnieper River remaining Polish. That outcome was determined by a series of wars between Muscovy and Poland, ending with the peace settlement of 1689.

Map 1-4   Russian expansion in Europe, 1618–1689

Under the early Romanovs western European influences grew steadily more important but were countered by traditional Greco–Byzantine values centering around the Orthodox Church. Western influences were introduced initially by the Muscovite state, which sought to satisfy its material and security requirements. The inadequacy of Muscovy's mounted militia and undisciplined musketeers *(streltsy)* grew increasingly evident when compared to the regular, disciplined infantry forces of western Europe. At first Muscovite rulers hired foreign commanders and mercenary troops, then sought to adopt European military structure, weapons, and manuals. European experts were invited to survey Muscovite natural resources and help create a basis for a Russian iron industry in order to prepare rifles, cannon, and shot for the Muscovite army. At the Romanov court a small "Westernizer" faction developed among Muscovite noblemen, some of whom donned European dress and copied Western fashions. Setting standards for this element was a Western Settlement *(Nemetskaia Sloboda)* just outside Moscow that grew into a prosperous, attractive town where life was gay and unrestrained. Therefore during the seventeenth century a minority of the Muscovite elite became westernized and advocated radical change in traditional values and institutions. That in turn stimulated strong opposition from conservatives, especially clergy, to a westernization they believed was evil and godless.

BUILDING A RUSSIAN EMPIRE, 1689–1815

Peter I, "the Great" (ruled 1682–1725), the first able and energetic Romanov ruler, was the true creator of a multinational Russian Empire spanning eleven time zones. Far-reaching reforms of the army, economy, administration, and society implemented during his imperious reign transformed Russia. His first major independent action was the siege and capture of the Turkish fortress of Azov aided by a fleet built on the Don River in 1696. Encouraged by friends in the Western Settlement, Peter visited western Europe in 1697–1698 to satisfy personal curiosity and negotiate an anti-Turkish alliance. That latter effort failed, but Peter returned with hundreds of European technical specialists, convinced that in order to become a great power Russia must follow the military, political, and economic patterns of Europe. His return home was spurred by a revolt of the obsolete musketeers *(streltsy)* who sought to remove Peter from power. His response was to complete a brutal crushing of the streltsy and to introduce compulsory European dress at his court. An iconoclast who broke with most traditions of old Greco–Byzantine Muscovy, Peter maximized Russia's exposure to western European influences symbolized by creating a new Russian capital, known as St. Petersburg, amidst the marshes near the Baltic Sea.

Russia was at war practically throughout Peter the Great's reign. Like his great contemporary, Louis XIV of France, war became his main concern, expansion and conquest his primary aim. Whether Petrine wars were truly necessary or beneficial to the development of Russia is still debated. Were they fought to defend genuine and legitimate Russian national interests, such

PETER I, "THE GREAT," RULED *1682–1725*

as free access to the seas and European markets, ethnic and defensible European frontiers, and normal diplomatic and commercial relations with other countries, or were they chiefly aggressive products of Peter's inordinate ambition? Was the huge price in lives and treasure that Russia paid to become a great European power worthwhile for the Russian people? That price included the virtual enslavement of the Russian masses into the service of an autocratic, centralized police state governed by a nobility itself harnessed into compulsory state service.

Seventeenth-century Muscovite statesmen had sought to solve the so-called Polish, Swedish, and Turkish (Crimean Tatar) "problems." It became clear to them, and to Peter, that they could not be "solved" simultaneously because Russia was not powerful enough to confront all its neighbors together. Poland, severely weakened by the wars of 1654–1689 and by internal dissension, was no longer a threat by Peter's time and could become

Russia's ally against its remaining rivals for eastern European predominance, Sweden and Turkey. After failing to form a European anti-Turkish coalition, Peter concentrated on achieving closer contact with Europe by defeating Sweden and securing control of the eastern Baltic. In 1699 a secret coalition of Russia, Poland, and Denmark, all of whom coveted Swedish territory, was formed. Peter plunged into the Great Northern War without significant preparation or any Swedish provocation. The initial result of Peter's aggression was disaster: at the Battle of Narva (1700) his army of some 40,000 Russians was totally defeated by 8,000 Swedes under their young warrior king, Charles XII. Most Russian troops fled in panic, abandoning their equipment, including all the artillery, to the triumphant Swedes. Undiscouraged, Peter spent the ensuing years building and training a new army while his chief commander, boyhood friend Prince Alexander Menshikov, gradually conquered Ingria and Livonia from the Swedes. St. Petersburg was founded in 1703 at the mouth of the Neva River on land then still belonging to Sweden.

The decisive showdown of the Great Northern War came in 1709 at Poltava in Ukraine. Late in 1707 Charles XII had invaded Russia, advancing into Ukraine to obtain the support of the Ukrainian Cossack chieftain, Mazepa. However, Peter crushed the Ukrainian revolt and destroyed an army of Swedish reinforcements at Lesnaia (1708). In June 1709, at Poltava, Peter's large new army defeated Charles' forces. The wounded Charles XII had to seek refuge in the neighboring Ottoman Empire. Although the Northern War dragged on for another decade, this devastating defeat of the chief Swedish army confirmed Russia's rise as the predominant east European power. A crucial factor in final Russian triumph over Sweden was a major naval victory at Hangö (1714) by Peter's newly built Baltic fleet. The Treaty of Nystadt (1721), which ended the Northern War, gave Russia a large "window to the West," including Livonia, Estonia, Ingria, and part of Karelia. These Baltic territories, retained until 1918, would supply many of imperial Russia's top administrators and generals, drawn from the Baltic German nobility. The treaty brought a better educated non-Russian elite into the growing Russian Empire. Nystadt encouraged Peter to assume the title of emperor (1721), a title recognized over the next forty years by other European powers.

However, Peter the Great's attempt to solve the "Turkish question" and win firm access to the Black Sea ended in failure. Overconfident after his triumph at Poltava, Peter in 1710 unwisely invaded the Ottoman Empire, partly to evict Charles XII from his refuge, after appealing unsuccessfully to Slav Christians of the Balkans to revolt against Ottoman rule. Peter's army was surrounded on the Pruth River by a far larger Turkish force. Forced to sue for peace, Peter had to abandon Azov and all pretensions to the Black Sea region. This grave setback damaged Russia's prestige and delayed its emergence as a Black Sea power for half a century.

Not content with his Baltic foothold, Peter the Great during the last years of his reign pursued an expansionist policy in the south and east.

Map 1-5   Russian expansion under Peter the Great, 1695–1725

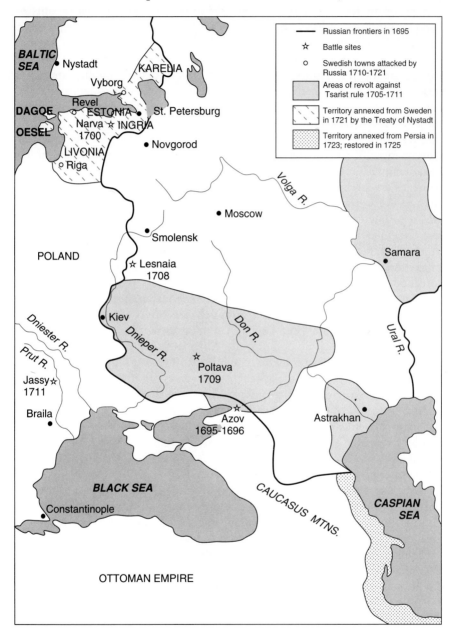

Adopting suggestions from Artemii Volynsky, governor of Astrakhan, Peter led an unprovoked attack on Persia, and conquered the western shores of the Caspian including the port of Baku. In 1700 he had granted Russian citizenship to the hard-pressed khan of Khiva in central Asia. Hearing that gold had been discovered along the Amu River, in 1717 Peter sent a military expedition to Khiva but the Khivans destroyed it.[3] Impractical dreams of conquering India and the abortive expedition to central Asia revealed that imperial Russia was not yet prepared for a major effort in that region.

During the subsequent Era of Palace Revolutions (1725–1762) Russian foreign policy was hampered by lack of governmental stability and by a series of weak or incompetent rulers. This deprived Russian policy of consistent purpose, and at times opened the way for foreign intrigue and bribery of Russian officials and even intervention in Russia's domestic politics (as in 1740–1741). The nationalist school of Russian historiography (for example, V. O. Kliuchevskii) assessed foreign policy in this period rather negatively although Soviet scholarship under Stalin regarded it as a period of necessary preparation for solving the Polish question by able diplomats such as Andrei I. Osterman and A. P. Bestuzhev-Riumin. By now Russia was a respected and permanent member of the great power club, which also included Prussia, France, Austria, and Great Britain. During the War of Austrian Succession (1740–1748), Russia joined Austria and Great Britain in an indecisive conflict with France and Prussia. In 1756 occurred the so-called "Diplomatic Revolution," by which Russia lined up with France and Austria in an effort to prevent Prussian expansion. In the ensuing Seven Years War (1756–1763), Russian armies repeatedly defeated the Prussian forces of Frederick the Great, even occupying Berlin in 1761. With Russia poised at the brink of victory, Empress Elizabeth died in January 1762, and her immature and impetuous successor, Peter III (ruled January–June 1762), an admirer of Frederick the Great, threw away all the gains Russia had scored and even concluded a military alliance with Prussia, Russia's former enemy. Russia's huge expenditures in these mid-eighteenth-century European wars, while consolidating Petrine conquests, produced few substantial results. Evidently, a stable government was a prerequisite for further imperial advances.

Catherine II, "the Great" (ruled 1762–1796), born Sophia of Anhalt-Zerbst, was Peter I's true successor in foreign affairs, which became her chief interest. Abroad, Catherine could operate wholly independently, in contrast with domestic affairs where, initially at least, she was restricted by a powerful nobility. Catherine's title to being "the great" rested formerly largely on her diplomatic and military achievements in making Russia a dominant European power. As in Peter I's case, should one accept a traditional definition of greatness linked closely with territorial expansion not in the interests of the Russian masses? It scarcely benefited Russia as a nation to incorporate millions of Jews and Poles who soon would become intensely alienated by Russian imperial rule.

Unlike her immediate predecessors in power—Anna Ivanovna and Elizabeth I—Catherine took a vital and direct role in the formation of foreign

---

[3]M. T. Florinsky, *Russia: A History and an Interpretation*, vol. I (New York, 1954), p. 354.

CATHERINE II, *"THE GREAT," RULED 1762–1796*

policy from the start. In a statement reminiscent of Peter the Great, she told her advisor and lover, Grigorii Potiomkin: "I wish to rule myself and let Europe know it!" From early youth Catherine had been schooled in intrigue and she had to be a master diplomat to win over Empress Elizabeth, remain married to the immature Grand Duke Peter (Peter III), and win the support of the regiments of the imperial guard. Through diplomacy an obscure German princess became an autocratic Russian empress. Catherine soon mastered the diplomatic techniques of eighteenth-century Europe, based as they were on pretense, deception, and intrigue. As a propagandist Catherine was unequalled among the rulers of her time, cloaking broad ambitions with liberal-sounding phrases typical of the European Enlightenment. Thus Poland was partitioned allegedly for the sake of "Polish freedom" and to secure rights for oppressed Orthodox believers. Russia's intervention in the Ottoman Empire was supposedly to emancipate unfortunate Balkan Christians suffering from Muslim tyranny. Realizing that Russia's greatness as a power would determine her own and lessen her dependence on the nobility, Catherine developed great self-assuredness in foreign policy. A hard and consistent worker with considerable knowledge of the European scene, she possessed the courage and determination to surmount problems and crises. Catherine permitted no important issue of foreign policy to be decided or even discussed without her and posed consistently as the defender of Russian national interests.

Catherine's subordinates in foreign affairs carried out the sovereign's will loyally. During the first half of her reign Catherine's main collaborator in foreign affairs was Nikita Panin, a spokesman for the nobility and architect of the so-called "Northern System." Succeeding him in 1780 was Prince A. A. Bezborodko, an able, hard-working official who drew up excellent reports but remained always merely a mouthpiece for Catherine. Prince Grigorii Potiomkin, the most influential of Catherine's favorites, also played a major role in foreign affairs in the latter portion of the reign, especially vis-à-vis the Ottoman Empire.

Initially, Catherine acted decisively to restore Russian prestige dangerously undermined by Peter III, her late and unlamented childish husband, whose madcap policies of breaking the alliance with Austria and allowing Frederick the Great to dictate peace in the Seven Years War had culminated in an expedition against Denmark in behalf of his native Holstein. Once peace had been concluded, Catherine announced that Russia would not follow in anyone's wake. Panin then arranged the Russo–Prussian alliance of 1764, which the nationalist historian V. O. Kliuchevskii later criticized as a disastrous error resulting in the destruction of Slav Poland. However, the Stalinist scholar V. P. Potiomkin (no relation to Catherine's favorite) affirmed that the alliance allowed Russia to dominate Polish affairs, restrained Turkey, and let Russia play a great power role at slight cost.

The outgrowth of this defensive alliance was the Northern System, whose purpose was to create a coalition of all non-Catholic north European countries and Poland under Russia's leadership against a southern alliance of France–Austria–Spain in order to guarantee a balance of power and European peace. Denmark was brought into this northern alignment in 1765 and an Anglo–Russian commercial treaty was signed. But northern European states proved too divided by political forms and national interests to cooperate effectively. Also, the alliance with Prussia alienated Austria unnecessarily from Russia.

Poland became the main focus of Catherine's attention in the 1760s. Since the time of Peter I, Russia had been steadily encroaching upon the independence of a Poland with an impotent central government. The liberum veto (allowing noble members of the Diet to veto elections of a king) placed the government at the mercy of a selfish Polish aristocracy willing to appeal to foreign powers for support of its "liberties." Soon after

Catherine's accession, the Polish king died and Catherine promptly wrote a former lover, Stanislas Poniatowski, supporting his claims to the throne because his gentle devotion to her would make him a perfect puppet. Catherine thus agitated for Poniatowski's election, bribing those Poles in a position to influence the Diet's election. Although Austria, France, and most of Poland backed the candidacy of the Elector of Saxony, Catherine relied on bribery, her secret agreement with Frederick of Prussia, and armed force to get her way. To ensure a "free election" by the Diet, Catherine ordered a Russian army into Poland. Poniatowski was then "unanimously" chosen king in a Warsaw ringed with Russian artillery (August 1764). Catherine retained a pretext for subsequent intervention by supporting equal religious rights for non-Catholics (mainly Orthodox). When the Diet refused to grant these, the Russian ambassador organized a confederation of dissidents and rebellious Catholic noblemen. Under pretext of aiding this confederation, Russian troops were ordered into Warsaw in 1767 and compelled the Diet to grant dissidents equality. A year later another Russian army invaded Poland and brought the country under almost complete Russian domination.

Austria and France, worried about growing Russian predominance in Poland, intrigued in Constantinople, bribed Turkish officials, and finally induced the Ottoman government to declare war on Russia late in 1768. Russia was unprepared for this conflict, but Catherine swiftly built up the army and navy. For the army she found able commanders, including the great Alexander Suvorov, and for the navy hired two British admirals and some Danish sailors. This motley force defeated the Turkish fleet, but an expected uprising of Balkan Christians against Turkish rule failed to develop. On land the Crimean Tatars were finally defeated and the Crimea conquered. By the spring of 1774 the invincible Suvorov, after a series of brilliant victories, compelled the Turks to sue for peace. The result was the Treaty of Küchük-Kainarji (1774), which confirmed the Crimea's "independence," provided free access to the Mediterranean via the Turkish Straits for Russian merchant ships, and accorded a vaguely worded right of Russian intervention in the affairs of the Orthodox Balkan Christians. This treaty marked a crucial turning point in Russo–Turkish relations, confirming Russia's emergence as a Black Sea power.

Before the Russo–Turkish war had ended, Austria and Prussia, alarmed over Russian victories over the Turks, sought to distract Catherine by proposing a partition of Poland. The First Partition of 1772 followed agreements among Russia, Prussia, and Austria. The three powers consumed their respective slices of the Polish ham despite the pitiful pleas of Poniatowski, Catherine's ex-lover. The Polish Diet was then bribed and coerced into accepting the partition. Russia's share was most of Belorussia, including the districts of Polotsk, Vitebsk, Mogilev, and a strip of Livonia. Although the nobility there was largely Polish, the mass of the population were Belorussian peasants, mostly Orthodox in religion.

The First Partition marked a high point in Russo–Prussian relations. The failure of Panin's Northern System induced Catherine to draw gradually

MAP 1-6   Partitions of Poland, 1772–1795

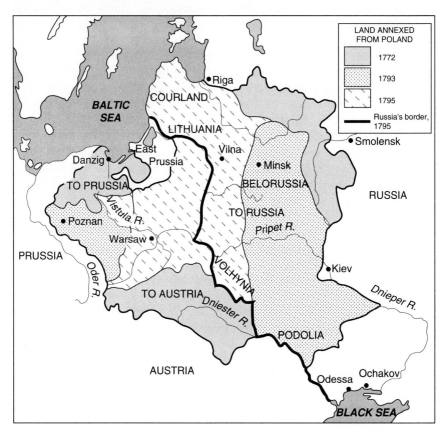

closer to Austria in order to permit both powers to act against the Ottoman Empire. During a Bavarian succession crisis that brought Austria and Prussia to the brink of war, Catherine mediated successfully, establishing a strong basis for Russian diplomatic intervention in German affairs; thereafter many German princelings appealed to her to arbitrate their disputes. In 1780 Catherine met with the liberal new Austrian ruler, Joseph II, and they agreed to a defensive alliance that would be invoked in case of war with the Ottoman Empire.

Buttressed with the Austrian alliance, Catherine and Potiomkin advocated the so-called "Greek Project," a vague scheme to expel the Turks from Europe and reconstitute a shadow Byzantine Empire under her grandson, who was appropriately named Constantine (after the great fourth-century Roman emperor and founder of Constantinople). Catherine and Joseph agreed, in case of Austro–Russian victory, to partition the Balkans into spheres of interest and set up a kingdom of Dacia (Romania). Preliminary steps in this ambitious campaign included Russia's incorporation of the Crimea (1783). That virtually completed Russia's southward expansion and was followed by the development of Sevastopol in the Crimea as the main base for an expanded Black Sea fleet. In 1787 Catherine and Joseph made a triumphant tour down the Dnieper River to the Crimea, which alarmed the Turks and induced them unwisely to force war with Russia and Austria. Russian unpreparedness, rivalry among her generals, and early setbacks failed to discourage Catherine, who insisted on victory. Although Austria left the conflict, Suvorov and other generals triumphed over the Turks. The Treaty of Jassy (1792) advanced the Russian frontier westward to the Bug River, giving Russia possession of the port city of Odessa and the Crimea. Catherine never abandoned the elusive "Greek Project," but could not achieve it because the Turks retained control over the Balkan Christians.

Russia's involvement in wars with Turkey and Sweden (1787–1791) provided the Poles with a final chance to reform antiquated political institutions. The Four Years Diet abolished the liberum veto, and the May Constitution (1791) confirmed this by abolishing elective monarchy and the nobility's right of confederation. These Polish reforms and the involvement of the other powers in war with revolutionary France gave Catherine a golden opportunity for further partitions of Poland. When a small group of Polish malcontents with the May Constitution (Confederation of Targowica) appealed to Catherine, she sent in 100,000 Russian troops to "defend Polish liberties," which broke Polish resistance. Secret Russo–Prussian negotiations then produced the Second Partition of 1793, giving Russia the regions of Vilna and Minsk.

That triggered a final desperate Polish uprising in 1794 led by General Thaddeus Kosciuszko, who appealed to the Polish peasantry for support. However, the poorly equipped Polish army was defeated. This time Russia, Prussia, and Austria participated in a final dismemberment of Poland. In this Third Partition, Russia obtained Courland, Lithuania, Podolia, and Volhynia. These territories remained part of a swollen Russian empire until 1917. Poland had disappeared from the map of Europe. Russian frontiers were advanced far into Europe, but most Russians remained serfs subject to absolute control of private landowners or state officials and providing cannon fodder for Catherine's "glorious" victories.

Catherine's death in 1796 brought to the throne her middle-aged and militaristic son, Paul I, who was slow to develop a coherent foreign policy. Initially, he proclaimed a policy of peace and reversed Catherine's commitments to fight against revolutionary France. While denouncing the French Revolution, Paul opposed a belligerent policy as ruinous and pointed to Russia's empty treasury. Renouncing the "Greek Project," he recalled Russian troops from Georgia and Persia. However, by 1798 Paul, renouncing his policy of non-intervention, joined the First Coalition against revolutionary France, partly under the influence of conservative French émigrés at the Russian court. Russia's participation in the warfare of 1798–1799 was highlighted by the aged Suvorov's final brilliant, but pointless, campaign.

Like Hannibal, Suvorov crossed the Alps with his army, but the coalition fell apart and he was recalled. After Napoleon Bonaparte achieved power by the coup of 1799, Paul reversed course once again to achieve rapprochement with France. At the time of Paul's murder (1801), Russia was drifting toward war with England. Indeed, Paul had dispatched 40,000 Cossacks across the deserts of central Asia in order to invade India. In foreign affairs Paul seemed to have lost direction and achieved little of consequence for Russia.

Under Paul's son, Emperor Alexander I (ruled 1801–1825) the Russian Empire reached its peak of power and influence, extending its sway deep into Europe and over the lowland Caucasus. Russia became more closely involved in European affairs than ever before, partly because of Alexander's education in the principles of the Enlightenment, but even more because of its vital role in the Napoleonic wars. Although as heir to the throne Alexander in discussions with his young liberal friends of the Unofficial Committee expressed sympathy for the principles of the French Revolution—liberty, equality, and fraternity—once he became emperor he guarded jealously his prerogatives as autocrat, generally acting as his own foreign minister and making major decisions himself. His rather vague desire for general peace was expressed initially by moves to prevent a breach with Britain and adopting a conciliatory stance toward other powers. Alexander's pacific policy in 1801–1804 coincided with a truce in a generation of warfare between France and Britain.

After 1804 Franco–Russian relations deteriorated because, as Emperor Alexander concluded, only a coalition of the other continental powers and Britain could thrust an expanding Napoleonic France back into its natural boundaries and bring about permanent peace. Instructions issued to Nicholas Novosiltsev, Russian special envoy to Britain, in November 1804, outlined an Anglo–Russian alliance to destroy the Napoleonic empire and announced rather ambitious Russian territorial objectives: 1) all of Poland; 2) Moldavia, Constantinople, and the Turkish Straits if possible; 3) Malta; and 4) reaffirmation of Russia's right to "protect" the Orthodox Christians of the Balkans. The result of Novosiltsev's mission was the Anglo–Russian Alliance (April 1805) to liberate all non-French territories seized by Napoleon. Russia agreed to provide the bulk of the land forces; Britain would keep them in the field with subsidies. In August 1805, Austria joined this coalition while Prussia remained neutral. Napoleon, who had planned an invasion of England, promptly moved eastward in order to knock out Austria before Russia could mobilize all its forces. At Austerlitz in December 1805, Napoleon defeated the main Austro–Russian army. Austria was compelled to make peace, but General M. I. Kutuzov was able to extract much of the Russian army.

A fourth anti-French coalition was formed among Russia, Prussia, and Britain in July 1806. Once again Napoleon moved swiftly to crush the Prussian army before the slow-moving Russian army arrived. Bitter struggles between the French and Russian forces proved indecisive during 1806, but

Map 1-7 Napoleonic Wars and Russia, 1805–1814

in June 1807 General Leon Bennigsen's Russian army was decisively defeated by Napoleon at Friedland, inducing Tsar Alexander to seek peace. His decision was based on the battered state of the Russian army, the loss of continental allies, an empty treasury, and inadequate English subsidies.

The two emperors, Napoleon and Alexander, met at Tilsit in June 1807, conferring without interpreters on a raft in the Niemen River, which separated French and Russian armies. Reportedly, Alexander declared that he hated the English as much as Napoleon did. "If so," Napoleon supposedly replied, "then peace is concluded." Besides the public peace treaty they agreed in secret accords to partition Europe into French and Russian spheres of influence. Prussian portions of Poland were to be reconstituted as a Duchy of Warsaw, a French vassal state. Alexander agreed to mediate between France and Britain and, if he failed to arrange peace, to declare war on Britain. In return Napoleon pledged to mediate between Russia and Turkey, at war since 1806, and if unsuccessful, join with Russia in an agreement to partition European Turkey. As the victor in the preceding wars, Napoleon received the lion's share at Tilsit. Most of Europe was consolidated under French domination including defeated Prussia. However, Russia exploited the pact to wrest Finland away from Sweden. Tilsit thus has often been compared with the Nazi–Soviet Pact of 1939, which divided Europe similarly and likewise encouraged Russian aggression against its neighbors. In both cases the alliances proved short-lived and contained the seeds of conflict.

Soon the interests of France and Russia proved incompatible. Russian accession to Napoleon's Continental System designed to bar British goods from the continent proved disastrous to Russian foreign trade and produced severe inflation and depreciation of the Russian ruble. Napoleon's demands of 1810–1811 to tighten the Continental System by closing Russian ports to neutral ships was evaded by Alexander, who renewed commercial relations with Britain and taxed French luxury imports. Napoleon's anti-Russian agitation in Constantinople and secret aid to the Turks added to Franco–Russian tensions. Above all, Napoleon's unlimited objectives of conquering all of Europe made conflict inevitable. Charles Talleyrand, Napoleon's foreign minister, secretly encouraged Emperor Alexander to lead a coalition against his master declaring, "You must save Europe!" Alexander prepared for war with France by concluding peace with Sweden and Turkey and signing an alliance with Britain.

On June 24, 1812, without a declaration of war Napoleon's huge Grand Army invaded the Russian Empire. Only about one-third of a total force of nearly 600,000 men was French; the rest were drawn from Poland, the Germanies, Italy, and elsewhere. The Russian defenders, numbering less than 200,000, were compelled to retreat into the interior. The Russian commanders, Prince Mikhail Barclay de Tolly and Prince Pyotr I. Bagration, joined forces at Smolensk, but wisely decided not to fight the pitched battle that Napoleon was counting on. After Smolensk was abandoned, Emperor Alexander named Fieldmarshal Mikhail I. Kutuzov supreme commander, but Kutuzov, too, found himself compelled to continue the retreat. Finally, in response to the terrible clamor by the court and country, Kutuzov stood and fought at Borodino on September 7, 1812, an indecisive encounter with huge casualties on both sides. At Fili, just outside Moscow, Kutuzov decided to abandon Moscow to the advancing French in order to preserve his army.

Napoleon occupied a Moscow abandoned by much of its population. Fire broke out from unexplained causes and destroyed three-fourths of the city, forcing Napoleon to evacuate the Kremlin. Napoleon had believed that the fall of Moscow would force peace, but Alexander courageously resolved to fight on. Rising national resistance by the Russians, disturbing news from Spain, and a lack of supplies compelled Napoleon to order a French retreat on October 19. Kutuzov's army prevented a French retirement along a more southerly route, so they retreated over the same route by which they had come, finding few supplies or food. Eventually, small remnants of the Grand Army escaped encirclement, but Napoleon's empire was doomed.

Fieldmarshal Kutuzov favored stopping at the frontier after clearing the invaders from Russian soil; he saw no point in shedding Russian blood for the liberation of Europe. However, Emperor Alexander, the good European, committed Russia to an all-out war of liberation. Thus Russia played a major role in defeating Napoleon in Germany during 1813 and in the successful invasion of France in 1814. Alexander assumed a leading part in negotiating treaties that provided for Napoleon's abdication and French surrender on relatively generous terms.

Potentially, Russia in 1814–1815 could have been the dominant European power, and Alexander seemingly had an opportunity to become the messiah of Europe. However, he lacked the necessary determination and powers of leadership, instead being converted to conservative principles and relinquishing real direction of the continent to Prince K. von Metternich, Austria's foreign minister. The Russian position was somewhat weakened by Napoleon's escape from exile on the island of Elba and the failure of Russian forces to participate in the final defeat of Napoleon at Waterloo. At the Congress of Vienna of 1814–1815, interrupted by Napoleon's escape and his "Hundred Days" in power, territorial struggles almost led to renewed conflict. Russo–Prussian demands nearly provoked a breach with Austria and Britain, but defeated France sided with these two powers and Alexander backed away from conflict. At Vienna Russia obtained control of most of Poland, and had her claims to Finland and Bessarabia confirmed by the powers. Russia stood as the dominant land power in Europe, but Emperor Alexander pledged to preserve the boundaries and conservative principles agreed upon at the congress. The Congress of Vienna marked a vital watershed in Russian foreign policy, confirming the completion of the ambitious imperial aims adumbrated centuries earlier by Ivan III after the unification of Great Russia.

Suggested Readings

Anderson, M.S. *Britain's Discovery of Russia, 1553–1815*. London, 1958.
_____. *The Eastern Question, 1774–1923*. London, 1966.
Bolkhovitinov, N. N. *The Beginnings of Russian–American Relations, 1775–1815*. Cambridge, MA, 1976.
Crummey, Robert. *The Formation of Muscovy, 1304–1613*. New York, 1987.
De Jonge, Alex. *Fire and Water: A Life of Peter the Great*. New York, 1980.

De Madariaga, I. *Catherine the Great*. New Haven, CT, 1991.

Donnelly, A. *The Russian Conquest of Bashkiria, 1552–1740*. New Haven, CT, 1968.

Fennell, J. L. *The Emergence of Moscow, 1305–1359*. Berkeley, CA, 1968.

Fisher, Alan. *The Russian Annexation of the Crimea*. Cambridge, England, 1970.

Foust, Clifford. *Muscovite and Mandarin: Russia's Trade with China, 1727–1805*. Chapel Hill, NC, 1969.

Grey, Ian. *Ivan III and the Unification of Russia*. New York, 1964.

Halperin, C.J. *Russia and the Golden Horde*. Bloomington, IN, 1985.

Palmer, A. *Alexander I: Tsar of War and Peace*. London, 1974.

Pelenski, J. *Russia and Kazan: Conquest and Imperial Ideology, 1438–1560*. The Hague, Netherlands, 1974.

Platonov, S. *Moscow and the West*. Trans. J. Wieczynski. Hattiesburg, MS, 1972.

Polanska-Wasylenko, N. *Russia and Western Europe, 10th–13th Centuries*. London, 1954.

Prawdin, M. *The Mongol Empire: Its Rise and Legacy*. 2nd ed. New York, 1967.

Presniakov, A.E. *The Formation of the Great Russian State*. Trans. A. Moorhouse. New York, 1971.

Rybakov, Boris. *Kievan Rus*. Trans. S. Sossinsky. Moscow, 1989.

Skrynnikov, R. G. *Ivan the Terrible*, Gulf Breeze, FL, 1981.

Subtelny, Orest. *Ukraine: A History*. Toronto, Canada, 1988.

Sumner, B. H. *Peter the Great and the Emergence of Russia*. London, 1951.

Vernadsky, George. *Kievan Russia*. New Haven, CT, 1948.

_____. *The Mongols and Russia*. New Haven, CT, 1953.

_____. *Russia at the Dawn of the Modern Age*. New Haven, CT, 1959.

Wieczynski, J. L. *The Russian Frontier: The Impact of the Borderlands Upon the Course of Early Russian History*. Charlottesville, VA, 1978.

Wood, Alan. *The History of Siberia*. London, 1991.

2

MUSCOVITE AND RUSSIAN DIPLOMACY TO 1815

The Russian state constituted more a political than a national unity, the Empire being, so to say, no more than a vast abstraction of a multitude of national realities. No strictly national policy imposed itself in an absolute manner; the greatest variations in the diplomatic program were permitted.
B. *Nolde,* L'alliance Franco-Russe *(Paris, 1936)*

If one scratched an eighteenth-century Russian, would one truly find an Asiatic underneath? Did Muscovite and later Russian diplomacy employ the values and methods of Byzantium, Asia, or Europe? Was Russian diplomacy truly mysterious, secretive, and inscrutable? Was there a conscious transition from the earlier Byzantine and Asiatic legacy of Muscovy to the pro-European orientation and policies of Peter the Great, Catherine the Great, and Alexander I? How successful was Russian diplomacy in promoting national interests? To suggest tentative answers to these questions, we must examine the development of Russian diplomatic institutions and Russia's changing role in world affairs. Here we will trace this process through the Congress of Vienna, which confirmed the virtual completion of the process of imperial construction in Europe.

MUSCOVITE DIPLOMACY

Even before the unification of Great Russia by Ivan III, the Muscovite court negotiated with the Golden Horde, the caliphs of Baghdad, and other Asian rulers. Muscovite princes won their diplomatic spurs first as intermediaries between their fellow Russian princes and the khan of the Golden Horde, then as leaders of a coalition of Russian princes that exploited growing Mongol fragmentation to defeat the Horde. Under Ivan III, Moscow, following its conquest of Novgorod and Tver, entered for the first time into significant relations with leading eastern European countries. Receiving the special envoy of the Holy Roman Empire, Nicholas Poppel, in 1486, Ivan III moved apart from his boyars in council in order to discuss secret matters since there was as yet no special Muscovite diplomatic institution. Three years later Iurii Trakhaniot, Ivan's special envoy to the Holy Roman emperor, upon his return to Moscow acknowledged the great honor accorded him when the emperor and his son met with Trakhaniot in person. Therefore when the emperor dispatched an envoy to Moscow, Ivan III was careful to receive him in the same manner. Crude Muscovite diplomats, regarded by some Europeans as "baptized bears," observed European diplomatic methods and ceremonies firsthand and began to copy them. Rejecting the German emperor's offer of a royal title, Ivan III, grand prince of Moscow in dealings with lesser Russian princes, began to refer to himself as tsar and sovereign of all Russia. In 1518 his son and successor, Vasilii III, described himself officially as tsar for the first time in a document sent to the Holy Roman emperor.[1]

In the mid-sixteenth century under Ivan IV, "the Terrible," Muscovy entered the diplomatic arena of eastern European politics. His foreign policy was directed primarily westward in an effort to smash the de facto blockade against Muscovy endorsed by its neighbors: Poland, Lithuania, and the Livonian Order. Consequently the establishment of direct relations with England after the Richard Chancellor expedition was hailed in Moscow as a major triumph. Nonetheless, Muscovy still sought an outlet to Europe through the Baltic Sea and equality in deciding the international problems of the Baltic region. Initially Ivan IV tried diplomacy, but when it failed he invaded Livonia in 1558. The Livonian War developed into a general eastern European conflict in which eventually Muscovy was defeated by superior forces.

The growing complexity of Muscovy's external relations required regular diplomatic institutions and etiquette. Under Ivan III foreign policy issues had been discussed and decided by the grand prince meeting with the Boyar Duma containing his principal servitors. Soon the task of receiving foreign envoys was given to grand princely treasurers *(kaznachei)* who also handled financial matters. Gradually certain grand princely secretaries *(diaki)* specialized in negotiations with foreign envoys. At first primarily foreigners in the grand prince's service—mostly Greeks and Italians—were selected as Muscovite envoys because they were more cultured than Muscovites and knew European conditions.

In 1549, early in Ivan IV's reign, an ambassadorial board *(Posolskii prikaz)* was created under a secretary *(diak)*, Ivan M. Viskovatyi; in 1561 he was given the title of chancellor *(pechatnik)*. This untitled secretary ran the foreign office while the tsar decided important questions with the Boyar Duma as before. As he drew into his capable hands all current diplomacy, Viskovatyi amazed foreign envoys with his intelligence and skill. However, when the Turks and Crimean Tatars entered the Livonian War against Muscovy, Ivan IV accused Viskovatyi of "Turkophilism" and had him executed in 1570. He was succeeded by the almost equally able brothers,

---

[1]V. P. Potemkin, ed., *Istoriia diplomatii*, vol. I (Moscow, 1941), p. 197.

Andrei Shchelkalov and Vasilii Shchelkalov, the former running the Ambassadorial Board for twenty-five years. As the seventeenth century dawned, the board remained small: besides the secretary and his assistant were only fifteen to seventeen lesser officials and a few translators and scribes.

As more and more foreign envoys entered Muscovy after the Time of Troubles, the question arose how and where to house them. In the sixteenth century special quarters *(dvory)* had been set aside for some; others lived in private homes. Early in the seventeenth century in the Kitai-gorod section of Moscow a separate Ambassadorial Court *(posolskii dvor)* was constructed. Under pretext of protecting foreign envoys, the Muscovite government sought to isolate them, not allowing them to leave their special quarters before they were received in audience by the tsar. Later in the seventeenth century this semi-prison regime gradually was relaxed. Meanwhile Muscovy's expanding commercial and political relations with Europe brought permanent foreign ambassadors and consuls to Moscow. In 1585 there was an acting English consul there, and, after 1623, the consulate was permanent and continuous. Dutch and Swedish representatives soon followed, but some other European countries were denied permanent representatives in Muscovy. Simultaneously Muscovite diplomacy was severely hampered by the lack of permanent missions abroad. Poorly informed about European events, Moscow had to make do with European newspapers translated in the Posolskii prikaz. Inadequate and belated information led Muscovite diplomats into major blunders: in 1687 a Russian envoy arrived in Paris to propose to Louis XIV an alliance against the Ottoman Empire only to discover that France had already aligned itself with the Turks.[2]

In the later seventeenth century, as Muscovy expanded into a large empire, the Posolskii prikaz underwent major growth. By 1689 it contained fifty-three sub-secretaries *(podiachykh)*, twenty-two translators, and seventeen interpreters. Directing foreign policy under the tsar's supervision, it also oversaw the affairs of foreign merchants in Muscovy as well as those of Don Cossacks and Tatars who entered the service of the Muscovite state after the fall of Kazan in 1552. The board initially administered newly acquired territories such as Siberia, Ukraine, and Smolensk, and collected funds to ransom prisoners. Several minor boards were subordinated to its authority. Such a mixture of functions complicated correct handling of business. One of its outstanding directors, Afanasii L. Ordyn-Nashchokin (1605?–1680) objected in vexation that one should not mix in the same agency "great affairs of state" with minor financial matters.

Revealing the growing importance of foreign relations in Muscovy was that, beginning in 1667, titled boyars, no longer simple secretaries, headed the Posolskii prikaz. Some of them were given as well the lofty title of chancellor. Perhaps the ablest of them was Ordyn-Nashchokin, a statesman of European caliber, who had helped negotiate the annexation of

---

[2]Potemkin, pp. 247–49.

left-bank Ukraine to Muscovy. Describing the Posolskii prikaz as "the eyes of all great Russia," he proclaimed its chief purpose: to expand Muscovy's frontiers. Often quarreling with Tsar Aleksei, Ordyn-Nashchokin had his own goals in foreign policy, which emphasized the vital necessity of Baltic seaports which could be acquired through an alliance with a weakened Poland.[3]

EIGHTEENTH-CENTURY IMPERIAL DIPLOMACY

Under Peter the Great (ruled 1689–1725) Muscovy became transformed into the Russian Empire and soon assumed the role of a leading European power. Peter's initial diplomatic foray into Europe was the so-called Grand Embassy of 1697–1698, which was designed to discover new European allies in order to continue the war with the Turks following Russia's conquest of Azov in 1696. When Peter realized that this objective had failed completely because Europe's attention then was focused on Spain, he shifted course with astonishing speed to revive Ordyn-Nashchokin's scheme of a "Northern alliance" against Sweden. The crudeness of Russian diplomacy during the Grand Embassy is suggested by the shambles left by Peter's entourage at a London home where it was quartered during the tsar's visit to England. This reflected an apparently deliberate flouting of Western conventions possibly to demonstrate Russian superiority. Still retaining certain Byzantine or Asiatic habits of thought and behavior, Russian foreign envoys had to be supplied by Moscow with detailed instructions as to how to act, what to say, and how to say it. Never given full authority, they could decide nothing without referring to higher authority at home. If new subjects were broached during negotiations, they had to seek new instructions from Moscow.[4] However, during Peter's reign many of these ancient traditions would be discarded.

During the lengthy Great Northern War with Sweden, Petrine Russia finally established regular diplomatic missions abroad in European fashion as its diplomats swiftly overcame their former crudeness. In 1699 A. A. Matveev was sent to Holland as "an extraordinary ambassador with plenary powers"; soon thereafter he became Russian ambassador to England. After Matveev was arrested in 1708 for debt and was mistreated and insulted in detention, Peter insisted on diplomatic immunity for his diplomats. With support from other foreign envoys, Matveev was soon released and a special law was enacted in England describing the rights of diplomats. Queen Anne expressed her personal regret at the incident and London dispatched a special mission to Russia to apologize; it was received by Peter with great ceremony. However, foreign envoys in Russia were sometimes mistreated. In 1718 Peter ordered the Dutch envoy in St. Petersburg arrested for

---

[3]Potemkin, pp. 234–35.

[4]Gordon Craig, "Techniques of Negotiation," in Ivo Lederer, ed., *Russian Foreign Policy: Essays in Historical Perspective* (New Haven, CT, 1962), pp. 352–54.

allegedly sending unfavorable reports home about Russia. His papers were seized and his recall demanded.[5]

An inefficient Posolskii prikaz proved inadequate to handle Russian foreign relations of growing complexity. During the Grand Embassy Peter was approached in England by Francis Lee, who proposed that he establish centralized administrative colleges in Russia with specified jurisdictions. Instead Peter set up a "field ambassadorial office" *(pokhodnaia)*, which gradually assumed the functions of Posolskii prikaz. In 1716 collegial organization and decision-making on the Swedish model was introduced into the Ambassadorial Board. Soon this was renamed the College of Foreign Affairs (1720) as one of eight administrative colleges created for the sake of "just government" and "good order" to replace the old *prikazy*.[6] Among the "office advisers" serving under its director, Count G. I. Golovkin and his assistant, was A. I. Osterman, later its extremely able director. Their tasks included drawing up documents to foreign rulers, memoranda to ministers, and other important secret state papers. Despite inexperience, Peter's young diplomacy scored quick successes, and in his last years a new generation of skillful, sophisticated diplomats emerged. Russia's outstanding triumph at the Treaty of Nystadt (1721) ending the Great Northern War testified to a new and capable diplomacy.

Setting an example to Russian diplomats was Peter himself. Controlling firmly all aspects of diplomacy, he participated personally in major negotiations and fulfilled at times the functions of ambassador and foreign minister. Twice he traveled abroad on diplomatic missions and concluded personally the agreement of 1698 for a northern alliance and a treaty in Amsterdam in 1717. Peter's instructions issued in 1718 to Russian envoys to the Aland Congress were models of diplomatic tact. In St. Petersburg, dealing directly with foreign ambassadors, Peter talked with them simply and openly. Rather than meeting with them in scheduled secret audiences, the tsar had to be sought out at parties. The Danish ambassador recalled: "I utilized a dinner at which I sat next to him to follow my ruler's instructions to discuss various matters with him. . . . The tsar listened graciously and gladly and replied to all I said to him." Peter hated all formality. When the ambassador went to a supposedly secret audience, Peter arrived at the Admiralty in a sloop and spoke loudly to the envoy about state affairs so everyone could hear. In foreign affairs Peter adhered to his own principles of political honesty, openness, and keeping promises. "It is better if our allies abandon us than we abandon them since one's word of honor is dearer than all else."[7] Unlike his predecessors and immediate successors, Peter I concentrated on a single foreign problem, such as access

---

[5]Potemkin, pp. 271–72.

[6]J. Cracraft, "Colleges of Peter the Great," in *Modern Encyclopedia of Russian and Soviet History*, vol. VII, p. 172.

[7]Potemkin, pp. 276–77.

to the Baltic Sea, subordinating to it all other diplomatic efforts. That technique helped account for his major victory over Sweden.

During the Era of Palace Revolutions (1725–1762) Russia continued to play a major role in European affairs, especially while Osterman, who had helped negotiate the Treaty of Nystadt, headed the College of Foreign Affairs. "A master in subtlety and dissimulation, he had perfect command over his passions and could even shed tears when the occasion required so great a display of feeling," wrote a contemporary, General C. H. von Manstein.[8] However, frequent changes of ruler and the lack of consistent policies in this period robbed Russian foreign policy of opportunities to score major gains. Thus at the end of the costly Seven Years War the immature newly enthroned ruler, Peter III, yielded all of Russia's conquests in that war to its former enemy, Prussia.

Catherine II employed some new diplomatic techniques during a long and triumphant reign. Greatly emphasized was foreign political propaganda, especially through her correspondence with such European intellectual leaders as Voltaire, Baron Friedrich Grimm, and Denis Diderot. Carefully following foreign publications that might damage Russia's reputation or her own, she succeeded in halting publication of a book criticizing the Coup of June 1762, which had elevated her to the Russian throne. She invited foreign envoys to accompany her in repeated trips around Russia during which complex international problems were discussed and alliances concluded. Like most Europeans, Catherine normally employed French as the language of diplomacy rather than Russian, which she spoke imperfectly.

The complex diplomacy of the late eighteenth century required a revamping of Petrine foreign policy institutions. In 1718 the College of Foreign Affairs had only 120 officials; by 1762 it employed 261. During lengthy sojourns of the imperial court in Moscow under Peter II and Elizabeth I, the colleges had accompanied the ruler; a separate office was left behind in St. Petersburg to handle current affairs. Under Catherine II, "the Great," the College of Foreign Affairs had a president, normally with the title of chancellor, and a vice president. It contained a secret department, or political section, divided between European and Asian affairs, and a public department where officials administered special funds, dealt with current affairs, and postal and commercial sections. Theoretically these affairs were conducted collegially (collectively), but in fact by then they were controlled by the president and his assistant. Nonetheless, in 1781 Catherine reminded college presidents by decree that all decisions should be made collectively.

ALEXANDER I AND THE FOREIGN MINISTRY, 1801–1825

In 1802, under the highly educated and idealistic Alexander I, eight ministries were established, including a Ministry of Foreign Affairs, to replace

---

[8]C. H. von Manstein, *Contemporary Memoirs of Russia from the Year 1727 to 1744* (New York, 1968, Reprint), p. 335.

the administrative colleges. The idea of centralized ministries of a European type developed during the brief reign of Paul I (1796–1801), Alexander's father, but he had lacked sufficient time to implement it. Theoretically a ministry represented the concept of one-man rule, unlike the supposedly collective decision making in administrative colleges; in fact the principle of one-man control had prevailed increasingly in the late eighteenth century. Throughout Alexander I's reign the term "college" *(kollegiia)* continued to be used and organizational changes remained insignificant. As its role gradually waned, the College of Foreign Affairs continued to handle ceremonial functions, such as the protocol of receiving foreign ambassadors.

Moreover, in the new Foreign Ministry, contrary to theory, backwardness and inefficiency prevailed. Russia's ambassador in London, S. R. Vorontsov, who regarded the British Foreign Office as the ideal, concluded that the Russian foreign service was in a "terrible state of disorganization."[9] Comprising over 300 officials in Russia alone, the Ministry was heavily bureaucratic and grossly overstaffed with many incompetents. Meanwhile the British Foreign Office in 1822 had a staff of only twenty-eight; the French Foreign Ministry in 1825 had but fifty-five employees. Functional distinctions between offices were often lacking and lines of authority were scrambled as in the old prikazy. Suffering from a corruption endemic in the Russian bureaucracy, the Foreign Ministry often leaked state secrets. Placement in the Foreign Ministry, as in most branches of the imperial Russian government at that time, was chiefly by imperial favor and nearly all appointees were from a pampered gentry class. Although diplomatic posts often carried high prestige, most gentry diplomats were poorly trained and underqualified. Until Ioannes Capodistrias after the Vienna Congress inaugurated a training program, their only preparation was normally a brief period as a copyist or office apprentice in the foreign service. In the absence of an educated and well-trained civil service—and because Emperor Alexander wished to "Westernize" Russian diplomacy and raise it to European levels—Russia's diplomatic service remained dominated by foreigners and military men.

The role of the Foreign Ministry was determined by its relationship with an autocratic emperor, relations with other ministries and internal agencies, and its ties with the outside world. Like other foreign ministries, its chief tasks were to conduct political relations with foreign countries, foster Russian trade, defend legitimate interests of Russians abroad, and respond to legal requests by foreigners about their affairs in Russia. The Foreign Ministry was headed by a minister, sometimes with the title of chancellor or vice-chancellor, and an assistant-minister *(tovarishch-ministr)*, both appointed and dismissed directly by the emperor. Within the Ministry were a council *(sovet)* to discuss matters submitted by the minister, the Asiatic Department, departments of internal relations, personnel and economic affairs, and archives. Its foreign agencies, which depended on the

---

[9]Patricia K. Grimsted, *The Foreign Ministers of Alexander I* (Berkeley, CA, 1969), p. 26.

importance and size of the country concerned, included embassies, missions, general consulates, and consulates. The minister's chancellery handled diplomatic correspondance. The activities and personnel of the Ministry were described annually in a Russian language *Ezhegodnik* (Yearbook) and a French language *Annuaire de l'empire de Russie*.

A decree of Emperor Alexander of April 19, 1819, created the Asiatic Department within the Foreign Ministry to deal especially with Asian countries with which Russia had diplomatic or commercial dealings and with Russia's Asiatic subjects. Its first section handled Turkish, Persian, and Georgian affairs; the second dealt with nomadic peoples of the Caucasus and Central Asia. An Asiatic Committee, designed to expand Russian trade with Central Asia, likewise functioned from 1819 to 1847. Because of Alexander I's pro-European orientation, the Asiatic Department remained of secondary importance during his reign.

From the unification of Muscovy in the sixteenth century until the revolution of March 1917 Russian foreign policy, to a greater extent than elsewhere in Europe, was determined primarily by the ruler. All five emperors of the nineteenth and early twentieth centuries—despite variations in character, ability, and degree of interest in and knowledge about foreign affairs—maintained this autocratic tradition. Thus the Austrian ambassador in Russia during Alexander I's reign, although representing an autocratic emperor, expressed surprise "how absolute the will of the sovereign is in this empire."[10] No other European ruler except Napoleon I took such a personal interest or played such a significant role in foreign affairs as did Alexander. Normally no other member of the imperial family exerted much influence over foreign policy. Typically the Foreign Minister executed his sovereign's will unquestioningly rather than formulating basic policies himself. Thus a French ambassador in Russia just after 1900 described Count V. N. Lamzdorf as "a minister of foreign affairs à la russe" who "did not have charge of the foreign policy but only of the diplomacy of Russia, with the mission of adapting the latter to the former."[11] Even under the constitutional monarchy of 1906–1917, the Fundamental Laws of Russia declared: "The emperor is the supreme director of the external relations of the Russian state with foreign powers; he also sets the course of the international policy of the Russian state."[12] Between 1802 and 1894 the Foreign Ministry served primarily as a technical aid and advisory body to autocratic emperors who claimed the personal right to formulate foreign policy. Nonetheless, during that span it regulated quite effectively relations between Russia and the outside world unless overridden by the emperor. However, from 1894 to 1917 its ability to perform this essential function

---

[10]Grimsted, p. 11.

[11]G. H. Bolsover, "Aspects of Russian Foreign Policy," in R. Pares and A.J.P. Taylor, eds., *Essays Presented to Sir Lewis Namier* (London, 1956), p. 328.

[12]Quoted in Robert Tucker, "Autocrats and Oligarchs," in Lederer, p. 172.

declined drastically because of rapid turnover of foreign ministers, the removal of essential authority from their hands, and the incompetence of Nicholas II.

Under Alexander I (ruled 1801–1825) imperial Russia reached its zenith of power and prestige. As the only continental European country able to resist Napoleon, Russia under Alexander led the armies of a European coalition into Paris in 1814. At the subsequent Congress of Vienna (1814–1815), which confirmed Russia's control over Finland, most of Poland, and Bessarabia, Russia's international influence set a standard that subsequent emperors and foreign ministers sought in vain to emulate. Emperor Alexander's alternating decisions for peace or war with Napoleon largely determined the destiny of Europe. Thus over the opposition of most of his generals, including the victorious M.I. Kutuzov, Alexander insisted on pursuing the war against Napoleon across Europe to final victory. Capable assistants such as Prince Adam Czartoryski and Ioannes Capodistrias, both foreigners, supplied advice, but Alexander often reached decisions and initiated policies without consulting them. Foreign diplomats sought direct access to Alexander, but usually they had to conduct business with the Foreign Minister. "The departure of the emperor leaves political affairs in complete stagnation," reported the French chargé d'affaires in 1819. "Nothing is done in this respect during his absence. . . ." Diplomatic affairs generally followed a formal procedure of notes through the Foreign Ministry accompanied by lengthy delays. "The absolute impossibility of hurrying the St. Petersburg cabinet even on the most ordinary . . . communications has always stopped me," complained an exasperated Austrian ambassador in 1805. In view of the prevalent tight secrecy in St. Petersburg, the French ambassador declared that there was "no other court where the diplomatic corps is less informed on political dispositions and proceedings than here."[13]

Alexander I possessed outstanding diplomatic ability and played a dominant role in determining Russian foreign policy. Intellectually able and extremely charming, he penned subtle dispatches and felt wholly at ease with foreign statesmen. However, he suffered from serious emotional imbalance. "His daily explosions of rage and frenzy" at the Congress of Vienna revealed qualities that impaired much of his diplomatic work. Furthermore, he was often vague, lacking in willpower, and frequently yielded to outside influences before making decisions. Alexander preferred to put affairs in the hands of a personal friend rather than a capable administrator. He approached foreign policy in an idealistic, utopian manner rather than with clearly formulated goals reflecting Russia's interests.[14]

Alexander I's foreign ministers, though mainly implementers not makers of policy, nonetheless ranked among the top officials of the empire and exercised great power. Despite frequent sessions with his foreign minister

---

[13]Grimsted, pp. 23–24.
[14]Grimsted, pp. 34 ff.

where they formulated policy jointly, Alexander delegated much responsibility to him. With a large staff, the foreign minister elaborated on the emperor's general guidelines and executed his policies, supervised only by an impractical and often preoccupied ruler. As the foreign minister sought the emperor's approval for his ideas on basic policy, their intellectual and psychological relationship outweighed institutional patterns.

Russian diplomats abroad, because of difficulties of communication, even though limited by detailed written instructions, remained relatively independent, determining much of the daily conduct of affairs. Wrote Alexander to one of his envoys in 1812: "Pay close attention to what I have written and make your decisions with reflection. I am too far away to be able to direct you at every moment; your own wisdom must supplement."[15] Excessive independence of envoys was countered by frequent resort to special emissaries and missions.

Of the eight men of sharply contrasting backgrounds, personalities, and ideas who directed the Foreign Ministry under Alexander I, seven served only briefly. Some departed after severe policy differences with the emperor, others as the course of Russian external policies fluctuated. Only Count Karl V. Nesselrode (minister 1812–1855) enjoyed a long and secure tenure of office. Descended from a family of Rhenish nobility, Nesselrode, unlike his predecessors, acquired Alexander's full confidence, joined him at European congresses, and signed all the major treaties of 1813–1815. Without personal opinions on foreign policy, Nesselrode did whatever the emperor ordered. Though lacking brilliance, he was "honest, loyal, hardworking, and willing to oblige,"[16] a well-trained, conscientious, and tactful spokesman of his imperial master. Only three of Alexander's foreign ministers—A. R. Vorontsov (S.R. Vorontsov's brother), A. Budberg, and N. P. Rumiantsev—bore the formal title of Foreign Minister, but there was always an effective "minister," regardless of his actual title, for the emperor to consult.

Suggested Readings

Bolsover, G. H. "Aspects of Russian Foreign Policy," in R. Pares and A.J.P. Taylor, eds., *Essays Presented to Sir Lewis Namier.* London, 1956.

Croskey, Robert. *Muscovite Diplomatic Practices in the Reign of Ivan III.* New York, 1987.

Dziewanowski, M. K. *Alexander I: Russia's Mysterious Tsar.* New York, 1990.

Grimsted, Patricia K. *The Foreign Ministers of Alexander I.* Berkeley, CA, 1969.

Kukiel, M. *Czartoryski and European Unity, 1770–1861.* Princeton, NJ, 1960.

Lederer, Ivo, ed., *Russian Foreign Policy: Essays in Historical Perspective.* New Haven, CT, 1962.

Madariaga, Isabel de. *Britain, Russia and the Armed Neutrality of 1780.* London, 1962.

---

[15]Grimsted, p. 18.
[16]Grimsted, p. 198.

Nicholson, Harold. *Diplomacy.* 3rd ed. London, 1963.
Palmer, Alan. *Tsar Alexander I: Paternalistic Reformer.* New York, 1970.
Tarle, Evgenii. *Napoleon's Invasion of Russia, 1812.* New York, 1942.
Tatishchev, Sergei S. *Iz proshlago russkoi diplomatii.* St. Petersburg, 1890.
Webster, C. K. *The Art and Practice of Diplomacy.* 2 vols. New York, 1962.

ERA OF SATIATION AND THE CRIMEAN WAR, 1815–1856

Victory over Napoleon Bonaparte following his invasion of Russia in 1812 made Imperial Russia temporarily the dominant European land power. Its generous frontiers, confirmed by the Congress of Vienna in 1815, established for the Russian Empire a most favorable position vis-à-vis Europe. By acquiring Finland, most of Poland, and Bessarabia, Russia had advanced westward far beyond the line of ethnic Russian settlement. Possession of two-thirds of Poland placed Russian armies within easy striking distance of Vienna and Berlin. Control of Finland solidified Russia's sway over the eastern Baltic Sea. The annexation of Bessarabia, acquired from Turkey by the Treaty of Bucharest (1812), provided a base for military operations into the Balkans and to dominate the Danubian Principalities (later Romania). Allied informally with the Austrian Empire and the Prussian monarchy until the Revolutions of 1848, and with France prostrate and Germany still divided, Imperial Russia with the largest army in Europe, enjoyed a highly enviable power position.

ALEXANDER I: THE LAST DECADE, 1815–1825

Russia's preeminent position provoked a major shift in the empire's aims and policies in Europe. Since the fifteenth century Muscovy had expanded outward from a central core in all directions to create a huge, multinational Russian Empire spanning two continents. Now Alexander I sought to preserve the leading position in European affairs gained in the Napoleonic Wars, to protect advantageous frontiers, and to maintain the partitions of Poland. In the "era of satiation" following Napoleon's defeat, both Alexander and his successor, Nicholas I, pursued basically conservative policies: to preserve legitimate divine-right monarchy in Russia, and if possible throughout Europe, defending it against potential challenges from the new forces of liberalism, nationalism, and socialism. Furthermore, they sought to maintain a balance of power highly favorable to Russia, prevent the hegemony of any single power in western Europe (such as France), and block the formation of any hostile coalition against Russia. Imperial Russia's aims during the nineteenth century remained limited as it sought to prevent

ALEXANDER *I*, RULED *1801–1825*

a general European conflict that might undermine its position. Generally, Russia from 1815 to 1914 acted as a charter member of the European community of powers and mostly in accord with its standards. Russian diplomats, like other Europeans except the English, generally employed the French language both orally and in their dispatches. The Romanov dynasty, closely linked by marriage and blood with other European royal houses, shared with them a common interest in self-preservation by avoiding adventurous and provocative policies. Russian imperial expansion in Asia, mostly during the second half of the nineteenth century, resembled that of other European powers, except that it was continental in nature. Viewed similarly by Asian states, this expansion was conducted in the name of spreading Christian European civilization to benighted and backward Asiatics. Imperial Russia's foreign policies in Europe during the nineteenth century differed fundamentally from the earlier aggressive, expansionist course pursued by the grand princes and tsars of Muscovy, by Peter the Great, Catherine the Great, and later by a Soviet regime that rejected European standards.

The final decade of Alexander I's reign traditionally has been considered an age of reaction marked by heightened autocracy, severe censorship, repression, and fear. By refusing to grant Russia proper a constitution despite immense sacrifices by its people, Alexander appeared to be turning his back on the liberalism of his youth. However, he did establish semi-constitutional regimes under his rule in the new Kingdom of Poland and Grand Duchy of Finland, and insisted on restoring a constitutional monarchy in defeated France. Actually, Alexander's final years represented a confusing combination of liberal intentions and reactionary behavior representing no sharp break with the era before 1812. Epitomizing the regime, 1815–1825, dominated by the sinister militarist, Count Aleksei Arakcheev, were military colonies established under his brutal supervision that combined the worst features of serfdom and the military barracks.

For seven years after the Congress of Vienna, Europe was supervised informally by the "Congress System" composed of the great powers, which effectively preserved peace. Its basis was the Quadruple Alliance of 1814 (Russia, Britain, Austria, and Prussia) created to defeat Napoleon; it was broadened in 1818 to include France among its members. Alexander I, in his idealistic and mystical quest for European peace and harmony, in 1815 composed for signature by his fellow monarchs a Holy Alliance to be based on Christian principles. Although signed eventually by most European rulers and symbolizing the unity of conservative European monarchies, it lacked real practical significance or power. Proving more substantial was the Concert of Europe, which brought together in periodic conclaves the rulers and foreign ministers of the great powers to deal with any threat to the general peace and the Vienna Settlement. However, at the Congress of Aix-la-Chapelle of 1818 Lord Castlereagh, the British foreign secretary, rejected proposals by Tsar Alexander for an international army to keep the peace, to admit some smaller European powers to the congress, and to institute regular and intimate great power cooperation. That congress then decided to withdraw Allied occupation troops from defeated France and grant her equality. Great Britain refused any commitment to suppress revolts against legitimate rulers and after 1818 largely withdrew from continental affairs.

Thus the Troppau Conference late in 1820 brought together only the three eastern conservative monarchies of Russia, Prussia, and Austria, marking the beginning of a split between a conservative east and a relatively liberal west in Europe. Alexander I offered a Russian army to the French and Austrians to suppress revolts in southern Europe, but they declined. At Troppau Alexander admitted to Prince Klemens von Metternich of

Austria that his earlier liberal views had been mistaken, adding: "I am here without any fixed ideas, without any plans. . . . Tell me what you desire and what you wish me to do, and I will do it."[1] This appeared to reflect Alexander's surrender of European leadership to the Austrian foreign minister. In November 1820 the Troppau Protocol legitimized intervention, both diplomatic and military, in the affairs of states that had changed their governments because of revolutions, and to restore legitimate regimes. Lord Castlereagh protested, rejecting the Holy Alliance's claimed right to crush revolutions in Europe and its colonies. At the Laibach Conference of January 1821, Alexander and Metternich agreed to authorize Austria to put down nationalist revolts in Italy.

Continuing during these years to control Russian foreign policy closely, Alexander pursued a flexible course of cooperation with France and Austria. In the foreign office, 1816–1822, he maintained both Ioannes A. Capodistrias, a liberal aristocrat from the Greek island of Corfu, and Karl Nesselrode, a conservative Austrophile and polished European diplomat. Capodistrias, a close friend of Alexander who overshadowed the self-effacing Nesselrode in the foreign ministry, favored constitutionalism and moderate reform, ardently espoused Greek independence, and remained committed to constructing a new European order based on independent national states. By contrast the obedient but capable Nesselrode established close ties with Europe's leading conservative statesman, Prince Metternich of Austria.

National revolts in the Balkans against Ottoman Turkish rule faced Alexander and his successors with tough choices over the so-called "Eastern Question." This involved the future of the Ottoman Empire, the Balkan Christians, the sensitive issue of control of the Turkish Straits—the Dardanelles and Bosphorus—and access to the Mediterranean for Russian merchant ships and warships. Should Russia stand forth resolutely as the protector of the Balkan Christians, especially the Orthodox majority of Serbs, Greeks, and Bulgars, against Turkish rule, or should it defend the sultan of Turkey as a legitimate monarch? Should Tsar Alexander seek to preserve the weakening Ottoman Empire and thereby ensure peace and stability, or should he reach agreements with other interested powers to partition European Turkey, or perhaps transform the Ottoman Empire into a Russian client state?

The Greek Revolt of 1820–1821 tested severely Alexander's precarious balancing act between liberal constitutionalism and status quo conservatism. Preoccupying European diplomacy during much of the 1820s, the Greek question threatened to involve Russia in war with the Porte.* Early in 1821 Alexander Ypsilanti, a Greek officer serving in the Russian army, left Russia illegally and invaded Turkish-ruled Moldavia, sparking revolts in Greece and

---

[1] Quoted in Frederick Artz, *Reaction and Revolution, 1814–1832* (New York, 1934), p. 164.

*A term commonly applied to the Ottoman government.

Greek appeals for Russian support. Some army officers and expansionists in St. Petersburg advocated a Russian war against the Porte, but Alexander realized that Ottoman collapse might well destroy the Concert of Europe and provoke dangerous opposition from other great powers. Therefore in 1822 Alexander, repudiating the Greekophile approach of Capodistrias, turned toward Austria and dispatched a secret mission to Vienna to reach agreement about Greece with Metternich. The latter persuaded the tsar to dismiss Capodistrias and refuse aid to the Greek rebels; this initial Greek national revolt was then suppressed by the Turks.

Friendly relations between Russia and the United States were achieved under Alexander I. The two countries had first exchanged ambassadors in 1809, drawn together by a common hostility to England as mistress of the seas. An admirer of the American Constitution, Alexander had corresponded with President Thomas Jefferson, whom he held in high esteem. During the War of 1812 Russia supported the United States as a naval rival of Britain. After 1815, however, basic socioeconomic and ideological contradictions between republican America and autocratic serf Russia appeared.[2] From Alaska, then Russian America, Russians had moved south to found Fort Ross (1812) near San Francisco Bay, and between 1815 and 1817 followed indirect Russian efforts to influence or control Hawaii. Alexander I's efforts on behalf of the Holy Alliance to restore Spanish rule in newly liberated Latin America provoked the United States to issue the Monroe Doctrine in December 1823, a policy backed by Great Britain. However, a confrontation between Russia and the United States was avoided: the treaty of April 1824 restricted Russian claims in Alaska to the region north of 54° 40′ latitude; Russia pledged to respect freedom of navigation and fishing in North American coastal waters; and renounced any intervention in Latin America. By renouncing any further expansion in North America, Alexander I facilitated the establishment of friendly relations between the United States and Russia, both of which remained antagonistic to the policies of Great Britain.

NICHOLAS I: GUARDIAN OF THE STATUS QUO, 1825–1852

The reign of Nicholas I (ruled 1825–1855), dubbed by contemporaries the "Iron Tsar" for his conservative and repressive policies and his formidable appearance, amounted in many ways to a continuation of trends evident during the last decade of his brother's rule but without Alexander's perplexing dualism. Nicholas assumed power following the abortive Decembrist revolt in which mostly liberal army officers aimed to achieve a constitutional monarchy and end serfdom. A few, such as Paul I. Pestel, son of the governor-general of Siberia, advocated a radical republic.

---

[2]N. N. Bolkhovitinov, *Russko-Amerikanskie otnosheniia 1815–1832* (Moscow, 1975), pp. 1–2.

NICHOLAS I, "THE IRON TSAR," RULED 1825–1855

Punishing the Decembrists harshly, Nicholas henceforth was suspicious of educated army officers. Far more conservative by education and inclinations than Alexander, Nicholas pursued similar policies abroad. He viewed Russia as a mighty fortress that would preserve and protect conservative principles by force if necessary and saw himself as its supreme commander to whom everyone owed unquestioning obedience. Lacking Alexander's idealism, vagueness, and mysticism, Nicholas adopted a direct, frank, and forceful approach in foreign policy. At times he acted boldly and won major initial gains, yet until some major miscalculations that contributed to the coming of the Crimean War, he sought consistently to avoid any general conflict and to maintain reasonable and peaceful relations with the Western powers. He was the unusual militarist who desired peace. While Nicholas usually acted as his own foreign minister, his foreign ministry executed his decisions without question. Count Nesselrode, continuing as foreign minister throughout the reign, served as the perfect foil for his imperious master: polished, European, and cautious, without ambition to play an independent role, he was also an extremely able diplomat.

As Nicholas I arrived in Moscow for his coronation in July 1826, he learned that the Persian army had invaded the Russian Caucasus and captured three towns. Late that year Nicholas dispatched General I. F. Paskevich to the Caucasus, where during the next two years he scored several decisive victories until Persia sued for peace. By the Treaty of Turkmanchai (1828) Russia secured most of Armenia with Erivan and advanced its frontiers to the Araxes River. Paskevich, whom Nicholas dubbed "the father commander," was named Count Paskevich-Erivanskii. Whereas the Caucasian lowlands had been conquered fairly easily, Russian control of the mountainous areas remained very insecure. In the late 1820s a strong Muslim resistance movement, known in Russia as Muridism, developed in rugged Daghestan. Its initial leader, Kazi Mullah, proclaimed a holy war on Russia. Religious and national hatred of Russians was fostered by Cossack occupation of mountain lands belonging to Muslim tribesmen. After Kazi Mullah's death in 1834, an able and successful commander, Shamil, led the mountaineers in guerrilla warfare and for two decades inflicted humiliating defeats on Nicholas' Army of the Caucasus. Nicholas considered that Shamil's victories endangered Russia's security in the south since the British, then predominant in Persia, afforded sympathetic support to the Muslim rebels. Nicholas' spit-and-polish, parade-ground army proved highly ineffective in the Caucasus fighting.

Nicholas I regarded state relations with the Ottoman Empire as far more important than those with Balkan peoples struggling for their independence. He remarked to the Austrian ambassador: "I abhor the Greeks, although they are my co-religionists; . . . I look upon them as subjects in open revolt against their legitimate sovereign; I do not desire their enfranchisement; they do not deserve it."[3] At times he dealt with the Porte unilaterally, but generally Nicholas proved willing to cooperate with the Western powers—Britain and France—in order to avoid conflict with them over the Balkan region. Thus the Protocol of St. Petersburg (1826) provided for Anglo–Russian cooperation in dealing with the Greek revolution, which resulted in the emergence of first an autonomous, then an independent Greece. In January 1826 Nicholas outlined clearly his views on the troublesome Eastern Question:

> I must without fail bring this matter to a rapid conclusion . . . I will be happy to reach an agreement with all of my allies on this question whose

---

[3]Quoted in W. Bruce Lincoln, *Nicholas I* (Bloomington, IN, 1978), p. 118.

importance . . . I vividly recognize. . . . I want peace in the East. . . . But . . . if even one of my allies should betray me, then I will be obliged to act alone.[4]

And the Emperor told Lord Aberdeen on a visit to England in 1844: "I do not claim one inch of Turkish soil, but neither will I allow that any other [power] shall have an inch of it."[5]

Thus it was not out of any love for Greeks or Serbs that Nicholas I in March 1826 issued an ultimatum to the Porte demanding Turkish evacuation of the Danubian Principalities (Moldavia and Wallachia) and fulfillment of Turkish pledges to Serbia included in the Treaty of Bucharest (1812). Lacking western support, the Turks had to yield, and by the Convention of Akkerman (October 1826) recognized the autonomy of Serbia and the Danubian Principalities and guaranteed free passage for Russian merchant ships through the Turkish Straits. However, the following year when the Turks refused to accept terms presented by the powers (Britain, France, and Russia) to settle the Greek question, the Turkish fleet was destroyed by an Allied naval force at Navarino Bay. The sultan promptly repudiated the Akkerman Convention and declared a holy war on Russia. Nicholas at first expected that the Porte would yield to a show of military force. Instead Russia had to fight a difficult and costly war with Turkey (1828–1829). After Fieldmarshal I. F. Paskevich captured Erzerum in Asia Minor and Russian forces approached Constantinople, the sultan, in the Treaty of Adrianople (1829), had to reaffirm the Akkerman Convention, make the Danubian Principalities a Russian protectorate, and cede Georgia and more Black Sea coastline to Russia. Nicholas thus assumed a position of preeminence in Ottoman affairs. From then until the Crimean War it became Russian policy to maintain the territorial integrity of a weak Porte under Russian protection. Foreign Minister Nesselrode, the architect of that policy, in a remarkable memorandum, declared that it was Russia's interest "in having a weak power [Turkey]—a state always menaced by internal revolt of its subjects—as our neighbor."[6]

The Porte's subservience to Russia increased further after the revolt of Mehemet Ali, pasha of Egypt, against the sultan in 1832. After France and Britain had refused to aid him, the sultan turned in desperation to Russia, which dispatched land and naval forces and prevented Mehemet Ali from capturing Constantinople and helped the European powers arrange peace. The Treaty of Unkiar-Skelessi (July 1833), marking the apogee of Russian influence in Turkish affairs, provided that Russia would aid the Porte militarily upon request and that the Turks would close the Dardanelles strait to foreign warships. This treaty safeguarded Russia's vulnerable Black Sea

---

[4]Quoted in Lincoln, p. 115.

[5]Quoted in Lincoln, p. 116.

[6]Vincent Puryear, *England, Russia, and the Straits Question, 1844–1856* (Berkeley, CA, 1931), p. 8.

coast and authorized Nicholas to protect European Turkey against external invasions. However, strong Anglo–French objections to Unkiar-Skelessi induced Nicholas to conclude the Treaty of Münchengrätz (September 1833), by which Austria and Prussia accepted the terms of Unkiar-Skelessi and pledged to preserve the Ottoman Empire against rebellious vassals. In effect this nullified any unilateral Russian protectorate over the Porte.

Because of Western agitation in Constantinople, Nicholas could not long keep the Porte in servile dependency. The British ambassador, Lord Ponsonby, counterbalanced Russian influence and helped the sultan regain considerable freedom of maneuver. While Nicholas and Nesselrode remained moderate, pacific, and defensive, Ponsonby and an English journalist, David Urquhart, whipped up anti-Russian feeling in Britain. A widespread movement of suspicion and hatred of Russia, known as Russophobia, swept through Britain and France, contributing importantly to eventual conflict. When Mehemet Ali revolted again, touching off another Near Eastern crisis in 1839–1840, Russia cooperated with the western powers to restrict him to Egypt and the Treaty of Unkiar-Skelessi lapsed. In 1841 the powers signed a Straits Convention with the Porte that barred foreign warships from the Straits while the Ottoman Empire was at peace. Russia thus remained secure unless the Ottoman Empire were a belligerent.

The European Revolutions of 1830 and a major revolt in Russian Poland challenged the conservative policies of Nicholas I. In France the July Days (July 28–30) overturned the reactionary regime of Charles X, which Nicholas was disinclined to defend. However, initially he refused to recognize the liberal July Monarchy of Louis Philippe because he believed that it violated the principle of legitimacy, a key pillar of the Vienna Settlement. But finding little support for such a course in Vienna or Berlin, Nicholas had to renounce any military intervention to restore Charles X and eventually followed Austria and Prussia in recognizing the regime of Louis Philippe. Nicholas likewise wished to intervene to suppress the Belgian revolt against the United Netherlands in order to protect the domains of a legitimist Dutch king, but the other powers opposed this. Reluctantly, Nicholas accepted the neutral Belgium negotiated by the powers. Then in November 1830 the Poles, inspired by ideals of nationalism and Romanticism, revolted against Russian rule symbolized by Nicholas' militaristic brother, Grand Prince Konstantin Pavlovich. After the latter's failure to act decisively, Nicholas appointed Fieldmarshal Paskevich to command the large Russian forces in Poland which, by August 1831, had crushed the Polish insurrection whose remnants sought refuge in Prussia. Ending the constitutional Kingdom of Poland, created by Alexander I in 1815, Nicholas replaced it with the Organic Statute of 1832, which divided Russian Poland into provinces.

A far graver challenge to the conservative system upheld by the three eastern monarchies were the Revolutions of 1848, which alarmed Nicholas I much as the French Revolution of 1789 had frightened Catherine the Great. The February Revolution in Paris was followed by the ouster of the formidable Prince Metternich in a March revolution in Vienna and riots in Berlin that induced the Prussian king to promise a constitution. Revolution had apparently triumphed throughout Europe except in Great Britain and the Russian Empire. But growing divisions among the revolutionaries enabled Nicholas and the conservatives to prevail eventually once again. From the fall of 1848 on, Habsburg and Hohenzollern troops reconquered power for conservative Austrian and Prussian regimes while Nicholas adhered reluctantly to military non-intervention. However, Hungary remained under liberal nationalist control, threatening to inflame neighboring Poland. To Nicholas the Hungary of the democratic nationalist Lajos Kossuth represented the center of a dangerous revolutionary contagion that might well infect his empire. In April 1849, responding to an urgent appeal from the Austrian Habsburgs, Nicholas sent a powerful Russian army into Hungary to defeat "the enemies of order and tranquillity in the whole world." The Hungarians were crushed, but bitter feeling developed between Austrian and Russian forces. The following year Austro-Prussian antagonism enabled Russia to intervene and arbitrate a settlement of the German question which insured Austrian predominance and the divided Germany that was in the interests of both Austria and Russia. Thus in 1850 the Russia of Nicholas I continued to stand as the apparently invincible champion of conservative and legitimate monarchy and the dominant military power in Europe.

THE CRIMEAN WAR, 1853–1856

The Crimean conflict, which pitted a diplomatically isolated Russia against the Ottoman Empire, Great Britain, France, and Piedmont–Sardinia, marked the disastrous denouement to Nicholas I's reign, altering significantly the European balance of power as well as Russia's foreign and domestic policies. The war was fought by the Western powers ostensibly to contain a Russia they viewed as threatening to dominate the Ottoman Empire, the Balkans, and perhaps Europe as well. Western scholars, such as Harold Temperley, have argued that the Crimean War represented a legitimate Anglo–French response to aggressive Russian expansionism first revealed to them by the Treaty of Unkiar-Skelessi; others, such as Norman Rich, question this view. Patriotic Soviet historians, denying indignantly any Russian aggressiveness, have portrayed the Crimean War as a just struggle in defense of legitimate Russian national interests. Each of these views contains some validity. The disintegration of the Concert of Europe, which even after British withdrawal had worked unofficially to resolve dangerous great power disputes through international conferences, was accelerated by strong new forces unleashed by the Revolutions of 1848 and by new forceful personalities. One of these was Napoleon III, the nephew of the great Napoleon, who named himself emperor of the French in 1852, sought legitimacy and domestic support for his imperial rule, and attempted to destroy the Vienna Settlement of 1815.

As a recent scholarly account emphasizes, the Crimean War was no mere accident, nor was it primarily the outcome of diplomatic bungling, although both sides committed serious errors. Preceding the war was a lengthy diplomatic crisis that provided abundant opportunities to resolve differences through negotiation. These efforts failed chiefly because neither the Turks nor some leading Western statesmen wished the negotiations to succeed and therefore blocked a peaceful solution. These leaders included Napoleon III of France and Lord Palmerston and Stratford Canning of Great Britain.[7] Nicholas I and his special envoy, Prince A. S. Menshikov, contributed to the end result by their arrogance and tactlessness.

A "quarrel of monks" was the immediate, apparently trivial, issue out of which three great European powers and the Ottoman Empire stumbled into a useless and fruitless conflict involving casualties of more than half a million men. About 1850 Latin and Greek Orthodox priests in Palestine, then under Ottoman rule, quarreled over their respective rights at the Holy Places. During the eighteenth and early nineteenth centuries the Orthodox had largely prevailed in that question. The issue was very important to Russia as the main protector of the Orthodox inasmuch as there were some 13 million Orthodox Christians in the Ottoman Empire and thousands of Orthodox pilgrims came to Palestine annually compared to a relative handful of Catholics. Napoleon III, having just established his Second Empire and needing Catholic support, aimed to destroy the Vienna Settlement of 1815, undermine Russian preeminence, and restore France to its former position of European leadership. Therefore he supported strongly Latin claims to the Holy Places and sought alliance with Britain. Confirming Napoleon's broader objectives, his foreign minister, Drouyn de Lhuys, declared in July 1852:

> The question of the Holy Places . . . was of no importance whatsoever to France. All this Eastern Question which provoked so much noise was nothing more for the [French] imperial government than a means of dislocating the continental alliance which had tended to paralyze France for almost half a century. When finally an opportunity presented itself to provoke discord within this powerful coalition, the Emperor Napoleon immediately seized it.[8]

In December 1852 the Turks, bowing to French threats and military demonstrations, conceded all that Napoleon III had demanded on behalf of the Catholics at the Holy Places.[9]

Nicholas I responded promptly by mobilizing two Russian army corps in southern Russia and alerting his Black Sea forces. Nicholas jotted down his ideas as to how Russia might counter Franco–Ottoman actions in order to secure Orthodox and Russian rights. Eschewing any drastic Russian move, Nicholas considered partitioning the Ottoman Empire among the major

---

[7]Norman Rich, *Why the Crimean War?* (Hanover, NH, 1985), pp. 4–8.

[8]Quoted in Rich, pp. 20–21.

[9]Ann Saab, *The Origins of the Crimean Alliance* (Charlottesville, VA, 1977), p. 10.

European powers as "the least bad of all bad possibilities."[10] Receiving the emperor's notes, Nesselrode urged Nicholas to abandon all schemes of partition noting that the emperor himself had stated previously "that the maintenance of the Ottoman Empire is closely linked with the true interests of Russia."[11] As "the least dangerous method" to secure Russian rights, Nesselrode suggested sending a prominent special envoy to Constantinople to remind the sultan of his previous pledges to Russia and the Orthodox.

Nicholas dispatched on this mission a personal aide and former navy minister, Prince Alexander S. Menshikov, whose manner was arrogant and threatening. He was accompanied by the commander of Russia's Black Sea Fleet, the chief of staff of the army in Bessarabia, and the son of Foreign Minister Nesselrode. The clear purpose of this formidable delegation was to frighten the sultan into submitting to Russian demands and to reassert slipping Russian prestige at the Porte. However, Menshikov proved indecisive and naive, allowing the Turks to play their favorite game of delay and procrastination for almost three months. Menshikov also was firmly bound by instructions, drawn up supposedly by Foreign Minister Nesselrode but reflecting Nicholas' own thinking, stipulating that the Turks must confirm previous Russian and Orthodox rights in a formal treaty. Opponents of Russia asserted that Turkish compliance would have reduced the Ottoman Empire to a Russian protectorate. Menshikov forced the replacement of the Turkish grand vizier with Reshid Pasha, who was supposedly favorable to Russia but actually cooperated with its enemies.

The effect of Nicholas' blustering diplomacy drew Great Britain and France together to oppose what they believed was the prelude to Russian aggression. Returning in April as British ambassador to Constantinople, Lord Stratford Canning, a convinced Russophobe, deceived Menshikov and helped persuade the Turks to reject scaled-down Russian demands to protect the Orthodox. Although a compromise solution of the Holy Places dispute was worked out, when Menshikov's demands, presented a second time as an ultimatum, were not fully accepted by the Turks, Menshikov left Constantinople angrily in May 1853 as his instructions dictated. Lord Stratford, rejoicing at the failure of the Menshikov mission, urged London to continue its hard line against Russia. Emperor Nicholas, furious over rejection of his terms, threatened to occupy the Turkish-ruled Danubian Provinces of Moldavia and Wallachia under Russian protectorate since 1829. After the British and French fleets were dispatched to Besika Bay near Constantinople, the Turks, on June 16, 1853, rejected a final Russian ultimatum. Russian troops thereupon occupied the Danubian Principalities. Nicholas' overconfidence and numerous diplomatic blunders on both sides had brought the two sides to the brink of war.

---

[10] Rich, p. 22.
[11] Rich, pp. 22–23.

Only then, belatedly, did the Concert of Europe seek a compromise diplomatic solution to avert conflict. The Vienna Note, drawn up chiefly by the French ambassador and agreed to by the four powers—Great Britain, France, Russia, and Austria—guaranteed the rights of Orthodox priests in the Holy Places, and would assuage Russian prestige and safeguard Ottoman sovereignty. Revealing his essential moderation and refuting assertions of his aggressiveness, Emperor Nicholas accepted the Vienna Note unreservedly. That should have ended the diplomatic crisis. But the Turks, encouraged by Lord Stratford, demanded amendments that would have altered the entire tone of the note. Russia refused to accept those changes and Count Nesselrode reaffirmed Russia's treaty rights to intervene in the Ottoman Empire to protect its coreligionists. The ambassadors of the powers in Vienna abandoned the Vienna Note in dismay.

A series of moves toward war followed. Rejecting Nicholas' continued conciliatory overtures, the British ordered their fleet through the Turkish Straits, thus violating the Straits Convention of 1841 and encouraging Turkish obduracy. In October 1853, spurning Western advice, the Turks demanded by ultimatum that Russia evacuate the Danubian Principalities; when no answer came, the Porte declared war on Russia. In November the Turks foolishly sent their fleet to Sinope in the Black Sea where the Russians destroyed it. This aggressive Turkish move was described in London as "the massacre of Sinope." When Nicholas sent an envoy to Vienna with more conciliatory proposals, Great Britain and France, brushing them off, demanded that Russia evacuate the Principalities, but Nicholas refused and the Western powers declared war. Austria and Prussia, while supporting the Western ultimatum, remained neutral. War had come because all parties had committed serious mistakes and misinterpreted the others' intentions. As the crisis deepened, the British public grew excited as the yellow press whipped up indignation over Sinope. The Concert of Europe was smashed beyond repair by a war that erupted, notes the biographer of British War Secretary Sidney Herbert, "because the Western powers had already determined on war in every case but that of absolute and unconditional submission on the part of Russia."[12]

As the Crimean War began, Nicholas I remained overconfident about his beloved army. Russian forces had gained overwhelming victories in earlier conflicts against Persians, Turks, and Polish insurgents. However, in those contests the Russians had possessed great numerical superiority and better artillery. More sobering should have been Russia's inability to subdue Shamil's Muslim guerrilla forces. As it headed into the Crimean conflict, Nicholas' army remained a force of serfs with noble officers in which brutal discipline and punishments prevailed. Nicholas proved unrealistic about Russia's diplomatic situation. Because Russia previously had cooperated

---

[12]From Lord Arthur H. Stanmore, *Sidney Herbert of Lea: A Memoir*, 2 vols. (London, 1906), quoted in Rich, pp. 105–06.

MAP **3-1**   **The Crimean War, 1853–1856**

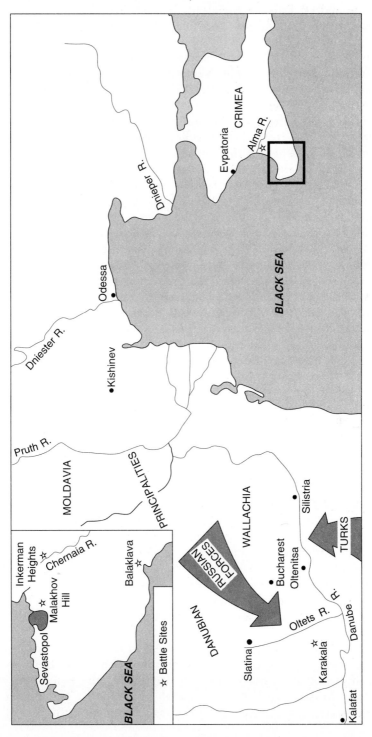

closely with Austria and Prussia, the emperor counted minimally on their neutrality and on Prussian friendship. Instead, the German powers allied with one another, mobilized, and compelled Nicholas to withdraw from the Danubian Principalities. Facing the constant threat of an Austrian invasion of Russian Poland and having to maintain considerable forces in the Caucasus to watch Shamil, Nicholas could employ only a fraction of his total forces against the Turks and Western Allies, thus preventing any major Russian invasion of Anatolia. In indecisive, small-scale battles early in 1854 in the Danubian Principalities the Russians fared poorly, then withdrew that summer behind the Pruth River.

The Crimean peninsula then became the focal point of conflict. Despite many warnings that the naval base at Sevastopol was the Allies' major objective, Nicholas at first sent few reinforcements there. With no railway lines south of Moscow, troops and supplies had to be sent by horsecart over muddy, rutted roads and few of them arrived in the Crimea. The initial Russian commander in the Crimea was Prince Menshikov, who lacked experience as a commander of land forces. Mistrustful of subordinates, he kept his own generals in the dark, and was cautious and indecisive. The Allies sent an expeditionary force to the Crimea, won the Battle of Alma against Menshikov, and besieged Sevastopol, hastily fortified by the able Colonel E. I. Todleben. A crucial battle at Inkerman Heights overlooking Sevastopol (October 1854) revealed other Russian shortcomings: no good map of the area was available to the Russian command, the chain of command was confused, and failure to commit reserves cost the Russians a probable victory.

On February 15, 1855, Emperor Nicholas removed the incompetent Menshikov and replaced him with the reputedly more energetic Prince M. D. Gorchakov. Exuding optimism on his arrival, Gorchakov soon concluded that the situation was hopeless and defeat inevitable. Three days later the "Iron Tsar," dismayed at the failure of his huge army to dislodge the Allies from the Crimea, died of pneumonia. His death scarcely affected the outcome of the war. In the continuing struggle at Sevastopol, the Russians were hampered by severe shortages of powder and supplies, insufficient and poorly trained troops, inferior weapons, and incompetent leadership. Late in 1855, after the Allies overran Malakhov bastion, a key position, Prince Gorchakov withdrew his forces across the bay and abandoned Sevastopol to the enemy. The final blow to Russia was diplomatic: Austria sent an ultimatum demanding that unless Russia accepted terms set by the Allies, she would join them in the war.

Nicholas' well-trained and realistic son had assumed power as Alexander II (ruled 1855–1881) with a flexible group of advisers who realized that Russia faced disastrous defeat unless the Allied terms were accepted. The Treaty of Paris (1856) ended the Crimean conflict on reasonable terms. The Allies insisted that Russia completely demilitarize the Black Sea, which meant no Russian battlefleet or coastal fortifications. The province of Bessarabia, annexed by Russia in 1812, was retroceded to the Porte. Russia had to relinquish its vague treaty rights to unilateral intervention on behalf of Orthodox Christians of the Ottoman Empire; those rights passed to the European Concert. However, these were limited reverses. No ethnically Russian territory had been lost nor had the main Russian army been defeated. Major Russian victories over the Turks in the Caucasus, including the capture of Kars, helped counterbalance the loss of Sevastopol.

Nonetheless, the Crimean War proved highly significant in Russian history and foreign policy. Temporarily reducing Russian prestige and power, especially in the Balkans and Europe, the Crimean defeat stimulated Alexander II's regime to seek to recover it elsewhere with victories. The defeat convinced Russian leaders of the necessity to emancipate the serfs and introduce other major reforms in order to save the regime, the Romanov dynasty, and Russia's role as a great power. Furthermore, the Crimean War undermined the strength of the European Concert and unleashed the powerful force of nationalism. By alienating Russia from Austria, the Crimean conflict ended, at least temporarily, cooperation among the three conservative east European monarchies and foreshadowed their subsequent fatal conflict over the Balkans. The Treaty of Paris, regarded in Russia as unnecessarily humiliating, made her a revisionist power. Russia's new leaders resolved to overturn humiliating peace provisions, such as demilitarization of the Black Sea (known as the "Black Sea clauses"), and to recover full freedom of action, essential for a great power.

Suggested Readings

Atkin, M. *Russia and Iran, 1780–1828*. Minneapolis, MN, 1980.

Bailey, Thomas A. *America Faces Russia*. Ithaca, NY, 1950.

Barker, A. J. *The War Against Russia, 1854–1856*. New York, 1971.

Barratt, G. *Russia in Pacific Waters, 1715–1825*. Vancouver, Canada, 1981.

Baumgart, W. *The Peace of Paris, 1856*. Trans. A. Saab. Santa Barbara, CA, 1981.

Curtiss, J. S. *Russia's Crimean War*. Durham, NC, 1979.

Grimsted, P. *The Foreign Ministers of Alexander I*. Berkeley, CA, 1969.

Ingle, H. *Nesselrode and the Russian Rapprochement with Britain, 1836–1844*. Berkeley, CA, 1976.

Lincoln, W. B. *Nicholas I: Emperor and Autocrat of all the Russias*. Bloomington, IN, 1978.

Marriott, J. A. R. *The Eastern Question*. Oxford, England, 1940.

Mosely, P. E. *Russian Diplomacy and the Opening of the Eastern Question in 1838 and 1839*. Cambridge, MA, 1934.

Presniakov, A. E. *The Emperor Nicholas I of Russia*. Ed. and Trans. J. Zacek. Gulf Breeze, FL, 1974.

Puryear, Vincent. *England, Russia and the Straits Question, 1844–1856*. Berkeley, CA, 1931.

Rich, Norman. *Why the Crimean War? A Cautionary Tale*. Hanover, NH, 1985.

Saab, Ann P. *The Origins of the Crimean Alliance*. Charlottesville, VA, 1977.

Seaton, Albert. *The Crimean War*. New York, 1977.

Webster, C. K. *The Foreign Policy of Palmerston, 1830–1841*. London, 1951.

Woodhouse, C. M. *Capodistrias: The Founder of Greek Independence*. New York, 1973.

4

RUSSIA AND EUROPE IN
AN AGE OF REFORM, 1855–1881

The death of the "Iron Tsar" and defeat in the Crimean War marked the end of the old Russian regime that had combined serfdom with unfettered autocracy. Under Alexander II, despite his basic conservatism, dawned a period of hope and optimism as Russian leaders pursued new directions. Far-reaching changes were implemented in many areas of Russian life by an able group of enlightened bureaucrats trained in the reign of Nicholas I. This internal transformation and a gravely depleted treasury compelled the regime of Alexander II to follow a cautious, pacific course in Europe. While seeking to restore Russia's prestige and place in European affairs, Alexander realized the necessity of avoiding conflict with major powers. Eventually, domestic reforms improved Russia's standing abroad as they overcame the negative effects of the Treaty of Paris.

THE "GREAT REFORMS"

Well-educated and well-prepared to assume control, Alexander II succeeded his father, Nicholas I, at age thirty-six. One of his tutors, the poet V. A. Zhukovskii, is often credited with inculcating humane attitudes in Alexander. However, while praising Alexander's intelligence and seriousness, his tutors noted his tendency to be easily halted by obstacles. As a youth he was the weakwilled, obedient son of an authoritarian father, inclined to be indecisive and emotional. Throughout his life Alexander fought hard against irresolution and developed a stubbornness which encouraged him to adhere to difficult decisions and carry policies through to completion. As heir to the throne Alexander had given no indication of liberal views, so serfowners were not worried by his accession.

Serfdom, with its low productivity and degradation of an ignorant population, had existed in Russia for about 250 years. Confirmed legally in 1649, it remained until 1861 the cornerstone of the entire Russian social structure. In the eighteenth century serfdom spread to Ukraine and western borderlands, becoming much more onerous for the peasantry. Roughly half of the Russian peasants in 1860 were private serfs living mostly on noble estates under conditions of near slavery. The other half were state and court

Alexander II, "the Tsar-Liberator," ruled 1855–1881

peasants enjoying considerably better conditions, especially after reforms under Nicholas I. Soon after his accession, Alexander II expressed the hope that Russia's "domestic order [might] be strengthened and perfected" and that everyone might flourish under the rule of law.

The emancipation of Russia's peasants during the 1860s—the greatest of the so-called "Great Reforms"—constituted Alexander II's courageous attempt to transform Russia into a more modern country capable of facing European powers on equal terms. Since 1790 members of the Russian intelligentsia had attacked serfdom as a moral and economic evil while rural unrest swelled dangerously. Defeat in the Crimean War had thrown a bright spotlight on Russia's socioeconomic, technological, and military backwardness.

Alexander II was persuaded by the warning of his new liberal war minister, Dmitrii A. Miliutin: "Serfdom does not permit us either to reduce the term of [army] service or to increase the number of unlimited leaves so as to diminish the present number of troops."[1] The tsar realized that Russia could not remain a great power unless the serfs were freed and the army completely reorganized. Even radicals believed initially that the Treaty of Paris had opened a new era of change and relied on the renovating power of a flexible autocrat. Both Alexander and his liberal brother, Grand Prince Konstantin Nikolaevich, played key roles of leadership and persuasion in the emancipation. They sought to enlist the cooperation of the nobility but constantly pushed the emancipation process forward. Freeing court and state peasants proved relatively simple: all land they had tilled previously was transferred to their ownership and former rents were converted into redemption payments for the land. Emancipating the private serfs proved arduous and lengthy since the regime aimed eventually to provide them with sufficient land for a livelihood. They were emancipated personally in 1861, but dividing the land between them and the nobility and their redemption payments continued until the Revolution of 1905.

Other reforms stemmed largely from the Emancipation. In 1864 began the process of establishing district and provincial assemblies *(zemstva)* elected by all classes in order to perform local tasks for which the central government lacked the personnel and desire, such as building roads and bridges, and setting up public schools and clinics. This newly established principle of local self-government conflicted inevitably with the theory of autocracy. Although the nobility dominated them, the zemstva became centers for liberal change and reform. However, the regime blocked efforts by their liberal leaders to extend self-government to the national level through a constitution or a parliament. The antiquated, repressive court system of Nicholas I was replaced partially with a modern European system featuring public jury trials, irremovable judges, and equality before the law, but peasants entered these courts only if involved in litigation with members of another class. In education, universities were allowed to teach all subjects and were freed from most of Nicholas' repressive controls. Secondary schools were reorganized and opened to all classes and creeds. Censorship was greatly relaxed; many new newspapers and periodicals appeared.

War Minister Miliutin transformed the Russian army. Under Nicholas I Russia had maintained Europe's largest standing army. The postwar financial crisis virtually compelled basic changes. Even before the Emancipation Alexander II, in 1859, reduced the term of compulsory army service from 25 to 15 years. In 1864 fifteen regional military districts replaced Nicholas' overcentralized, bureaucratic system. Most brutal punishments were abolished, military schools were reformed and opened to all social

---

[1] Quoted in Alfred Rieber, *The Politics of Autocracy: Letters of Alexander II to Prince A. I. Bariatinskii 1857-1864* (Paris, 1966), p. 25.

classes, and military justice was greatly liberalized. Miliutin's crowning achievement was the universal military training law of January 1874, which proclaimed that "the defense of the fatherland forms the sacred duty of *every* Russian citizen." At age twenty Russian youths of all social classes would be drafted into the army for from six months' (for university graduates) to six years' service (for those without education). These reforms gave Russia a smaller, better-trained standing army with large reserves and much improved morale.

At the heart of these "Great Reforms" was the all-class principle, which lowered class barriers and began to develop a sense of common citizenship. Unfortunately, the autocracy and bureaucracy guarded their powers jealously and interfered constantly with new institutions. Conservative noblemen and officers managed to halt the reforms short of completion. Russia remained a country half reformed, half traditional.

THE MAKING OF FOREIGN POLICY UNDER ALEXANDER II

For centuries the ruler had controlled Russian foreign policy, altering it at his whim, declaring war, concluding treaties, and hiring and firing ministers at will. Often headstrong and overconfident, Nicholas I had personally dominated foreign relations. Alexander II was less knowledgeable about foreign affairs than either Nicholas or Alexander I and left its day-to-day conduct to subordinates. Less self-confident, Alexander II was also more flexible and often accepted sound advice. Alexander, revealing laudable caution and common sense, avoided great risks or dangerous adventures and possessed a sound, overall grasp of Russia's position in the world. However, at times he displayed a lamentable lack of decisiveness and proved susceptible to various elements and interest groups. At key junctures—in Central Asia in 1865 and in the Balkans in 1877–1878—Alexander lost overall control of Russian foreign relations, allowing nationalist or pro-Slav elements to impose their policies. Evident especially after 1871 was a strong and growing personal link between the tsar and his uncle, King William I of Prussia, who became emperor of Germany in 1871.

Other members of the imperial family exercised no direct or major influence over foreign policy and played minimal roles in its formulation. However, the heir to the throne, the future Alexander III, in the 1870s aligned himself chiefly with the pro-Slav element. Alexander II, like other Romanov rulers, carefully guarded his autocratic powers; thus he permitted no cabinet to debate or help determine decisions in foreign policy. Under Alexander II foreign policy remained that of the tsar.

In November 1855, nine months after Alexander II's accession to the throne, the aged foreign minister, Count Karl Nesselrode, submitted his resignation. As his political testament, Nesselrode in February 1856 submitted a detailed memorandum outlining the policies he believed Russia should pursue once peace had been concluded. Russia, argued Nesselrode, must concentrate primary attention on domestic affairs and on recovery.

Russian foreign policy, he admonished, must remain both monarchical and anti-Polish. He warned against the dangers of an alliance with France which he feared that his successor might adopt.[2]

In April 1856 Alexander II appointed as his new foreign minister, Alexander M. Gorchakov, the first native Russian to hold that office in many years. As the scion of a prominent Russian noble family who was responsible to the emperor alone, Gorchakov soon raised the foreign ministry to new importance. He had spent a lengthy career abroad as a diplomat, largely in Germany, and had participated successfully in the negotiations which ended the Crimean War. With his perfect command of French and the techniques of diplomacy, intimate knowledge of Europe and its leaders, Gorchakov proved excellent at maneuver and in developing felicitous formulas. He described his role modestly as being "a sponge which yields at the pressure of the imperial hand the liquid with which it is filled." Thus the transition from Nesselrode to Gorchakov produced no sharp break or reversal, but merely a change in emphasis. As Gorchakov was taking office, Alexander II was telling Alexis Orlov, a fellow diplomat: "After her recent trials, Russia must concentrate on her own affairs and seek to heal by domestic measures the wounds inflicted by war." In a famous circular later that year, Gorchakov expressed a similar approach: *"La Russie ne boude pas. La Russie se recueille."* ("Russia is not sulking. Russia is simply withdrawing within herself.")[3]

Gorchakov proved able, like Nesselrode before him, to collaborate closely and harmoniously with Alexander II. However, his own lack of forcefulness and decisiveness when added to Alexander's own often robbed Russian policies abroad of decisiveness and clarity. Gorchakov's shortcomings, which became more pronounced with age, included extreme vanity, superficiality, and almost complete ignorance about non-European areas and remarkable unconcern for what transpired there. His subordinates in the foreign office, notably A. G. Jomini and A. F. Hamburger, were competent but second-rate and unoriginal. Gorchakov was too vain to permit anyone with real dynamism around him.

The Foreign Ministry under Alexander II split into two major factions advocating rather different approaches toward foreign affairs. The Diplomatic Chancellery consisted chiefly of Gorchakov's own entourage and the officials who staffed the chief posts at the courts of the great European powers—in London, Paris, Vienna, and Berlin. They were mostly men of foreign origin or foreign names and high social status. Initially, Baltic Germans such as Meyendorff, Osten-Sacken, and Mohrenheim were prominent. Later, Russians with polish, culture, and social influence like P. A. Shuvalov, E. P. Novikov, and P. A. Saburov occupied these key ambassadorial

---

[2]W. E. Mosse, *The European Great Powers and the German Question 1848–71* (Cambridge, England, 1958), p. 70.

[3]Mosse, pp. 73–75.

A. M. GORCHAKOV, FOREIGN MINISTER, 1856–1882

posts. They were mostly pro-European in outlook and often were rather ignorant of Russia and even of the Russian language. Conducting their diplomacy and writing their dispatches in French, which Gorchakov preferred, they usually favored solutions reached through negotiation with other European powers at conferences. They were willing to play the complex game of European power politics according to definite, agreed-upon rules and formulas.

The Asiatic Department had been created within the Foreign Ministry in 1819 to handle Russia's relations with all non-European areas. Included within its purview were the affairs of European Turkey and its Balkan Christians. Under Alexander II the Asiatic Department exercised far more influence than previously because of its greater autonomy under the able and dynamic Count N. P. Ignatiev (1861–1864) and his successor, P. N. Stremoukhov (1864–1875). Containing none of Gorchakov's cronies, the Asiatic Department tended to regard the Diplomatic Chancellery men as effete, artificial, gilded, excessively Europeanized, and thus insufficiently patriotic. The Asiatic Department drew its personnel chiefly from native Russians, middle-class professionals, and people of Balkan or Asiatic origin, who conducted their correspondence mainly in Russian. Usually they possessed special training in Oriental languages and were strongly nationalistic in outlook. Scorned by the snobs of the Diplomatic Chancellery, Asiatic Department men were rarely promoted beyond the consular level. Generally, the work of the department was coordinated by its highest ranking member, Russia's ambassador in Constantinople. This was especially the case under Count Ignatiev, who served as ambassador in Constantinople, 1864–1877. Advocating a decisive, Russia-first policy very different from that of Gorchakov, Ignatiev proved a formidable foe and rival of the foreign minister. Able, ambitious, and difficult to control, Ignatiev followed a semi-independent course, especially in the 1870s, which gave Russian foreign policy a perplexing duality. While Ignatiev served in Constantinople, the Asiatic Department was directed by Stremoukhov, likewise a Russian nationalist but a moderate one. In 1875 he was replaced by N. K. Giers, a capable professional who became Gorchakov's assistant and eventual successor.

Among other agencies with significant influence upon Russian foreign policy under Alexander II was the War Ministry. Its direction by an intelligent, dynamic minister, D. A. Miliutin, with much influence over the emperor, gave the War Ministry sometimes decisive importance. Miliutin favored cautious policies in Europe and the Balkans and moderate expansion in Asia while avoiding any major conflict. The War Ministry controlled governors and governor-generals in far-flung frontier regions as well as military commanders who frequently disregarded decisions of the Foreign Ministry and committed the government to risky, unwanted policies.

Public opinion, despite the "Great Reforms," exerted generally slight influence on decisions in foreign policy. Until 1906 Russia lacked a national parliament that might exercise control, limit appropriations, or subject officials to questioning. Despite a liberalized censorship, the press was sharply restricted in discussing foreign policy issues, although it often managed to do so, and had to be very cautious in criticizing official policies. With a few exceptions, public attention was focused on domestic issues, and there was almost no way to make public pressure effective. The most significant exception to this rule was the powerful public sympathy for the Balkan Slavs expressed during the Eastern Crisis of 1875–1878. Through the Slav Committees and pro-Slav newspapers this was translated into public pressure on the government and emperor for decisive action. That campaign proved unusually effective partly because of the indecisiveness of the emperor and the Foreign Ministry. However, generally the tradition of absolutism in foreign affairs persisted to a greater degree in Russia than in other European countries. This was partly because Russia lacked really

Count N. P. Ignatiev, Ambassador to Turkey, 1864–1877

vital interests abroad and its foreign trade remained relatively small. Thus, as historian Boris Nolde pointed out,[4] foreign policy issues were treated generally as abstract problems of state which could be improvised, changed, and goals quickly abandoned. Thus foreign and domestic policies in Russia normally were widely separated. The government could conduct its foreign policy with little regard for domestic considerations, mainly for reasons of state.

The humiliating and painful Crimean defeat left Alexander II determined to avoid war with a major European power and above all with a

---

[4]Baron Boris E. Nolde, *L'Alliance franco-russe: Les origines du système diplomatique d'avant guerre* (Paris, 1936), pp. 166–68.

European coalition. This made the Russian leadership more anxious than previously to negotiate solutions to major problems with European governments. During Russia's relative power eclipse, 1856–1870, Alexander II sought to maintain its favorable European boundaries while restoring the country's prestige and equality in European affairs.

What were the chief problems in Russia's overall relationship with Europe under Alexander II and his successors? One crucial issue was the Polish question. The partitions of Poland (1772–1795) tended normally to draw together in their defense the three conservative monarchies of central and eastern Europe: Russia, Prussia–Germany, and Austria. On the other hand, Polish aspirations to freedom and independence attracted much ideological and humanitarian sympathy in France and Britain. Paris remained the chief center of Polish émigrés, highly influential in this era under the direction of Prince Adam Czartoryski, former assistant Russian foreign minister. Second, the German question became transformed during Alexander II's reign by the aggressive and successful policies of the outstanding Prussian statesman, Otto von Bismarck. Prior to the 1860s Germany had remained fragmented among numerous petty states that tended to look either to Prussia or Austria for leadership, creating the famous German dualism. For almost two centuries Russian preeminence in eastern Europe had been based partially on a sharply divided Germany. Were the German dualism to be replaced by a unified and powerful Germany on its western borders Russia's power position might well be imperiled. However, this danger did not seem great as long as Prussia was ruled by Alexander II's beloved uncle, William I. Finally, Russia and Great Britain were rivals in world politics. As Russia expanded in central Asia toward India and attempted to enhance its position in the Near East and at the Turkish Straits, its imperial rivalry with Britain increased and at times, as in 1878, threatened to lead to war.

FRANCO–RUSSIAN ENTENTE, 1856–1862

During the first years after the Crimean War, Russia's main alignment in Europe was an informal and partial entente, or understanding, with France based on some similar interests. Napoleon III of France had become a spokesman for the rights of smaller and oppressed nationalities against the conservative Austrian Empire. Already at the Paris Congress of 1856, a friendly understanding had developed among Russian, French, and Sardinian representatives, united by common hostility to repressive Austrian rule in northern Italy. Afterwards Russian leaders sought to exploit potential divergences between Britain and France in order to break up the Crimean coalition. In that endeavor Foreign Minister Gorchakov, emotionally pro-French, proved to be an able tactician.

In early 1857 the Crimean conflict seemed to be a fading memory as France and Sardinia actively sought Russian support on the Italian question. The Russian envoy to Sardinia, Count Ernst Stackelberg, at a dinner given for him by Count Cavour, Sardinia's leading statesman, declared: "Our two countries must be good friends since there are no interests which divide them and they have common grudges (that is, against Austria) which bring them together."[5] In the fall of 1858 Napoleon III sought to arrange Franco–Russian cooperation in the approaching Austro–Sardinian War he had helped to plan. The following year while Napoleon aided Piedmont–Sardinia militarily to expel the Austrians from Lombardy, Russia remained benevolently neutral as its leaders gloated at Vienna's discomfiture. This promoted Russia's long-term aim of splitting the Crimean coalition and ending her isolation. The limits of this new Franco–Russian relationship were set by Alexander II who restrained an enthusiastic Gorchakov out of the former's continuing distrust of Napoleon III's eventual aims. However, the result proved favorable to Russia: a unified Italy by 1861 friendly to Russia and a weakened Austrian Empire. Furthermore, Napoleon III, during his negotiations with Russia, had indicated that, for him, the neutralization of the Black Sea under the Paris Treaty was a negotiable affair.

Common hostility to Austrian domination of the Danubian region stimulated Franco–Russian cooperation in southeastern Europe. Thus, in 1860, France and Russia sponsored the achievement of the partial unification of the Danubian Provinces, subsequently Romania, and their autonomy within the Ottoman Empire. Again partially motivated by Austrophobia, both powers fostered the Greater Serbian policies of Prince Mihailo Obrenović and his foreign minister, Ilija Garašanin. Similarly they collaborated in the expulsion of King Othon from Greece. Russian policy under Alexander II thus differed markedly from that of the "Iron Tsar" in its willingness to sanction armed revolts against legitimate rulers, sometimes in actions contrary to international agreements.

The Polish Insurrection of 1863 against Russian rule revealed the fragility of this Franco–Russian entente drawing the Crimean allies together in common condemnation of Russian tyranny and repression. The defiant Poles received diplomatic support from Napoleon III and the British government, backed strongly by Anglo–French public opinion. As Austria joined their joint diplomatic protests, this three-power intervention seemed to threaten a new Crimean war. Later in 1863, as the crisis deepened, Napoleon III advocated military intervention, and a French landing on the Baltic coast loomed as a definite possibility. However, British opposition to military involvement helped restrain a French emperor who was deeply involved already in Mexico. The French attitude was partly a traditional one of opposing Russian predominance in Poland and partly a protest against the mistreatment of Catholic clergy.

COOPERATION WITH PRUSSIA AND GERMAN UNIFICATION, 1863–1871

As Russia's relations with France and Britain deteriorated, Alexander II looked somewhat desperately to Prussia for assistance against the Poles and

---

[5]W. E. Mosse, *The Rise and Fall of the Crimean System, 1855–71* (London, 1963), pp. 117–18.

for diplomatic support. The Alvensleben Convention of February 1863 with Prussia provided for common action against the Poles. Meanwhile Foreign Minister Gorchakov won a rather undeserved reputation as a fiery Russian patriot by his sharp diplomatic notes to the Western powers refusing any concessions to their demands. His success in defying France and Britain on the Polish question did much to restore Russian prestige and self-confidence.

For the next twenty-five years Russia was aligned primarily with Prussia, then with Germany, and contributed significantly to German unification. The reasons for this renewed Russo–Prussian alliance were both historical and sentimental. The two powers had cooperated during the period from the Congress of Vienna until the Crimean War. Alexander II found the Prussian tie very satisfying for dynastic and ideological reasons. Otto von Bismarck, the conservative Junker who achieved power in 1862 as minister-president of Prussia, helped pave the way for Russo–Prussian cooperation during his ambassadorship in St. Petersburg (1859–1862). He found that the Russian court shared his conservative political convictions and feared a possible triumph of Prussian Liberals. An alliance with Prussia, Alexander told Bismarck in 1862, was dear to his heart and was in the true interests of Russia.[6]

The Russo–Prussian alliance aided Russia greatly in weathering the Polish crisis of 1863; Russia repaid its partner during the Austro–Prussian War of 1866 with a benevolent neutrality that tied down Austrian forces on the Russian frontier. Oblivious to the long-term significance of a unified Germany, Gorchakov calculated that Prussia's support and a weakening of Austria and France would aid him in revising the Treaty of Paris by abrogating the "Black Sea clauses." Assured once again of Russia's benevolent neutrality, Bismarck helped provoke the Franco–Prussian War of 1870 as the final stage in his successful campaign for German unification. Initially, Gorchakov worked on behalf of Prussia to ensure both Austrian and Danish neutrality. Then after the decisive Prussian victory at Sedan and the capitulation of Napoleon III, Gorchakov sought Bismarck's support to eliminate the "Black Sea clauses." Assured of Prussian support, in October 1870, with French resistance to Prussian armies weakening, Alexander II informed his ministers that he had decided to denounce the "Black Sea clauses." Gorchakov thus dusted off his circular drawn up the previous year and sent it to Russian envoys abroad: Russia, it argued, could not be expected to observe all provisions of an oft-violated Treaty of Paris. Gorchakov's circular was soon published and received enthusiastic support from the Russian public. However, the British press almost unanimously denounced Russia's de-nunciation of the "Black Sea clauses"; some papers demanded immediate war with Russia. Fortunately, Prime Minister William Gladstone, skillfully holding British public anger in check, worked for a peaceful compromise. In 1871 the European powers at a conference in London ratified this

---

[6]*Immediatbericht* of Bismarck, April 8, 1862, cited in Mosse, *The European Powers*, p. 96.

arbitrary Russian action since it had become clear that they could not keep the Russian Black Sea demilitarized permanently. Repudiation of the "Black Sea clauses" brought Foreign Minister Gorchakov to the zenith of his career as he was rewarded with the title of chancellor of the empire by a grateful Alexander II. However, the price which Russia paid for this symbolic liberation was exorbitant: a unified and powerful German Empire right on its frontiers. Actually, for decades Russia could not afford either to rebuild its Black Sea fleet or its coastal fortifications.

THE THREE EMPERORS' LEAGUE AND ITS BREAKDOWN, 1871–1881.

With the Black Sea's deneutralization in 1871, the Crimean system designed by Lord Palmerston to block Russian expansion lay moribund. Still lingering on was the Triple Treaty of April 1856 by which Great Britain, France, and Austria had pledged to protect and enforce the territorial integrity of the Ottoman Empire. But when the Turks in 1870 had inquired what London would do in case of Russian aggression, Gladstone realized that prospects of support from either of its Crimean partners were remote. Knowing that a great power could not be held permanently in humiliation and inferiority, the Austrians had long since reconciled themselves to abrogation of the "Black Sea clauses." By 1871 the Crimean system had lapsed in the face of major changes in the European power balance confirmed by Prussia's victory over France. Also, Russian leaders had never wavered after 1856 in their determination to revise the Paris Treaty.[7]

Having seen his goal of German unity confirmed at the hall of mirrors in Versailles, Bismarck attributed the highest importance to maintaining the alliance with Russia in order to safeguard the new imperial Germany. Alexander II's friendship seemed to him the most reliable element in the new European situation created by the unifications of Italy and Germany. He sought to play off Russia against Britain while reinforcing the Russian alliance. Germany soon assumed European leadership with Chancellor von Bismarck as the dominant figure in diplomacy. To make Germany fully secure, Bismarck realized the necessity of establishing a solid relationship as well with Austria–Hungary. In August–September 1871 the German and Austrian emperors agreed to cooperate to maintain the status quo, and the new Austro–Hungarian foreign minister, the Magyar Count Gyula Andrássy, urged close ties with Germany in the face of the potential danger he perceived from Russia.

This prepared the way for the conclusion in 1873 of the League of the Three Emperors *(Dreikaiserbund)*. Ideological bases for cooperation of the three conservative monarchies were weaker than in 1815, although the Polish question still united them. Worried by growing Austro–German intimacy, Alexander II virtually invited himself to an imperial reunion in

---

[7]Mosse, *Crimean System*, pp. 190 ff.

Berlin in 1872. Bismarck told the British ambassador: "It is the first time in history that the three Emperors have sat down to dinner together in the interests of peace. I wanted these three Emperors to form a loving group like Canova's three graces. . . . All three think themselves greater statesmen than they are." Their foreign ministers also attended. While Bismarck was charmed by Count Gyula Andrássy, "but as for that old sot of a Gorchakov, he gets on my nerves with his white cravat and his pretensions."[8] Although the agreements of the three sovereigns were too vague to prove binding, until 1875 the Dreikaiserbund kept France effectively isolated in Europe. The alliance was a reaffirmation of the old dynastic politics where rulers determined policy rather than responsible ministers.

The war scare that erupted in the spring of 1875 revealed the fragility of the Dreikaiserbund. On April 8, 1875, the Berlin *Post* published a bellicose article entitled, "Is War in Sight?" which emphasized the danger to peace represented by French rearmament. Reports circulated in France, which was wholly unprepared for war, of German plans for a preventive war before France could recover fully from the Franco–Prussian conflict. Much alarmed, the French foreign office alerted other European governments to the alleged danger. Gorchakov assumed leadership in moves to prevent war by organizing Anglo–Russian support for France. He reassured the French ambassador, "Bismarck cannot make war upon you when he has the moral opinion of Europe against him, and he will have" and affirmed that "France, strong and powerful, is necessary to Europe."[9] With typical vanity Gorchakov then took all the credit for preserving peace when Bismarck disavowed any idea that Germany intended making war on France. Embroiling Gorchakov with Bismarck, the "war scare" incident foreshadowed the coalition which defeated Germany in World War I.

Three months later revolts by Slav Christians erupted in Turkish-ruled Bosnia and Hercegovina which developed into the Balkan Crisis of 1875–1878.* Bismarck welcomed this crisis for taking the heat off Germany and distracting European attention from Franco–German tensions, but by promoting Austro–Russian hostility, it shattered the Dreikaiserbund. Bismarck cooperated with Austria's Andrássy and Gorchakov in seeking a compromise diplomatic solution to the crisis by pressuring the Turks to grant reforms to their Balkan Christian subjects. When such efforts failed at the Constantinople Conference, partly because of British support for the Turks, Bismarck acted as arbiter between Austria–Hungary and Russia in order to prevent them from fighting and thus destroying his entire diplomatic system. Once Austria and Russia, by the Budapest Convention of early 1877, had

---

[8]N. Japikse, *Europa und Bismarcks Friedenspolitik* (Berlin, 1927), pp. 29-31, citing dispatches from the Public Record Office, London.

[9]William Langer, *European Alliances and Alignments 1871–90*, 2nd ed. (New York, 1956), p. 39.

*For the Balkan Crisis see Chapter 5.

set certain limits to Russian action in the Balkans, Bismarck then encouraged Russia to make war against the Porte. Following victory, Russia dictated peace to Turkey at San Stefano (March 1878) on terms unacceptable to both Austria–Hungary and Britain. Russia faced the probability of war with both and Alexander II and his advisers realized there was little hope of winning. In May 1878 Russia and Great Britain reached a compromise agreement that scaled down Russian gains. At that point Chancellor Bismarck agreed to host the Congress of Berlin (June–July 1878), where he sought to act as "honest broker" between the contending powers, and a European solution to the Balkan Crisis was worked out. This dismayed Russian nationalists, who viewed its terms as a betrayal of the Slavs.

Russia emerged from the Berlin Congress virtually isolated diplomatically. Already, in April 1878, Austria–Hungary and Germany had reached a secret agreement for cooperation; Great Britain remained hostile. In 1879 a formal Austro–German alliance was concluded after Bismarck overcame Emperor William's desire to continue reliance on Russia. However, Russia's reaction, instead of drawing closer to republican France as Bismarck feared, was to go begging to Bismarck hat in hand. This led directly to the revival of the Dreikaiserbund in 1881, although Austro-Russian relations remained cool. The assassination of Alexander II in March 1881 by members of the People's Will organization found Russia aligned firmly with Germany internationally.

Suggested Readings

Bury, J.P.T., ed., *The Zenith of European Power.* London, 1966.

Corti, Egon. *The Downfall of Three Dynasties.* London, 1934.

Gall, L. *Bismarck: The White Revolutionary.* 2 vols. London, 1986–1987.

Holborn, Hajo. "Russia and the European Political System," in I. Lederer, ed., *Russian Foreign Policy: Essays in Historical Perspective.* New Haven, CT, 1962, pp. 377–415.

Langer, W. L. *European Alliances and Alignments, 1871–90.* New York, 1956.

Leslie, R. F. *Reform and Insurrection in Poland.* London, 1963.

Lincoln, W. B. *The Great Reforms: Autocracy, Bureaucracy and the Politics of Change in Imperial Russia.* Dekalb, IL, 1990.

Medlicott, W. N. *The Congress of Berlin and After: A Diplomatic History of the Near Eastern Settlement 1878–1880.* London, 1938.

Millman, R. *British Foreign Policy and the Coming of the Franco–Prussian War.* London, 1965.

Mosse, W. E. *The European Powers and the German Question, 1848–1871.* Cambridge, England, 1958.

———. *The Rise and Fall of the Crimean System, 1855–71.* London, 1963.

Rich, Norman. *The Age of Nationalism and Reform, 1850–1890.* London, 1970.

Simpson, J. Y. *The Saburov Memoirs.* Cambridge, England, 1929.

Sumner, B. H. *Russia and the Balkans, 1870–1880.* Oxford, England, 1937.

Taylor, A.J.P. *The Struggle for the Mastery of Europe, 1848–1918.* Oxford, England, 1954.

5

RUSSIA AND THE BALKANS, 1855–1881

If Russia comes to liberate, she will be received with great sympathy, but if she comes to rule, she will find many enemies.

Liuben Karavelov, a Bulgarian leader, in 1870

Under Alexander II Russian policy toward the Balkan peninsula was dualistic and confused. Radically different approaches were advocated by Foreign Minister Alexander M. Gorchakov and his chief rival, Count N. P. Ignatiev, Russia's ambassador in Constantinople. Peaceful assurances from St. Petersburg were challenged repeatedly by bellicose pronouncements from Panslav spokesmen and newspapers in the 1860s and 1870s. Russia failed to pursue consistent, well-conceived policies toward Balkan countries because the Gorchakov–Ignatiev rivalry reflected fundamental differences in principle. Both the St. Petersburg government and the Panslavs—that is, those advocating some type of Slavic unity and cooperation—tended to "play favorites" in the Balkans, which contributed to their fragmentation. It remained unclear whether the Panslavs aimed to unite Balkan Slavs under Russia's aegis or keep them divided in order to control them and the Turkish Straits.

From Peter the Great onward Russian leaders sought to dominate the Balkan region and the Straits for strategic, economic, and ideological reasons. Prior to the Crimean War, St. Petersburg viewed the Balkans primarily as a land bridge to Constantinople. Direct or indirect control over the Straits linking the Black Sea with the Mediterranean remained an important objective of Russian diplomacy to the end of the imperial regime. Furthermore, the Russian government considered itself the natural protector of Balkan Slav and Orthodox peoples, viewing them as natural allies against the German powers. Friedrich Engels, Karl Marx's collaborator, wrote prophetically in 1890:

> Russia needed only to proclaim its mission to protect the oppressed Greek Church and enslaved Slavdom and the terrain for conquest—under the cover of liberation—was already prepared.[1]

---

[1] Friedrich Engels, "The Foreign Policy of Russian Tsarism," in Paul W. Blackstock and Bert Hoselitz, eds., *The Russian Menace to Europe; A Collection of Articles, Speeches, Letters and News Dispatches by Karl Marx and Friedrich Engels* (Glencoe, IL, 1952), p. 28.

Nineteenth-century Russian emperors, aiming usually to preserve the Ottoman Empire and avoid wars with European states, also encouraged incipient Balkan liberation movements in Serbia and Greece. However, Nicholas I regarded semi-independent Serbia and Montenegro as mere tools of Russian policy, ignored their national interests, and overestimated their willingness to obey his dictates. Thus, on the eve of the Crimean War, the "Iron Tsar" forced from office Ilija Garašanin, premier and foreign minister of Serbia, for pursuing critical and independent policies toward Russia.[2] During that war Nicholas was gravely disillusioned by the Serbian states' refusal to side openly with Russia.

Tsarist Russia had few direct economic interests in the Balkans. Both regions, producing primarily agricultural products and raw materials, required capital resources and imported finished goods from western Europe. Therefore Russia could do little to promote Balkan economic development or to compete effectively there with European countries and their capitalists. Thus in 1880 Baron A. G. Jomini of the Russian Foreign Ministry warned his colleague, N. K. Giers, that Russia "has nothing to buy or sell in Bulgaria," which was equally true for other Balkan countries.[3] Nevertheless, when political considerations dictated it, Russia extended short-term credits to Serbia (1867–1878) and Bulgaria (1878–1885).

RECOVERING PRESTIGE AND INFLUENCE, 1856–1875

The Treaty of Paris (1856), by revoking Russia's claimed right of unilateral intervention on behalf of Balkan Christians and retroceding southern Bessarabia to Turkey, sharply reduced Russia's prestige in the Balkans for a time. Although Alexander II and Gorchakov considered the restoration of Russian influence there a high priority, they had to devise policies providing Russia with a lengthy breathing spell to enable Russia to recover militarily and financially from the Crimean defeat. In the meantime Russia's freedom of maneuver in the Balkans and Straits was limited severely by the provisions of the Paris Treaty and by military and political problems in the Caucasus, Poland, and Central Asia. Although Russia continued support to Balkan national liberation struggles against the Porte, a Foreign Ministry memorandum of March 1856 emphasized the need for restraint. However, in that very year, Russia and France raised the issue of the future of Moldavia and Wallachia and secured the withdrawal of Austrian occupation forces. In 1859 the union of the two provinces under Prince Alexander Cuza's rule represented the first major step in creating a national Romania.

Russia and France likewise aided Montenegro's continuing struggle for independence from Turkey. Following the Turkish invasion of Montenegro

---

[2]See David MacKenzie, *Ilija Garašanin: Balkan Bismarck* (Boulder, CO, 1985), chap. 8.

[3]Charles Jelavich, *Tsarist Russia and Balkan Nationalism: Russian Influence in the Internal Affairs of Bulgaria and Serbia, 1879–1886* (Berkeley, CA, 1958), p. 69.

early in 1858, Russia protested strongly. After the Turkish military defeat, a conference of European powers extended Montenegro's boundaries somewhat. In 1862 an anti-Turkish uprising broke out in neighboring Hercegovina; Montenegro assisted it. When the Turks invaded Montenegro, Russia and France supported her diplomatically. Montenegro met defeat, but Franco–Russian diplomatic pressure preserved its territorial integrity.

Meanwhile St. Petersburg was strengthening its influence in vassal Serbia. In December 1858 the abdication of Prince Alexander Karadjordjević and the restoration of Prince Miloš Obrenović represented a victory for Franco–Russian influence and a defeat for Austria. Foreign Minister Gorchakov first supported Miloš, then his Europeanized but autocratic son Prince Mihailo Obrenović and his Foreign Minister Ilija Garašanin. In November 1860 Gorchakov affirmed to Russia's consul in Belgrade that Serbia, because of its strategic position "has become the center and point of support for other Slav areas of Turkey." Six years later, writing his consul in Bucharest, Gorchakov reaffirmed that policy:

> Bearing in mind that our policy in the East is directed mainly toward strengthening Serbia materially and morally and giving her the opportunity to stand at the head of the movement in the Balkans, the Foreign Ministry has decided to subordinate to this plan all of its further activities in regard to arming the Slav peoples in Turkey.[4]

In the 1860s Russian Panslavs, advocating South Slav unification under Russian leadership, welcomed Serbia's leadership of the Balkan Slavs. In January 1858 had been formed a private but officially approved organization, the Moscow Benevolent Committee to foster Slav cultural and religious activities under Ottoman rule and to educate Slav students in Russia. An early statement by its leaders, A. S. Khomiakov's *Epistle to the Serbs from Moscow* (1860), warned the Serbs to spurn western European institutions and ideas and to follow their "elder brother," Russia, along the correct path of Orthodoxy. Its arrogance and paternalistic tone alienated many Serbs. Another leading Russian Panslav and later chairman of the Moscow Committee, Ivan Aksakov, expressed dismay at the "European poison" allegedly infiltrating the Balkans. Appalled by the Francophile atmosphere of the Montenegrin court, he also denounced Serbia's adoption of parliamentary institutions as an attempt to "imitate the external forms of European civilization."[5]

In 1867 the Moscow Committee sponsored a Moscow Slav Congress attended by distinguished scholars from western and southern Slav lands. Before it began, Ivan Aksakov proclaimed in his newspaper, *Moskva:*

---

[4]A. Popov, "Russkaia politika na Balkanakh, 1860–1878 gg.," in *Avantiury russkogo tsarizma v Bolgarii* (Moscow, 1935), pp. 197–98.

[5]I. S. Aksakov, *Polnoe Sobranie Sochinenii*, vol. 1 (Moscow, 1886), pp. 23–29.

... God has assigned a lofty task [to the Russians]: to serve the liberation and rebirth of its enslaved and oppressed brethren. There is in Russia no desire for usurpation, no thought of political domination. It desires but the freedom of spirit and life for those Slavic peoples which have remained faithful to the Slavic confraternity.[6]

But when the hosts suggested using Russian as the Slavs' common literary language, a leading Serbian delegate, Dr. Vladan Djordjević objected, stressing that the Serbs belonged to European civilization.[7] While stimulating pro-Slav activity in Russia, the Slav Congress foreshadowed the manifold difficulties obstructing genuine Slav brotherhood.

Count N. P. Ignatiev, the leading Panslav in the Russian government, as minister in Constantinople in 1864 (ambassador, 1867–1877), urged an immediate solution of the "Eastern Question" by Russia and the Balkan peoples. After negotiating the Treaty of Beijing (1860),* Ignatiev had been named an aide-de-camp to the tsar and henceforth exerted great influence over Russian foreign policy. Ignatiev advocated a Russo–Slav war against the Porte. Once the Turks had been defeated, a Serbo–Bulgarian state ruled by Serbia's Prince Mihailo should be formed under Russian guidance. It could then annex Bosnia while neighboring Hercegovina might join Montenegro.[8]

Following Prince Mihailo's accession in 1860, official Russia gave him strong diplomatic support. Russia and France soon agreed to seek removal of all Turkish garrisons from Serbia and to enable it to build up its own army. After the Turks bombarded Belgrade in June 1862, a special European conference convened at Kanlidze near Constantinople at Russia's urging. Thanks to this Russian backing and the efforts of the Serbian leaders, Garašanin and Jovan Ristić, in 1867 the Turkish garrisons were all withdrawn, leaving Serbia virtually independent.

Both the Russian Foreign Ministry and Panslav leaders supported strongly the efforts of Prince Mihailo and Garašanin in 1866–1868 to create a Serbian-led Balkan League in order to liberate the Balkan peoples from Turkish rule. Encouraged by Russia, Serbia established military alliances with Montenegro and Greece, a friendship pact with Romania, and informal ties with Croatian and Bulgarian nationalists. Russia subsidized Serbia's war preparations, but a Russian military mission sent to inspect the Serbian army found it poorly organized and prepared. Late in 1867 Prince Mihailo reached agreement with Austria, backed away from war, and removed the militant Garašanin as foreign minister. Russia thereupon suspended war credits.

---

[6]*Moskva*, March 28, 1867, quoted in M. B. Petrovich, *The Emergence of Russian Panslavism, 1856–1870* (New York, 1956), p. 201.

[7]Petrovich, pp. 228–29.

*See Chapter 7.

[8]N. P. Ignatiev, "Zapiski, 1864–1874," *Izvestiia Ministerstva Inostrannykh Del*, no. 1 (1914), pp. 93 ff.

Prince Mihailo's murder in June 1868 by Pavle Radovanović merely confirmed the end of close Serbo–Russian cooperation and the collapse of the first Balkan League.

Nonetheless, the pro-Slav movement in Russia continued to grow. In 1868 a St. Petersburg section of the Moscow Benevolent Committee was founded, which included as members high army officers and government officials such as Count Ignatiev. Other Slav committees were formed in Kiev (1869) and Odessa (1870). To be sure, the committees' practical achievements remained modest. A number of Balkan Slav students, chiefly Bulgarians, were educated in Russia, and were later prominent in Bulgaria's liberation. However, they were inspired largely by radicals like N. G. Chernyshevskii rather than by conservative Panslavs. Sending minor financial aid to Balkan churches and schools, the Slav committees stimulated Russian interest in the Balkan Slavs.

The Balkan region remained generally calm from 1868 to 1875. The League of Three Emperors (formed 1873) aimed to preserve the status quo and prevent disruptive revolts or conflicts. Foreign Minister Gorchakov, accepting the European balance of power concept, emphasized peaceful negotiation to resolve differences. St. Petersburg gave clear priority to great power relationships over its Balkan interests while encouraging the Balkan Slavs nevertheless to view Russia as their political protector.

Continuing to challenge Gorchakov's pro-European and pacific course was Count Ignatiev's Russia-first, Panslav, and aggressive approach. Operating from the influential Constantinople embassy, he coordinated the activities of Russian consuls in the Near East and Panslav agitation in Russia and the Balkans. Later, Ignatiev explained that his diplomatic aims had resembled Gorchakov's but his means had been more radical. He sought to destroy the Paris Treaty, recover southern Bessarabia, and control the Turkish Straits either directly or indirectly through Russian agreement with a dependent Turkey. Ignatiev believed Russia was destined to lead the Slav peoples and dominate the Balkans and Porte without concessions to other European powers:

> All my activities in Turkey and among the Slavs, 1861–1877, were inspired by . . . the view that Russia alone could rule in the Balkan peninsula and Black Sea so that Austria–Hungary's expansion would be halted and the Balkan peoples, especially the Slavs, would direct their gaze exclusively to Russia and make their future dependent upon her.[9]

Through his consuls Ignatiev sought to foster chiefly Russian political influence, as expressed in his statement of 1877: "Austrian and Turkish Slavs must be our allies, the weapons of our policy against the Germans [Austrians]," Russia's chief opponents in the Balkans.[10]

---

[9]Ignatiev, "Zapiski," *Istoricheskii vestnik* (1914), vol. 135, p. 56.
[10]Quoted in L. S. Stavrianos, *The Balkans Since 1453* (New York, 1938), p. 292.

Despite his brilliant diplomatic skills, Ignatiev damaged Russia's prestige and future political position in the Balkans by helping to divide its peoples. The Bulgarian national movement had been developing more slowly than that of Greeks or Serbs, but the Bulgars looked chiefly to Russia for aid. In 1870 Ignatiev intervened to foster creation of a separate Bulgarian Orthodox church (Exarchate), complicating the explosive Macedonian question that would embroil Bulgarians, Serbs, and Greeks for generations. Ignatiev was seeking to enhance his, and Russia's, leverage at Constantinople. Anxious to divide the Balkan peoples, the Porte granted the Bulgarians very favorable terms for a separate church thereby deepening the rift between them and the Serbs and Greeks.[11] Both Ignatiev and official Russian policy stimulated Bulgarian separatism and Montenegrin rivalry with Serbia.

From 1868 to 1875 semi-independent Serbia and Montenegro remained absorbed in domestic problems and mutual rivalry. Montenegro then was Russia's main Balkan foothold and its Prince Nikola became Alexander II's protégé. Despite Regent Jovan Ristić's proclaimed goal of unifying the Serbs, Belgrade's role eroded under the regency while Montenegro and the Vojvodina in Hungary emerged as rival Serbian centers. As the Balkan League of 1867 dissolved, ties linking Serbia with other Yugoslavs weakened. Ristić's initial overtures to Russia were dismissed coldly by Gorchakov. But then in 1871 the Serbian regency and St. Petersburg, alarmed at revolutionary and liberal challenges posed by Svetozar Marković's socialists in Serbia and Svetozar Miletić's liberals in the Vojvodina, achieved a limited rapprochement. Alexander II received the young Prince Milan Obrenović in Livadia while Ristić sought stronger Russian support for the embattled Obrenović dynasty.

THE BALKAN CRISIS, 1875–1878

In July 1875 Slav Christians in southern Hercegovina revolted against Turkish misrule; this was soon followed by larger uprisings at Nevesinje further north, and by mid-August uprisings spread northward into Bosnia. After initial efforts at suppression failed, the Turks and the great European Powers (Britain, France, Germany, Austria and Russia) were confronted with a major crisis. As this movement threatened to become a Balkan struggle for liberation, relations between Russia and the Balkan Slavs again became crucial. At the urging of Russia and Austria–Hungary, Prince Milan of Serbia agreed to remain neutral unless Montenegro intervened. But returning to Serbia from Vienna, Milan was confronted by powerful national agitation for armed intervention. Taken by surprise but believing the Dreikaiserbund could restore peace, Alexander II denounced the Hercegovina insurgents as "bandits," while a Panslav newspaper, supporting the rebels, predicted Serbia would unify the Turkish Slavs.

---

[11]G. Trubetskoi, "La politique russe en Orient, le schisme bulgare," *Revue d'histoire diplomatique*, vol. XXI (1907), pp. 185 ff.

Official Russia advised Serbia and Montenegro not to aid the insurgents militarily. If Prince Milan were compelled to take responsibility for his actions, agreed the tsar and Baron A. G. Jomini, acting head of the Russian Foreign Ministry, he might be restrained. Thus Alexander instructed his consul in Belgrade, A. N. Kartsov, to warn the prince that if Serbia attacked the Turks, Russia would abandon him. However, Kartsov urged Prince Milan privately to take Serbia into war; Count Ignatiev too apparently urged the Serbs to fight. In September when Jovan Ristić's "action cabinet" took office in Serbia, St. Petersburg disapproved. The tsar and Gorchakov refused to deal with "dangerous radicals and warmongers" like Ristić.

Meanwhile Russia's press and public displayed increasing sympathy for the embattled South Slavs. General M. G. Cherniaev, editor of the Panslav *Russkii mir,* predicted that the insurgents aided by Serbia and Montenegro could liberate the Balkan Christians, and that Europe could not preserve the Balkan status quo. Most leading Russian newspapers backed the official policy of peace, but the Slav Committees grew ever more active. The St.

MAP 5-1   **Russia and the Balkans, 1876–1885**

Petersburg Committee won permission to collect contributions for civilian victims in Hercegovina throughout the Russian empire, but not to recruit volunteers.

After Ristić's "action cabinet" fell in October 1875, the Three Emperors' League warned that incursion of armed bands from Serbia into Ottoman territory would be considered aggression. Backed by that League's diplomacy, Prince Milan had rid himself of a bellicose cabinet he detested.

But only three months later Serbia moved again towards intervention. When Jovan Marinović, leading conservative opponent of war, withdrew from Serbian politics, Prince Milan could not resist the pro-war Ristić Liberals. If the insurrection resumed in the spring, warned the Austrian consul, fear of losing his throne would force Milan to act. In February 1876 Milan declared: "My decision has been made; war is inevitable." When the Austrian consul protested Serbia's war preparations, Milan pledged that Serbia would fight only if the insurgents resumed operations, Montenegro declared war, and the powers did not intervene.[12] Predicted *Russkii mir*'s correspondent in Serbia:

> Speak but one word, Russia, and not only the entire Balkan peninsula . . . but all the Slav peoples . . . will rise in arms against their oppressors. In alliance with her 25 million fellow Orthodox, Russia will strike fear into all of western Europe.[13]

St. Petersburg's policy toward the South Slavs remained unclear until in December 1875 Foreign Minister Gorchakov accepted the compromise Andrássy Plan and rejected Ignatiev's advice that Russia settle up directly with the Turks. Avoiding a full commitment to either Andrássy, the Austro–Hungarian foreign minister, or Ignatiev, Alexander II told the latter that a direct Russo–Turkish agreement would breach the Three Emperors' League. The tsar and Baron Jomini adhered to a middle course. Russia's official newspaper, reiterating Russia's support for the Three Emperors' League, also encouraged the South Slavs. In St. Petersburg Consul Kartsov could not obtain clear directives; Jomini confided that Gorchakov had no program. Returning to Belgrade, Kartsov advised Prince Milan officially to avoid warlike action. Receiving conflicting Russian messages, Prince Milan refused to halt Serbian rearmament or pledge neutrality. Officially Russian leaders advocated non-intervention, but privately the tsar, heir, and Gorchakov all sympathized with the insurgents while Russian public support for them increased. Thus Baron Jomini told a member of the St. Petersburg Committee in January 1876: "Do anything you like provided we know

---

[12]Austrian State Archives, report from Austrian consul in Belgrade (Haus-, Hof-, und Staatsarchiv (Vienna), P.A., Konsulat Belgrad), Wrede to Andrássy, January 15 and February 25, 1876, Nos. 3 and 19.

[13]*Russkii mir*, no. 1, January 1, 1876.

nothing about it officially."[14] While increasing public aid went to the insurgents, officialdom looked the other way.

In neighboring Bulgaria, still firmly under Turkish rule, young radicals led an abortive uprising in September 1875. Encouraged by insurgent successes in Bosnia and Hercegovina, a Bulgarian revolutionary group in Bucharest, supported by members of the St. Petersburg Slav Committee, prepared a general revolt for the spring of 1876. Poorly planned and implemented by inexperienced radicals, this April Uprising merely provoked massacres of Bulgarian peasants by Turkish irregular troops. Eventually, these massacres caused an outcry in Great Britain, but since the St. Petersburg government declined to intervene, the hour of Bulgaria's liberation had to be deferred.

That spring of 1876 tension escalated between the Serbian states and Turkey. A war psychosis dominated Serbia, which sought to revive the Balkan League of 1867 in order to liberate and unify all Serbs in Turkey into a single national state. Serbia's belligerence imperilled the Three Emperors' League since Russia would not compel Serbia to remain at peace. Foreign Minister Gorchakov's growing support for the autonomy of Bosnia-Hercegovina and for aggrandizement of Montenegro enhanced Russia's prestige in the Serbian world.

The unauthorized arrival in Belgrade in April 1876 of the retired Russian Panslav officer, General M. G. Cherniaev, conqueror of Turkestan,* heightened Serbia's bellicosity since that Russian firebrand repeatedly had advocated a Greater Serbia. When Cherniaev boasted of corresponding with an aide to the Russian heir, Serbian leaders realized his potential value to their war plans. Nullifying Russia's previous support of the pacific Andrássy Plan, Cherniaev's sudden arrival tilted the scales towards war: Serbian hawks concluded that Russia could be involved in a conflict with Turkey. On May 24 Prince Milan proclaimed Cherniaev a Serbian citizen and commander of its eastern armies. Quickly he requested a Russian loan of 500,000 rubles. Generously offering Serbia's mines and forests as collateral, Cherniaev claimed that Serbia would soon become an obedient dependency of Russia.[15]

Once Serbia and Montenegro allied, a war with Turkey became inevitable. The pro-Russian Metropolitan Mihailo of Serbia declared: "We count on the love of Russia and its brotherly sympathy for Orthodox and Slav sufferers. . . ."[16] As Russia's leaders hesitated, its Balkan consuls grew perplexed. Thus Alexander II ordered Kartsov in Belgrade to sever all ties

---

[14]Lenin Library (Moscow), Manuscript Division, "Dnevnik A. A. Kireeva," (diary) vol. VI, p. 114.

*See Chapter 6.

[15]David MacKenzie, "Panslavism in Practice: Cherniaev in Serbia (1876)," *Journal of Modern History,* vol. 36 (1964), pp. 282 ff.

[16]N. N. Durnovo, "K istorii serbskoi-turetskoi voiny 1876 g.," *Istoricheskii vestnik,* vol. 75 (1899), pp. 536–37.

MAP 5-2   Growth of Serbia, 1856–1913

with General Cherniaev and prevent Serbia from going to war, but Foreign Minister Gorchakov told the consul confidentially: "Do not forget that although the Tsar is opposed to war, his son, the heir to the throne, stands at the head of the [Slav] movement."[17] Gorchakov gyrated between the heir's "war party" and the tsar's peace faction. Meanwhile the Russian press

---

[17]A. N. Kartsov, "Za kulisami," *Russkaia starina*, vol. 134 (1908), pp. 70–71.

reflected growing Russian public support for war by the Serbian states. Thus Russia shared responsibility for the outbreak of the Serbo–Turkish War in June 1876. While Russia did not actually push the Serbian states into conflict, a split Russian leadership with clear pro-Slav sympathies robbed Gorchakov's diplomacy of credibility. Once Cherniaev arrived, Serbia's war party concluded that Russia could be dragged into a South Slav war of liberation.

Initially, Russian Panslavs and the Serbian states cooperated closely in the Serbo–Turkish War, but that conflict soon ended in defeat, disillusionment, and mutual alienation. Crossing the Turkish frontier General Cherniaev proclaimed: "We are fighting . . . for the holy cause of Slavdom . . ., for freedom. . . . Long live the unity of the Balkan peoples!"[18] He hoped to reach Sofia, Bulgaria, and solve the Eastern Question without the Russian army. More realistically, Ristić viewed Serbia's militia army as a Slav vanguard to drag Russia into war.

Displeased at the outbreak of war, Russian leaders resisted involvement in an unwanted conflict fostered by pro-Slav opinion. Refusing aid to the Serbian states, official Russia joined Austria–Hungary in proclaiming nonintervention. Alexander II instructed the Third Section, his political police, to recall the disobedient Cherniaev. Since Belgrade had spurned his advice, stated the tsar, Russia could not be blamed for leaving the Serbs to their fate. Strongly opposing a Russo–Turkish war, War Minister Dmitrii A. Miliutin declared it would be "a terrible misfortune."[19]

The Serbo–Turkish War tested the Three Emperors' League severely. In July 1876 at Reichstadt, Austria and Russia, reaffirming non-intervention, agreed secretly to regulate any postwar settlement but to allow the Serbian states territorial gains if they triumphed. Renouncing support for a large South Slav state, official Russia opposed a Greater Serbia. Gorchakov warned that if Serbia won, she would not obtain Bosnia but only a rounding of frontiers. Viewing the war as a crusade against Islam, Russian Panslavs predicted a Serbian victory provided Russian society aided the Serbs financially. That summer the pro-Slav movement in Russia "seized hold of all layers of society and thrust all other interests into the background."[20] Such a popular movement had scarcely been seen before in Russian history.

The unquestioned leader of this pro-Slav movement was Ivan S. Aksakov, chairman of the Moscow Slav Committee. He wrote K. P. Pobedonostsev:

> The Serbian cause has now become a Russian affair. . . . Russians . . . cannot lay down their arms without ruining Russian honor until they obtain something for Serbia.[21]

---

[18]H. Schulthess, *Europäischer Geschichtskalender 1876* (Nördlingen, Germany, 1877), p. 508.

[19]D. A. Miliutin, *Dnevnik* (Moscow, 1947–1950), vol. II, pp. 51–54.

[20]A. D. Gradovskii, *Sobranie sochinenii*, vol. VI (St. Petersburg, 1901), p. 227.

[21]Aksakov, 228 ff.

In vain Aksakov warned Cherniaev to reject partisan Serbian views on Bulgaria: "You are a Russian and we Russians must stand above Bulgarians and Serbs and adopt a broader view." Following Serbia's defeat, Aksakov cautioned him: "Only Russia can solve the Slav question, not even Russian society . . ., but Russia as a whole, as a *state* organism headed by the government."[22] Unofficial Russian financial aid to the South Slavs, although substantial, failed to meet their needs. Slav committees dispatched roughly 5,000 Russian volunteers of whom about 3,000 actually fought with Cherniaev's Serbian army.

Official Russia's relationship with the Slav committees and their volunteer movement remained ambiguous though the imperial court encouraged them. When Cherniaev reported an early victory at Šumatovac, Russian court leaders rejoiced. St. Petersburg vacillated over the volunteers when it could easily have prevented their dispatch. Commented War Minister Miliutin:

> . . . In this whole affair of the volunteer movement to Serbia the Tsar himself has acted in a dual manner and partly himself contributed to the spread of the conviction that the government encourages this movement. . . . The agitation from the Heir's residence goes entirely counter to accepted official policy; the Tsar knows this . . . and closes his eyes to it. With such duality can there be any definite system in our actions or any clear plan?[23]

General Cherniaev's role in Serbia reflected Panslav goals and methods. His slogan of South Slav liberation cloaked his Panslav aim to make Serbia a tool of Russia. His thorny relations with the tsar and Foreign Ministry revealed official coolness towards Panslavism; his program to solve the Eastern Question disregarded Russia's urgent need for amity with the German powers. Cherniaev's military and political failure in Serbia revealed Panslavism's bankruptcy in action. When he proclaimed Prince Milan "King" of Serbia, St. Petersburg repudiated him and his influence in Belgrade faded. However, his support of Greater Serbian nationalism endeared him to the Serbian public.[24]

Panslavism's chief philosopher, N. Ia. Danilevskii, tracing intra-Slav differences mainly to European influences, predicted they would disappear in a common struggle against non-Slavs. But the Slav Committee's envoy in Serbia wrote: "In Serbia collided two wholly different social structures and there was no connecting element which could facilitate their mutual understanding."[25]

As Cherniaev's Serbo–Russian army faced final defeat in southern Serbia at Djunis in October 1876, war fever spread to Russian official circles as

---

[22]David MacKenzie, *The Lion of Tashkent* (Athens, GA, 1974), pp. 160, 171.

[23]Miliutin, p. 70.

[24]MacKenzie, "Panslavism in Practice," pp. 296–97.

[25]G. Devollan, *Serbskii vopros pered sudom russkogo obshchestva* (St. Petersburg, 1877), pp. 15 ff.

shown by the mood at the tsar's palace in Livadia. A war plan by General N. N. Obruchev of the General Staff predicted that Russian armies could defeat the Turks and occupy Constantinople within three months and prevent formation of a hostile European coalition. Even the Foreign Ministry grew bellicose: Baron Jomini viewed this as Russia's best chance to crush the Turks. Russia responded swiftly to Cherniaev's and Prince Milan's desperate pleas to arrange an armistice; both Gorchakov and Ignatiev claimed full credit for the ultimatum to the Porte, which saved Serbia from destruction.

Serbia's debacle showed that the Serbian states with unofficial Russian aid could not defeat Turkish regulars. Russia's ultimatum reasserted official leadership, relegating the Slav committees and press to the backseat. However, Cherniaev's crusade committed official Russia to take decisive action. Russia's ultimatum and subsequent partial mobilization made a Russo–Turkish war virtually inevitable. Serbs and other Balkan Slavs still looked to Russia for their salvation.

At the great power Constantinople Conference (January 1877) Russia tried to resolve the Eastern Question by peaceful compromise. Count Ignatiev, treating Serbia like a poor relation, fostered Montenegrin and Bulgarian claims, but the Porte rejected even his minimum terms. In March Serbia made a separate peace with Turkey which caused Russian Panslavs to shift support to Montenegro and Bulgaria. Russia signed a secret convention with Austria insuring the latter's neutrality in a Russo–Turkish conflict, but Russia had to pledge not to create a large South Slav state and to concede Bosnia and Hercegovina to Austria–Hungary. Most Panslavs were prepared to sacrifice the western Balkans to Austria if Russia could dominate Bulgaria and control the Turkish Straits.

Declaring war on Turkey in April 1877, Alexander II scrupulously avoided inciting a Balkan war of national liberation. Nonetheless, Russian Panslavs rallied behind the government. As the Slav committees became obedient auxiliaries of the government, Panslav generals were assigned obscure posts. Whereas the Russian command wanted the small Balkan states to enter the war, the Foreign Ministry opposed it as complicating the peace settlement and increasing dangers of European intervention. Initially, the tsar accepted Gorchakov's insistence on a localized war fought for limited aims. Thus Russia rejected initial offers of military cooperation from Serbia, Romania, and Greece. In May Ambassadors P. A. Shuvalov (London) and E. P. Novikov (Vienna) persuaded Alexander II to avert complications with Great Britain by concluding peace with the Turks when Russian armies reached the Balkan Mountains.

But when he reached Russian military headquarters in the Balkans, the tsar repudiated that idea. By June most top Russian leaders were urging creation of a great, undivided Bulgaria and making Constantinople a free city. The Foreign Ministry yielded. When Serbian leaders met with the tsar at Ploesti, they learned that when the Russian army crossed the Danube River, Serbia would be urged to reenter the war. On June 28, crossing the

Danube, Grand Prince Nikolai Nikolaevich summoned Serbia to declare war and independence from Turkey. When the Serbs demanded large Russian subsidies, Alexander II told Serbia's envoy:

> Tell Milan I love him like a son, that he can count on my protection under any circumstances, and that Serbia's national future depends on her participation in the war. . . . *If Serbia does not cross the frontier within a twelve-day period, she is lost and her national future will be compromised forever.* . . .[26]

But subsequent Russian reverses at the fortress city of Plevna made Belgrade coy and evasive. Meanwhile, Romania, joining Russia in mid-May and proclaiming its independence, supplied large forces for the Russians besieging Plevna.

Plevna's fall (December 10) was followed by a triumphant Russian advance on Constantinople. Serbia now hastily joined the conflict alongside Russia, Romania, Montenegro, and the Bulgarians. The Russo–Turkish War finally became a Greek Orthodox war against Islam and a Slav war of national liberation, although under its Budapest Convention with Austria, Russia had to restrict sharply its cooperation with the Serbian states; also the Tsar had promised the British not to seize Constantinople. However, victory prodded Russian ambitions. A bellicose Russian press demanded the final solution of the Eastern Question. Entering Adrianople on January 21, 1878, Grand Prince Nikolai Nikolaevich wrote the tsar: "We must go to the center, to Tsarigrad [Constantinople] and finish there the holy cause You have assumed."[27] Such a course, bound to provoke war with Great Britain, was averted by Alexander II and War Minister Miliutin who vetoed the seizure of Constantinople or the Straits.

RUSSIA MAKES PEACE IN 1878; THE AFTERMATH

In framing peace terms Russian leaders were caught between European limitations and their Balkan allies' territorial demands. The Armistice of Adrianople of late January 1878 contained bases of peace by which Serbia, Montenegro, and Romania would receive independence and Bulgaria and Bosnia–Hercegovina autonomy. The "maximum" proposal of Count Ignatiev, Russia's chief negotiator, called for a fully independent, greater Bulgaria, Russian control of the Straits, and large gains for other Balkan allies. Alexander II rejected this "maximum" as too drastic to win European approval. Top Russian leaders then approved Ignatiev's "minimum," providing substantial concessions to the Serbian states, almost without discussion. Foreign Minister Gorchakov, sharing Ignatiev's preference for Bulgaria and Montenegro over Serbia, instructed the ambassador:

---

[26]Catargi to Prince Milan, report, July 15/27, 1877, *Ristić Papers*, 19/2, Archive of the Historical Institute (Belgrade).

[27]M. Hasenkampf, *Moi dnevnik, 1877-1878 gg.* (St. Petersburg, 1908), pp. 342, 360.

Especially adhere stubbornly to everything that affects Bulgaria and hasten peace negotiations so as to confront the Powers with a maximum number of *faits accomplis.*[28]

Unable to satisfy the Serbian states fully, Ignatiev wrote Gorchakov on February 15: "No matter what concessions we may succeed in extracting from the Turks for the Principalities, we can be sure in advance that they will invariably appear insufficient . . . ."[29] Later, Ignatiev claimed he had favored a Greater Serbia but had been stymied by errors at military headquarters and a weak-kneed Foreign Ministry. Meanwhile the Austrian emperor warned the tsar against seeking an independent Bulgaria and insisted that Serbia's territorial gains be restricted.

Count Ignatiev's Treaty of San Stefano (March 1878) rewarded Bulgaria and Montenegro richly, but not Russia's other allies. It proposed a large, united tributary Bulgaria under Russian military occupation, turning over to the Bulgars most of the area occupied during the war by the Serbian army. Russian leaders were definitely pro-Bulgarian, concluded Serbia's envoy to St. Petersburg: "Russia . . . is not seeking to secure Bulgaria from the Turks . . ., but purely to guarantee it from Serbia."[30] Montenegro would be almost tripled in size while Serbia and Romania would receive little. G. I. Bobrikov, Russia's military envoy to Serbia, deplored San Stefano's provisions:

> By this treaty we armed against ourselves not only the western great powers, but all of the peoples for whose interests we had taken up arms. By the Treaty of San Stefano we laid the basis for quarrels among the peoples of the Balkan peninsula and foreshadowed our humiliation in Berlin.[31]

However, because of vehement opposition to the treaty's terms—especially over Bulgaria—by Austria and Great Britain, San Stefano would never be implemented. St. Petersburg, having to focus on its great power relationships, yielded at the Balkan Slavs' expense in order to avoid a coalition war which Russia could not afford to fight militarily or financially. For most Russian leaders sacrificing Serbian aspirations in the western Balkans was essential in order to assuage Austria–Hungary. Only Ignatiev, sent to Vienna in late March 1878 to defend his treaty and consolidate the Three Emperors' League, found Austrian terms unacceptable. Vienna, he realized, would become the major beneficiary of the Russo–Turkish War, deprive Russia of future influence over the Balkan Slavs and prevent their independent development:

---

[28]Ignatiev, *Istoricheskii vestnik*, vol. 139 (1916), p. 51.

[29]Ignatiev, *Istoricheskii vestnik*, vol. 139 (1916), pp. 58, 62; S.A. Nikitin, ed., *Osvobozhdenie Bolgarii ot turetskogo iga*, vol. II (Moscow, 1961-1967), pp. 484-89.

[30]Protić to Ristić, telegram, February 8/20, 1878, (report of March 2/14) *Ristić Papers*, Archive of the Historical Institute (Belgrade).

[31]G. I. Bobrikov, *Zapiski G. I. Bobrikova* (St. Petersburg, 1913), pp. 84 ff.

My whole soul rebelled against destroying with my own hands my . . . work of fifteen years, killing all the hopes of the Slavs and strengthening Vienna's predominance in the east. . . . I considered granting Bosnia and Hercegovina to Austria to be a crime against the Slav population and shameful to Russia.[32]

After his mission failed, Ignatiev was removed from office.

The compromise hammered out in May 1878 by the Marquis of Salisbury and Count P. A. Shuvalov, Russia's ambassador in London, helped Russia avert war with Great Britain. Alexander II had to agree that all of San Stefano's provisions could be debated at the great powers' Congress of Berlin in June. The leading Panslav journalist, M. N. Katkov, predicted that that congress would bring war or humiliation to Russia. Conflict with Austria and Great Britain, he affirmed, would be preferable to yielding on Bulgaria. However, official Russia had resolved to make the necessary concessions.

Doddering Chancellor Gorchakov, Russia's official chief delegate at the Berlin Congress, declared: "Russia brings her laurels here and hopes the Congress will convert them into olive branches."[33] Instead it was Shuvalov, the second delegate, who by hard work and great skill preserved some Russian wartime gains. Only Russia's minimum aims could be achieved, Shuvalov warned St. Petersburg. "Whoever wishes to go beyond this, wants war."[34] War Minister Miliutin cautioned Shuvalov: "You know the situation. We cannot fight any more. . . . Better yield everything so as not to break up the congress."[35] Encountering solid Anglo–Austrian opposition over Bulgaria, Shuvalov had to agree to split San Stefano's "Big Bulgaria," reduce its frontiers, and shorten Russia's military occupation. Shuvalov told the Serbian delegate to reach agreement with Austria and do nothing at the congress without her approval. General Bobrikov deplored this virtual surrender of Serbia to Austria:

It was strange to see our own diplomats turn their backs on the Serbs and act disdainfully. They turned their backs on our stake in the strengthening of the Serbian nationality, on the balance of power in the Balkans.[36]

Nonetheless, Serbia, unable to secure territory in Bosnia–Hercegovina, obtained its independence and more territory than she had been promised at San Stefano.

---

[32]Ignatiev, *Istoricheskii vestnik*, vol. 143 (Feb. 1916), pp. 376–77.

[33]H. von Kremer-Auenrode and Hirsch, eds., *Das Staatsarchiv: Sammlung der officiellen Actenstücke der Geschichte der Gegenwart*, vol. 30, no. 6753 (Protocol of June 13, 1878), (Leipzig, 1878).

[34]B. Bareilles, ed., *Le rapport secret sur le Congrès de Berlin* (Paris, 1919), pp. 119–21.

[35]V. Khvostov, "P.A. Shuvalov o Berlinskom Kongresse 1878 g.," *Krasnyi Arkhiv*, vol. 59 (Moscow, 1933), pp. 100–01.

[36]Bobrikov, p. 95.

GORCHAKOV   BEACONSFIELD   ANDRÁSSY   BISMARCK   SHUVALOV

THE CONGRESS OF BERLIN, JUNE–JULY 1878

Montenegro emerged disgruntled from the congress. To obtain the port of Bar, she had to accept Austrian tutelage, abandon the rest of the Adriatic coast and claims to Hercegovina. Her boundaries were extended considerably but far less than had been promised at San Stefano.

Dismayed at the outcome, nationalist opinion in Russia and the Serbian lands interpreted the Berlin Treaty as Russia's betrayal of Slav interests. Wrote Russia's Panslav newspaper, *Russkii mir:* "We have the right to dispose of our own gains, *but in no case do we have the right to sacrifice others—those who trusted us with the defense of their interests.*"[37] Ivan Aksakov's famous speech to the Moscow Slav Society on July 4, 1878, expressed well the Russian nationalists' anger and sorrow at the treaty:

> We meet now . . . to attend a funeral . . . of whole countries—to attend the burial as it were of all the hopes of liberating the Bulgarians and of securing the independence of the Serbs. Are we not burying the cause which all Russians have at heart?

Russia's concessions, added Aksakov, amounted to formal abdication of its role as the leader of Slav and Orthodox peoples. War would have been preferable to such a dishonor, though Aksakov doubted that Britain and Austria would have dared to fight Russia.[38] The Russian government responded by closing the Moscow Society and exiling Aksakov to the provinces.

Russian leaders expressed shock and dismay at the outcome of the Berlin Congress. Chancellor Gorchakov, who avoided sessions where Russia had to yield, declared: "I only regret having had to add my signature to such a transaction." He told Alexander II: "I consider the Berlin Treaty the darkest page in my life." Commented the tsar: "And in mine too."[39] Shuvalov's sponsorship of the treaty wrecked his brilliant diplomatic career. Uncompleted domestic reform and shaky finances, noted War Minister Miliutin, had required peace in the Balkans and with Europe. Nonetheless, Russia's victory in the Turkish war had represented a big step forward:

> We could not expect to solve the whole Eastern Question in one campaign and it is better to accept the results of the Congress than go to war. Whatever limits the Congress sets on southern Bulgaria, northern Bulgaria will serve as a nucleus for the future unification of the entire Bulgarian people.[40]

Noting strong public hostility in Russia to the treaty, Miliutin commented: "The Berlin Treaty arouses general dissatisfaction because people expected

---

[37]"Pregled ruske štampe," *Istok* (Belgrade), June 21/July 3, 1878, p. 3. (Italics in original.)

[38]Aksakov, pp. 297–308.

[39]D. MacKenzie, *The Serbs and Russian Panslavism, 1875–1878* (Ithaca, NY, 1967), p. 327.

[40]Miliutin, pp. 72–73.

something colossal."[41] Echoing the war minister, the official Russian newspaper regretted that the powers had compelled Russia to abandon the San Stefano Treaty, which would have left Balkan peoples freer to develop:

> But each of our wars [against Turkey] has seen an additional step toward the final goal . . .: deliverance of the Christian East. However incomplete, the work of the Berlin Congress marks a fresh step along that path.[42]

Alexander II's final years, however, seemingly confirmed the verdict of Russian nationalist opinion. Austria–Hungary consolidated its political and economic hold over the western Balkans by occupying Bosnia–Hercegovina with Russia's blessing. Russian power and prestige in the Balkans declined significantly. The Serbia of Prince Milan became an obedient satellite of Vienna as Austria exploited Serbo–Montenegrin jealousies to keep them apart. Baron Jomini of the Russian Foreign Ministry predicted correctly that Austria–Hungary would attract the Balkan Slavs increasingly into its orbit:

> Its industrial and commercial superiority [over Russia] is evident. The material interests of the Slavs are all directed to that side. . . . With the aid of railroads, their ties with Austria and the West will soon become indissoluble, and from this time forward ties of race, language and faith will be only weak arguments. The only thing which attaches the Slavs to us is the oppression from which they suffer and the hope which they place in our assistance.

Once that factor ceased to operate, predicted Jomini, the Balkan Slavs would all spurn Russia.[43] Such a pessimistic appraisal appeared justified until the revival of Russian influence after 1906.

What were the results of Russia's Balkan policies under Alexander II? Few of the high hopes of Russian diplomats and Panslavs early in the reign were realized. Despite an improved image from domestic reforms, Russia's influence and prestige in the Balkans in 1881, except in Bulgaria, was no greater than in 1855 despite the costly Russo–Turkish War, which delayed Russia's economic development. Count Ignatiev's imperial dream of securing control of the Turkish Straits and dominating the Balkans and Ottoman Empire had vanished. To be sure, Chancellor Gorchakov's minimum objectives were achieved: abrogating the humiliating "Black Sea clauses," recovering southern Bessarabia, and restoring Russia as an equal member of the European concert. Even those gains had been purchased at the extravagant price of fostering the unification of a powerful German Empire right next to Russia. Panslav goals of creating a large South Slav state as

---

[41]Miliutin, p. 82.

[42]*Pravitelstvennyi vestnik*, cited in O. A. Novikova, *Russia and England from 1876 to 1880* (London, 1880), pp. 107–09.

[43]Jomini to Giers, October 9/21, 1878, cited in C. Jelavich and B. Jelavich, eds., *Russia in the East* (Leiden, Netherlands, 1959), pp. 86–87.

a Russian client and base from which to control the Straits, or building a Slav federation under Russia's aegis had failed miserably. Instead Balkan Slav and Orthodox peoples remained fragmented, embroiled in dangerous rivalry over Macedonia, and attracted increasingly westward toward Europe.

Suggested Readings

Bismarck, Otto von. *Reflections and Reminiscences.* 2 vols. London, 1898.

Cecil, G. *Life of Robert, Marquis of Salisbury.* 2 vols. London, 1921.

Geyer, Dietrich. *Russian Imperialism: The Interaction of Domestic and Foreign Policy, 1860–1914.* Trans. B. Little. New Haven, CT, 1987.

Harris, David. *A Diplomatic History of the Balkan Crisis: The First Year.* Stanford, CA, 1936.

Jelavich, Barbara. *The Ottoman Empire, the Great Powers, and the Straits Question, 1870–1887.* Bloomington, IN, 1973.

_____. *Russia and the Formation of the Romanian National State, 1821–1878.* Cambridge, England, 1984.

Jelavich, Charles. *Tsarist Russia and Balkan Nationalism: Russian Influence in the Internal Affairs of Bulgaria and Serbia, 1879–1886.* Berkeley, CA, 1958.

Jelavich, Charles, and Barbara Jelavich, eds., *Russia in the East, 1876–1880.* Leiden, Netherlands, 1959.

Kohn, Hans. *Pan-Slavism: Its History and Ideology.* Notre Dame, IN, 1953.

MacKenzie, David. *The Serbs and Russian Pan-Slavism, 1875–1878.* Ithaca, NY, 1967.

_____. *The Lion of Tashkent: The Career of General M. G. Cherniaev.* Athens, GA, 1974.

_____. *Ilija Garašanin: Balkan Bismarck.* Boulder, CO, 1985.

Medlicott, W. N. *The Congress of Berlin and After: A Diplomatic History of the Near Eastern Settlement, 1878–1880.* London, 1938.

Morley, John. *The Life of W. E. Gladstone.* 3 vols. London, 1903 (vol. 2 on Eastern Crisis, 1875–1880).

Novikova, O. A. *Russia and England from 1876 to 1880.* London, 1880.

Petrovich, Michael. *The Emergence of Russian Panslavism, 1856–1870.* New York, 1956.

Rupp, G. H. *A Wavering Friendship: Russia and Austria, 1876–1878.* Cambridge, MA, 1941.

Seton-Watson, A. W., ed., "Russo–British Relations during the Eastern Crisis," *Slavonic Review* (London), vols. 3–6 (1924–28).

_____. *Disraeli, Gladstone and the Eastern Question.* 2nd ed. London, 1962.

Stead, W. T. *The M.P. for Russia: Reminiscences of Madame Olga Novikoff.* 2 vols. London, 1909.

Stojanović, Mihailo. *The Great Powers and the Balkans, 1875–1878.* Cambridge, England, 1939.

Sumner, B. H. "Ignatyev at Constantinople, 1864–1874," *Slavonic Review*, vol. 11 (1933).

_____. *Russia and the Balkans, 1870–1880.* Oxford, England, 1937.

Wirthwein, W. G. *Britain and the Balkan Crisis, 1875–1878.* New York, 1935.

6

CONQUEST OF THE CAUCASUS AND TURKESTAN, 1855–1881

The decade following the Crimean War saw the completion of the subjugation of mountainous areas of the Caucasus and the conquest of the large region of southern central Asia known then as Turkestan. These operations were conducted by an impoverished Russian regime with little money to spare for imperial adventures. However, the results seemed at the time to justify the military efforts required.

PACIFICATION OF THE CAUCASUS

The treaties of Turkmanchai (1828) and Adrianople (1829) had extended Russia's hold over the lowland Caucasus region inhabited chiefly by Georgians and Armenians, who acquiesced peacefully to Russian rule in order to safeguard themselves from the greater danger of Turkish or Persian rule. The borders of the Russian Empire were thereby extended to the upper Euphrates River valley, an advance that caused considerable British concern about an eventual Russian move on British India. However, the formal annexation of the Caucasus by Russia according to treaty was succeeded, as we have seen, by a generation of difficult and frustrating conflict with Caucasian mountain tribes, mainly Islamic, under Kazi Mullah and then Shamil, an able warrior who was chosen their leader in 1834. Repeated large-scale military expeditions during Nicholas I's reign had failed to pacify the uplands. The mountaineers' resistance endangered Russian control over Georgia and Armenia. The guerrilla-style warfare, comparable to the subsequent British defeats at the hands of the Boers, produced losses damaging to Russian prestige.

In 1846 Nicholas had named Prince M. S. Vorontsov viceroy of the Caucasus with plenary powers. Vorontsov worked out a cautious but systematic plan to pacify the entire Caucasus through colonization with Cossacks, building roads and forts, and cutting down forests. This program had begun to achieve significant results before the end of Nicholas' reign, but large Russian forces remained tied down in the Caucasus region. Two able men serving in the army of the Caucasus during those years, Dmitrii A. Miliutin—subsequently Russia's war minister—and Prince A. I.

Bariatinskii, concluded that only effective guarantees that the religion, customs, and lives of Muslim mountaineers would be protected and respected would deprive the militants around Shamil of support and produce genuine pacification. During the Crimean War Miliutin and Bariatinskii drew up plans for the final conquest since Vorontsov's gradual tactics had weakened the mountaineers. Shamil's failure during the war to shake the Russian grip brought many defections from the mountaineers of Daghestan.

Prince Bariatinskii, a boyhood friend of Alexander II who enjoyed the new tsar's confidence, persuaded him to name him viceroy of the Caucasus in the summer of 1856 and requested that Miliutin be named as his chief of staff. Alexander obliged and gave them extraordinary powers, allowing Bariatinskii to maintain almost 300,000 men in the Caucasus until the task was completed. Bariatinskii's military plan was flexible and emphasized granting guarantees to the mountaineers. In 1857 General N. I. Evdokimov broke into the Argun valley, systematically cutting forests and constructing forts, which gave the Russians mountain ridges near Shamil's fortress at Vedeno. In April 1859 Vedeno was captured as Shamil and a few followers retired to their last stronghold on Mount Gunib. As the tribes of Daghestan one after another surrendered to Evdokimov, Shamil finally gave up in August 1859. Bariatinskii treated him generously and he resided peacefully and honorably in Russia until dying in Mecca in 1871.

Shamil's capture allowed Evdokimov to complete the pacification of the Circassians along the Black Sea coast. The western Caucasus was also subdued 1861–1864, and Bariatinskii was made fieldmarshal for his successful efforts. The entire Caucasus now became a secure Russian base for operations in the Transcaspia and central Asia. Most Russian troops could be withdrawn from the Caucasus, making a highly trained, efficient force of high morale available for other duties. This completed the expansion of the Russian Empire southward. About 400,000 tribesmen, amounting to over half the Circassian population, emigrated to Turkey.

CENTRAL ASIA: THE FIRST PHASE, 1730–1850

The Russian advance into central Asia can be regarded as a counter-offensive against the Mongols who earlier had moved into Rus from the borders of China. This Russian drive created an Eurasian empire as the Mongols' successors and involved the establishment of Russian rule over millions of Asian Muslims.

After the failure of Peter the Great's expedition under Prince Alexander Bekovich-Cherkasskii in 1717, the vast Kazakh steppe lying east of the Ural Mountains and south of Siberia was conquered by official expeditions against little resistance from its nomadic inhabitants. Its tribes were mainly engaged in cattlebreeding, moving seasonally from place to place in the steppe seeking adequate pasturage and water. The Kazakhs, who were Muslim, possessed primitive tribal organizations but lacked political unity. They were ruled loosely by the khans of three *ordy* (hordes), which represented mainly a division of grazing lands. Bitter struggles between the Kazakhs and the

Kalmuks encroaching upon their lands from the east weakened both peoples and opened the way for easier Russian penetration. Strife with the Kalmuks helps explain the decision of the khan of the Lesser Horde in 1730 to request Russian rule and place himself under Russian protection. The fortress of Orenburg (established 1734) just to the north of the Kazakh steppe became the main Russian base of operations in central Asia and remained the region's chief administrative center.

Russia's conquest of the Kazakh steppe (now Kazakhstan) only became final after a desperate Kazakh revolt which had been touched off by Orenburg's division of it into Russian administrative units and the confiscation of pasture lands. Exploiting widespread Kazakh dissatisfaction with Russian penetration, Khan Kenesary Kasimov led a mass uprising between 1837 and 1847. Temporarily uniting the Kazakhs, Kasimov boldly attacked the West Siberian and Orenburg defense lines, and brought Russian trade with central Asia to a standstill. Eventually, Kasimov was defeated by the rival Kirghiz tribes from the Issyk-Kul region. Kasimov, himself, was tortured and killed. But even his captors regarded him as a legendary steppe hero, and to many Kazakhs he remains so to this day. Kenesary Kasimov was to the Kazakhs what Shamil was to the mountaineers of Daghestan. Initially, Soviet historians portrayed him as a hero of national liberation, but under Stalin he was castigated as an obstacle to the much touted "friendship of peoples." Recently, his reputation has been refurbished by central Asian scholars. In any event, by 1850 Russian rule had been consolidated firmly over the entire steppe region.

To the south of the steppe in a region of desert interspersed with rivers and fertile oases lived millions of Muslims, mostly speaking Turkic languages. They were divided in the early nineteenth century into three native khanates of Bukhara, Khiva, and Kokand. These khanates resembled politically the feudal principalities of twelfth-century Europe, indicating why they proved unable to resist the Russian advance. Of the three khanates, the most dynamic and aggressive was the Emirate of Bukhara, founded in 1753, which became the chief center of Islam in central Asia. The emir was a supposedly all-powerful Asiatic despot, and the emirate was divided into provinces ruled over by despotic governors. Bukhara conducted a brisk commerce and produced cotton and silk by primitive methods, but basically it had a feudal economy with low productivity. The Muslim faith and its leaders exercised powerful influence, dominating education and often holding back economic and political development. The emirs built a professional army with some foreign advisers, but poorly equipped and without any national feeling, its morale was most uncertain, and the population generally was not warlike. In the mid-nineteenth century Bukhara had a population of some 3 million.

The remaining khanates were smaller and weaker. Kokand khanate, founded in 1798, resembled Bukhara but was far less unified. Its attempted expansion beyond its chief city, Tashkent (meaning "stone city"), into the steppe region provoked a series of wars with Bukhara and the Kazakhs.

Indeed, in the region rivalry and conflict between nomads and city dwellers was a persistent theme. By 1850, as the Russians approached, Kokand had already begun to disintegrate, and Tashkent had become semi-independent. South of the Sea of Aral lay the khanate of Khiva which, with a weak army and only 700,000 inhabitants, posed no threat to the others or to giant Russia. Known as Khorezm until the nineteenth century, it had been ruled by powerful Uzbek nobles descended from the family of Chingis-khan. The revolt of Kasimov induced General V. A. Perovskii, governor general of Orenburg, to launch an expedition against Khiva to deprive the Kazakhs of potential support. Perovskii moved through the desert with 5,000 men and 10,000 camels, but fierce desert heat forced him to retreat minus many of his camels. This gave Khivans undue confidence in the strength of their natural desert defenses.

Why did the Russians wish to expand into the thickly populated Muslim river valleys of southern central Asia after the Crimean War? The most obvious factor was geographical: Russia was contiguous with the southern oases. The region lacked all natural barriers or frontiers short of the formidable Hindu Kush mountain range. It might be considered only natural for Russia to fill this power vacuum in the heart of Asia in order to prevent its being filled by the British moving northward from India. Theories of Russia's manifest destiny were elaborated to justify expansion southward as far as the Hindu Kush.

More controversial were economic causes of Russian expansion. Soviet historians especially have stressed these as having been primary and decisive: the search for raw materials for a growing Russian textile industry, and the urge to obtain markets and control of trade routes leading to the Orient. All of these things, argued Soviet scholars, goaded the greed of a rising Russian bourgeoisie of merchant-capitalists. Thus Soviet historian N. A. Khalfin argued that Russian commercial and industrial leaders pressured the tsarist government to undertake the conquest of the region. I. A. Gage-meister, a leading Russian economist and official of the Finance Ministry, in 1857 stressed the brilliant prospect of eastern markets for Russia, the potential for navigation of the Syr-Daria River, development of cotton-growing, and of extensive trade between Russia and the khanates, but only if the latter were conquered and their institutions reformed. Other economists, including P. P. Semenov, pointed to central Asia as a key external market for a Russia that could not yet compete effectively with more advanced European countries but could supply backward central Asia with textiles if it moved in quickly before the British did. However, there is little evidence that Russian industrial leaders or merchants had much of a financial interest in central Asia. They possessed too little capital even to develop European Russia. Actually, they had to be subsidized and pushed by the politicians to enter central Asia.

Military arguments and justifications for Russian expansion were important. Tsarist administrators and military men asserted that Russian advances constituted an inevitable and justified response to attacks by nomads on Russian caravans from the territories of the khanates and on natives under Russian rule or protection. The military thus raised the security issue: the need to protect peaceful Russian citizens. They argued for the necessity to establish shorter, more easily defensible frontiers by advancing to natural boundaries. Franker military leaders affirmed the desirability of winning positions and bases which would enable Russia to exert pressure on the British in India during crises elsewhere. A key military reason was that local Russian administrators and commanders sought glory, adventure, and promotion by winning easy victories over disorganized native forces.

The factor of prestige likewise bulked large in Russian thinking in the post–Crimean era. It proved tempting to the imperial family and military leaders to compensate for the humiliating defeat in the Crimea by adding major new territories to the empire, which would redound to the credit of the Romanov dynasty and promote popular confidence in its competence to rule. Central Asia seemed destined for Russia to win cheap victories and refurbish its military laurels without much danger of conflict with a great power. Ideological justifications were readily supplied for expansion, such as the concept that it was inevitable and desirable for advanced European powers to rule over contiguous backward native populations. Wasn't it the "white man's burden" to spread Christian Russian civilization to benighted and backward "natives" living in squalor and tyranny under the despotic grip of Islam?

Together these factors and justifications account for a cautious imperialism authorized by the Russian government. This was a continental colonialism, the counterpart of the overseas imperialism of advanced European powers in Africa and Asia. Whereas the government generally advocated gradual, cautious advances, individual administrators and generals sometimes pushed ahead recklessly. Those closest to the scene usually were the most militant and impatient imperialists, often to feather their own nests. The War Ministry, administered by the patriotic and able Miliutin, favored moderate expansion but not to the point of provoking conflict with Britain. Frontier generals and administrators received orders from his ministry but did not always obey them. In the Foreign Ministry A. M. Gorchakov had an exaggerated fear of British reactions to Russian advances and cautioned restraint and setting demarcation lines beyond which Russia would not move. Finance Minister Mikhail Reitern, noting the Treasury's impoverished condition, opposed any major expenditures in central Asia and his agency constituted another restraining force. Alexander II, who at least theoretically made the final decisions, generally favored Miliutin's moderate expansion and sought to keep expansionist and anti-expansionist elements in balance. However, Alexander repeatedly lost control of the situation in the mid-1860s as reckless frontier generals pursued independent and unauthorized policies. Tempted by the glory and prestige provided by victories and annexations, Alexander and the imperial family generally rewarded the Turkestan generals as long as they were successful even if they violated their instructions.

THE CONQUEST OF TURKESTAN

In 1854, in the midst of the Crimean War, Nicholas I's government decided that the remaining gap in steppe defense lines should be closed, but Russia's absorption in that war delayed implementation. However, the previous year Count V. A. Perovskii, the governor general of Orenburg, had captured the Kokanese fortress of Ak-mechet on the right bank of the Syr-Daria River. Rebuilt and renamed Fort Perovsk, it became the anchor for a new advanced line of forts along that river, which pointed southward toward the khanates. This so-called Syr-Daria Line demarcated an unofficial frontier with Kokand and constituted one pincer of any potential operation to close the gap in steppe defenses. It was placed under a separate commander subject to the governor general of Orenburg.

During the late 1850s ensued a number of probing operations and reconnaissance moves as St. Petersburg refused to authorize impatient frontier commanders to undertake major operations until the Caucasus had been pacified. Meanwhile Prince Bariatinskii warned Alexander II of alleged British plans to dominate the Caspian Sea region. He advocated constructing a railway eastward from the Caspian for commercial and military purposes; this was the seed of the subsequent Transcaspian Railroad. Youthful Count N. P. Ignatiev was sent on a diplomatic mission to Khiva and Bukhara late in 1857. His reports confirmed the weakness of these khanates and urged his superiors to authorize a Russian advance. This advice was reinforced by the governor general of Orenburg and members of his military staff. In 1859 the governor general dispatched a small expedition under a Captain A. I. Butakov of the Aral Flotilla to navigate the Amu River through Khiva to Bukhara. On the eastern flank in Siberia the construction of Fort Vernoe and a Russian reconnaissance along the Chu River provoked a major Kokanese attack which was repelled. This demonstrated the vast Russian superiority in firepower and was followed by Russian occupation of Pishpek and the Issyk-Kul region. Finally, in 1863 Colonel M. G. Cherniaev was authorized to explore the upper Syr region with a Cossack detachment. As he approached the Kokanese fortress of Suzak, his men were fired upon. When he bombarded the city in retaliation, its garrison surrendered in terror. This expedition of 1863 helped convince the authorities in St. Petersburg to authorize a line-closing operation in Turkestan. Foreign Minister Gorchakov agreed with War Minister Miliutin that joining the Syr-Daria and west Siberian steppe lines would improve Russia's commercial position in the east and shorten frontiers, thus permitting financial savings.

The "closing of the lines" was implemented swiftly in the spring of 1864 by Colonel N. A. Verevkin from the Syr-Daria and Colonel M. G. Cherniaev from the west Siberian command. After they had linked up, Cherniaev decided on his own hook, citing arguments of security, to seize the fortress of Chimkent on the edge of Tashkent oasis. To await orders from distant Omsk, he argued, would endanger the region. If European governments protested, declared Cherniaev:

Map 6-1   **Central Asia: "Closing the Lines," 1864**

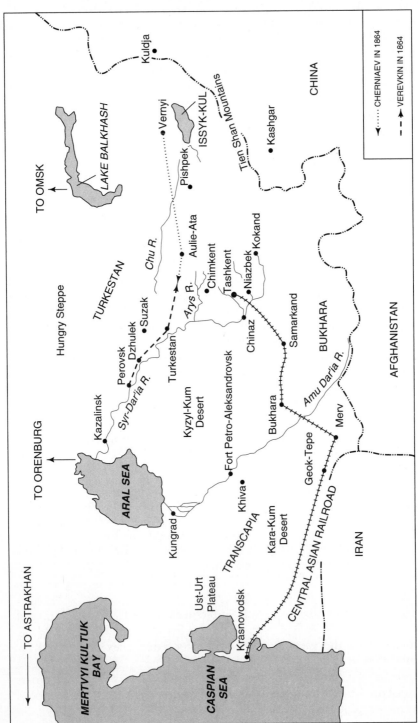

Chimkent is scarcely known to Europeans even by name, and its conquest cannot cause much noise, and having some 5,000 natives with me, we can pose as defenders of an exploited people. This argument, it seems to me, is sufficient to justify our actions to the English who have not justified their actions in India to us.[1]

His superior, General Miliutin, agreed that Chimkent was important strategically, but he wondered: "Who will guarantee that after Chimkent Cherniaev won't consider it necessary to take Tashkent, then Kokand, and there will be no end to it."[2] Miliutin had raised the crucial problem of how St. Petersburg could control frontier commanders over a thousand miles and weeks of travel away.

After the fall of Chimkent, the Russian Foreign Ministry submitted a report to Emperor Alexander and later a circular to the European powers arguing that Russian expansion in central Asia was similar to that of the United States against the American Indians and of Britain and France in Africa and Asia. Gorchakov added that "the insistent demands of our commerce and some kind of mysterious but irresistible attraction to the Orient" had been responsible for the Russian advances. The circular defended the expansion that had already occurred while providing assurances that Russia had no intention to move beyond Chimkent into the oasis region. War Minister Miliutin deplored such assurances, which tended to bind Russia's hands. Unexpected events often contradicted diplomatic promises and would give Russia's opponents "a pretext to accuse our policy of perfidy."[3]

After the government decided to combine the forward lines under a single command, Cherniaev was made military governor of Turkestan in February 1865 and promoted to major general. But neither St. Petersburg nor Orenburg prescribed any clear plan for him to follow except to consolidate control over the region already occupied. Foreign Minister Gorchakov opposed any further annexations unless Russian territory or commerce were directly threatened by Kokand:

As to Tashkent we have decided not to include it in the [Russian] Empire believing it much more advantageous to exert indirect influence over it.[4]

The new governor general of Orenburg, N. A. Kryzhanovskii, planning to visit Turkestan, urged General Cherniaev to take no action until he arrived. However, Cherniaev had no desire to see the laurels of victory snatched from his hands by an ambitious superior. Knowing that despite Miliutin's

---

[1]Quoted in David MacKenzie, "The Turkestan Generals and St. Petersburg, 1863-1866," *Canadian Slavic Studies*, vol. III, no. 2 (1969), p. 293.

[2]MacKenzie, p. 293.

[3]Gorchakov's circular of Nov. 21, 1864, in S.S. Tatishchev, *Imperator Aleksandr II: Ego zhizn i tsarstvovanie*, vol. II (St. Petersburg, 1903), pp. 115-16.

[4]MacKenzie, p. 297.

hesitations about expansion, he had much support within the War Ministry, as well as from the heir to the throne, Cherniaev decided to advance on the great commercial city of Tashkent, informing his superiors of this only during his advance. With only 2,000 men Cherniaev defeated the main Kokanese army, blockaded Tashkent, then assaulted the city defended by 30,000 Kokanese and captured it after two days of street fighting. His report of July 7 concluded:

> Please call the emperor's attention to this band of fearless warriors creating prestige for the Russian name in central Asia commensurate with the dignity of the empire and the power of the Russian people.[5]

Alexander II responded warmly: "Present rewards to those who distinguished themselves," and he wrote on Cherniaev's dispatch: "A glorious affair."[6] Almost alone Cherniaev insisted on Russian annexation of Tashkent, arguing that it was impossible to relinquish it to Asiatic rule. His policy became that of imperial Russia: once an Asian city had been occupied, it must not be evacuated. Cherniaev then followed up the conquest of Tashkent by a wholly unauthorized invasion of the khanate of Bukhara, but had to renounce it when his army ran short of supplies. By then, 1866, his superiors in Orenburg and St. Petersburg had combined to remove him from his post for repeated insubordination. However, Cherniaev's unilateral actions had advanced Russian power into the midst of the oasis region. Despite the reluctance of the Foreign Ministry, Russia became committed to remain and to continue its expansion southward. Cherniaev demonstrated that reckless action by a frontier general could commit his government to unwanted territory and responsibilities. General D. I. Romanovskii, Cherniaev's successor as governor of Turkestan and a close colleague of Miliutin, found himself compelled to continue Cherniaev's work by defeating Bukhara, humiliating the emir and forcing him to make peace.

Tashkent's annexation in 1866 compelled St. Petersburg to reach a decision as to how it and Turkestan should be administered. Since it was no longer practicable to run a large region from distant Orenburg, the decision was reached to create in July 1867 the new governor generalship of Turkestan under another Miliutin understudy, General K. P. fon-Kaufman, and to accord him awesome powers as imperial viceroy. To cope with vast problems of administering an alien and distant region and having to build an administration from the dregs of the imperial bureaucracy, Kaufman was given command of all troops, complete control of all revenues, ran the civil government subject to the War Ministry, and was made responsible for diplomatic relations with the khanates. It is no wonder that awestruck Uzbeks called him the semi-tsar.

---

[5]*Russkii Turkestan*, vol. 3 (Moscow, 1872), pp. 91 ff.
[6]MacKenzie, p. 299.

Kaufman's organization of a new administration for Turkestan was stimulated by his smashing military victories over Bukhara after the emir refused to accept his peace offers. Kaufman then refused to return the captured city of Samarkand to the emir. "I could not commit such sacrilege against the prestige, honor, and rights of Russia," declared this avowed imperialist.[7] Traveling to St. Petersburg to counter efforts of the Foreign Ministry to restore that fabled city to Bukhara, Kaufman warned Alexander II that Asians only respected force and that the maintenance of Russia's position in central Asia depended solely on the country's prestige and respect for its might:

> Asia knows that Turkey and England are watching us. The slightest concession and we will . . . risk losing all that we acquired earlier. . . . We are few here and England will aid the entire Muslim world to rise against us in Asia.[8]

Russia, Kaufman continued, should rejoice at expressed British anger over the fate of Samarkand. "England is Russia's enemy and can only be reached in Asia [by threatening British India]." The Russian proconsul apparently exaggerated British hostility at Russian advances, but his stubbornness was vindicated: Russia retained Samarkand. Actually, at this time British leaders in India believed that further expansion would merely burden Russia. Asserted the viceroy, Sir John Lawrence, that if India were invaded:

> We will have the advantages of terrain and knowledge of it. The further she [Russia] extends her power, the greater area she must occupy, the more vulnerable points she must expose, the greater danger she must incur of insurrection, and the larger must be her expenditures.[9]

After 1867 debate raged in Russia as to whether newly acquired Turkestan was worth keeping. Eugene Schuyler, an American diplomat, wrote in 1874 that, according to figures of the hostile Finance Ministry, deficits in Turkestan's budget were increasing, trade was declining, and its few resources could never repay administrative costs. Had Russian leaders known this earlier, they would never have occupied Turkestan, Schuyler asserted, but now for prestige reasons Russia could not withdraw.[10] Concluded the Finance Ministry: Turkestan "represented the unusual case of a colony supported by the mother country."[11] But General Kaufman realized

---

[7]E. Tolbukhov, "Ustroitel Turkestanshogo kraia," *Istoricheskii Vestnik*, vol. 132 (June 1913), pp. 904-07.

[8]Quoted in David MacKenzie, "Turkestan's Significance to Russia (1850-1917)," *The Russian Review* (April 1974), p. 172.

[9]Lawrence to Northcote, report to Foreign Office, Sept. 3, 1867; cited in MacKenzie, p. 172.

[10]Eugene Schuyler, *Turkistan*, vol. II (New York, 1876), p. 208 ff.

[11]Quoted in MacKenzie, "Turkestan's Significance," p. 174.

Turkestan's vast potential for trade and production of cotton. A leading liberal daily newspaper, *Golos (The Voice)*, defended Kaufman's administration of the region and predicted: "Russia's attention to [Turkestan's] needs and interests will find it one of the most precious and productive areas of our broad country."[12] Regardless of deficits, affirmed the military writer L. F. Kostenko, Russia must remain in Turkestan: "Because of its natural resources, central Asia possesses more revenue possibilities than any part of European Russia."[13] With little support from St. Petersburg, Kaufman persevered in developing Turkestan's resources and created a European portion of Tashkent as the center of Russian influence in Asia.

Further expansion of Russian Turkestan by Kaufman during the 1870s enhanced its strategic importance. The Khiva expedition of 1873 made that khanate a Russian protectorate and advanced Russian control to the Amu River. Turkestan now could be supplied directly from European Russia and British India became more vulnerable to Russian threats. In 1876 the conquest of Kokand khanate brought Russia closer to shrunken Bukhara and India. Annexed as Fergana province, it became the richest portion of Turkestan. Rejoiced Kostenko: "Each victory flourish sounded by the Russian army in Turkestan reverberated painfully in the hearts of our ill-wishers [the British] who looked enviously at our political and military progress."[14]

The Balkan Crisis of 1875–1878 confirmed Turkestan's strategic value and the linkage of the central Asian and Straits questions. Early in 1878, until blocked by orders from St. Petersburg, Kaufman planned to include Bukhara and Afghanistan directly in Russia's sphere, and he made plans for a demonstration on India's frontier in order to compel Britain to make concessions in Europe. General M. D. Skobelev, a leading expansionist and Turkestan general, regarded Turkestan valuable primarily as a base from which to threaten India and thus resolve the "Eastern Question" in Russia's favor.[15] Russian advances toward India were designed not to conquer that British possession but to apply military and political pressure on London.

Between 1879 and 1881 the Russians advanced in Turkmenia just north of Persia and Afghanistan. General Skobelev's campaign against the main Turkmen fortress of Geok-Tepe resulted in its capture after bitter fighting. To aid Skobelev's campaign, the War Ministry began to construct a Transcaspian Railroad, which when completed unified Russian central Asia and made the khanates of Bukhara and Khiva dependent upon Russia. The conquest of Geok-Tepe brought Russian domains to the frontiers of Persia and increased the pressure on that vulnerable country as well as British India.

During Alexander II's reign, at insignificant cost in lives and treasure, Russia, unopposed by any major power, acquired a vast oasis and desert

---

[12]*Golos* (St. Petersburg), January 24, 1875.
[13]Quoted in MacKenzie, "Turkestan's Significance," p. 174.
[14]Quoted in MacKenzie, "Turkestan's Significance," p. 175.
[15]H. S. Edwards, *Russian Projects Against India* (London, 1885), p. 285.

region twice the size of Texas and filled the major power vacuum in central Asia. In his fourteen years as governor general of Turkestan, General Kaufman, one of the most successful of Russian imperial pro-consuls, built a solid administration out of mostly inferior materials, won the respect and awe of the Uzbek population, and created a center of Russian power in the heart of Asia.[16] Russian military victories and expansion in central Asia helped the Romanov dynasty compensate to some degree for the sale of Alaska and failures in the Balkans.

Suggested Readings

Allworth, Edward, ed., *Central Asia: A Century of Russian Rule.* New York, 1967.

Baddeley, John. *The Russian Conquest of the Caucasus.* London, 1908.

Becker, Abraham. *Russia's Protectorates in Central Asia: Bukhara and Khiva, 1865–1924.* Cambridge, MA, 1968.

Brooks, W. E. "Nicholas I as Reformer: Russian Attempts to Conquer the Caucasus, 1825–55," In Ivo Banac, ed., *Nation and Ideology: Essays in Honor of Wayne S. Vucinich.* Boulder, CO, 1981.

Donnelly, Alton. "The Russian Conquest and Colonization and Kazakhstan to 1850," In M. Rywkin, ed., *Russian Colonial Expansion to 1917.* London, 1988, pp. 189–207.

Edwards, H. S. *Russian Projects Against India.* London, 1885.

Holdsworth, Mary. *Turkestan in the Nineteenth Century.* London, 1959.

Khalfin, N. A. *Russia's Policy in Central Asia, 1857–1868.* Trans. H. Evans. London, 1964.

Khan, M. A. *England, Russia and Central Asia, 1859–1878.* Peshawar, Pakistan, 1963.

MacGahan, J. A. *Campaigning on the Oxus and the Fall of Khiva.* London, 1874.

MacKenzie, David. "Kaufman of Turkestan: An Assessment of His Administration, 1867-1881," *Slavic Review.* vol. 26, no. 2 (June 1967), pp. 265-85.

———. "Expansion in Central Asia: St. Petersburg vs. the Turkestan Generals (1863-1866)," *Canadian Slavic Studies.* vol. 3, no. 2 (1969), pp. 286-311.

———. *The Lion of Tashkent: The Career of General M.G. Cherniaev.* Athens, GA, 1974.

Marvin, Charles. *The Russian Advance Toward India.* London, 1882.

Pierce, Richard. *Russian Central Asia, 1867–1917.* Berkeley, CA, 1960.

Schuyler, Eugene. *Turkistan.* 2 vols. New York, 1876.

Wheeler, Geoffrey. *The Modern History of Soviet Central Asia.* London, 1964.

---

[16]See D. MacKenzie, "Kaufman of Turkestan: An Assessment of His Administration, 1867-1881," *Slavic Review,* vol. 26, no. 2 (June 1967), pp. 265-85.

7

RUSSIA IN ASIA AND AMERICA TO 1881

Russian imperial expansion in the Far East was preceded by the conquest of vast Siberia from 1580 to 1689 by Cossack adventurers, entrepreneurs seeking gold, and fur trappers. Advancing from one river valley to the next, these enterprising Russians, with sporadic support from their government, moved rapidly against minimal resistance from small and scattered tribes until they reached Okhotsk on the northern Pacific coast in 1639. By 1650 Russia controlled virtually all of Siberia, thus transforming itself into a huge Eurasian empire. During the 1650s explorer Erofei Khabarov's expedition moved into the Amur River valley but few settlers followed. There were sporadic clashes with the Chinese in the 1680s that preceded and triggered a diplomatic settlement with China at the frontier settlement of Nerchinsk.

SINO–RUSSIAN RELATIONS TO 1881

The Treaty of Nerchinsk (1689) confirmed Russia's possession of Siberia and established treaty relations with the Chinese. Negotiated by Jesuits, the treaty left the strategic Amur River valley under Chinese sovereignty. But until the mid-nineteenth century the St. Petersburg government displayed little interest in vast, remote, and frigid Siberia, except as a penal colony. There was little free Russian settlement, and the few Russian seaports on the northern Pacific remained frozen most of the year.

From Nerchinsk, until about 1800, vast expanses of almost uninhabited territory separated the chief centers of Russia and China, and they remained almost wholly ignorant of one another. Meanwhile, the military balance of power shifted gradually in favor of Russia. Prior to Peter the Great, China had been the stronger; during the eighteenth century Russia's strength increased greatly, although it was not brought to bear upon China until the mid-nineteenth century. Until almost 1900 Chinese emperors regarded Russia as an inferior and barbarous country, considering it only a vassal state that posed no real threat to the Celestial Empire and whose representatives must bow down *(kowtow)* to the emperor, thereby confirming their inferiority. These Chinese beliefs were reflected in a Sino–Russian Convention of 1792, whose wording suggested a virtual edict from the Manchu emperor to a subordinate. However, the accelerating decline of the Manchu dynasty, evident from the late eighteenth century, swung the military balance clearly towards Russia, a fact about which Chinese leaders remained oblivious. As corruption burgeoned inside China, its army and navy became obsolescent, and the country was wracked by frequent internal rebellions.

In Russia knowledge about China gradually increased. Under terms of the Treaty of Kiakhta (1727) Russia secured Chinese permission to station a permanent mission of the Orthodox Church in Beijing, which served in lieu of regular diplomatic representation. Until 1800 this Orthodox mission did not prove very useful because the Russian priests there were not very knowledgeable, made few Chinese contacts, and often were corrupt or drunken. That changed with the ninth mission led by Father N. Ia. Bichurin (served 1806–1821) who learned Chinese and brought home an extensive library that required fifteen camels to transport across Mongolia.[1] Some members of this mission were employed by the new Asiatic Department of the Russian Foreign Ministry, formed in 1819, and subsequent missions with better prepared personnel provided Russia with much information on China and experts on its affairs. Therefore, by the time of the Crimean War, Russia could deal quite knowledgeably with China, whereas the Chinese remained woefully ignorant about Russia. Prior to 1850 Sino–Russian relations remained rather inactive, although Russian advances in the Kazakh steppe in central Asia provoked sporadic but ineffective Chinese protests. Communications between the two countries remained poor, and there was little significant Russian interest in fostering a more active relationship.

Meanwhile western European powers were penetrating the declining Chinese Empire and exposing its impotence. In the 1830s European private entrepreneurs entered China, chiefly through the opium trade conducted by British and Indian traders. When the Chinese government tried to halt this trade, Great Britain and France declared war on China. This first "Opium War" (1838–1842) ended in humiliating Chinese defeats. Under the Treaty of Nanking (1842) between Britain and China, five Chinese ports were opened to unrestricted foreign commerce, establishing a basis for a treaty system of extraterritorial rights for Europeans in China. European merchants and missionaries, beginning to open China forcibly, enjoyed superior status, and were subject only to their own laws and courts. That treaty system worked poorly and soon produced a second "Opium War" (1857–1858) in which France and Britain again defeated and humiliated Manchu China. The Chinese were compelled to open additional ports to European business. That second defeat provided imperial Russia with a golden opportunity to establish control over the Amur region and the so-called Maritime Province.

Why this occurred requires some explanation. European penetration of and trade with China affected negatively the long-standing Sino–Russian

---

[1] R. K. I. Quested, *The Expansion of Russia in East Asia, 1857–1860* (Kuala Lumpur, Malaysia, 1968), p. 24.

trade via the frontier town of Kiakhta which had grown rapidly in the first half of the nineteenth century. Now Europeans and Americans could bring their goods in by sea more cheaply than the Russians could overland, so the Kiakhta trade dwindled. That in turn stimulated Russian interest in the possibility of navigating the Amur River, colonizing its valley, and obtaining direct access to the Pacific Ocean there. Siberia's growth during the first half of the nineteenth century made such a sea outlet vital for its future development. The population of Siberia increased from about 1.5 million in 1815 to almost 3 million forty years later; in the same period the number of Siberia's merchants increased fivefold.[2] Eastern Siberia now had the capacity to supply settlers for the Amur region and a much greater need to develop adequate sea outlets and external trade.

Russian penetration of the Amur region and the development of seaports on the Pacific was largely the work of Nicholas N. Muraviov, subsequently dubbed "Amurskii" for his conquest of the Amur valley. In 1847 the energetic and ambitious Muraviov was named governor general of Eastern Siberia and the concept of Russian expansion at the expense of China gained an enthusiastic advocate. Cut off almost wholly from St. Petersburg, some 5,000 miles and weeks of travel away, Muraviov acquired almost unlimited authority. He played in the Far East a role similar to those of M. G. Cherniaev and K. P. fon-Kaufman in central Asia. However, unlike the conservative conquerors of Turkestan, Muraviov was a political liberal and admirer of the United States. He was also a firm opponent of British Asian imperialism. Under the guise of conducting trading activities for the Russian–American Company, Muraviov led a penetration of the Amur valley with small numbers of troops encountering no resistance from the Chinese. In 1850 Muraviov established a settlement at Nikolaevsk (named after the then Emperor Nicholas I) at the mouth of the Amur. Two years later the Russians moved across a narrow strait to Sakhalin Island, and occupied more and more of the coastline on the mainland. Sailing up the Amur River, a Russian force established a fort at Khabarovsk, named for the earlier Russian explorer. In Muraviov's wake followed thousands of Russian settlers who by 1856 had taken de facto control of the entire region. Foreign Minister Karl Nesselrode, cautioning about the need to "avoid extreme danger" from China, worried about international reactions.[3] But there was no way to stop Muraviov, and Nicholas I and his War Ministry rejoiced at this Russian expansion. The colorful and impulsive Muraviov was soon awarded the title of Count Muraviov-Amurskii.

Under Alexander II Russia exploited Chinese helplessness to obtain formal Chinese recognition of these advances. Initially, Alexander continued Nicholas' role as arbiter between Nesselrode and Muraviov on relations with China, but soon he backed Muraviov. In May 1858, by threats and persuasion

---

[2]Quested, p. 22.
[3]Quested, p. 31.

Muraviov induced a local Chinese commander to sign the Treaty of Aigun confirming Russian sovereignty over the left bank of the Amur from the Aigun River to the Pacific seacoast; the Ussuri region was placed under joint Sino–Russian rule. In June, Count E. V. Putiatin, sent as special Russian envoy to China, secured by the Treaty of Tientsin all advantages previously gained by treaty by Britain, France, and the United States, including extraterritorial rights. However, the Beijing government refused to ratify the Treaty of Aigun or formally cede the Amur region to Russia until reduced to helplessness by the Taiping Rebellion and the occupation of Beijing itself by Anglo–French forces. Meanwhile Russian forces continued moving southward along the Pacific coast, founding near the Korean frontier in July 1860 a city that confirmed Russia's imperial dreams in this region: Vladivostok, meaning "ruler of the East." Vladivostok was destined to become the chief Russian naval base and commercial seaport on the Pacific.

In November 1860, Russia's new envoy to China, the youthful general and imperialist, Count Nicholas P. Ignatiev (subsequently ambassador to Constantinople), first revealed his outstanding diplomatic talents by negotiating the Treaty of Beijing. Ignatiev kept his negotiations secret, so the

Map 7-1   Russia in the Far East to 1914

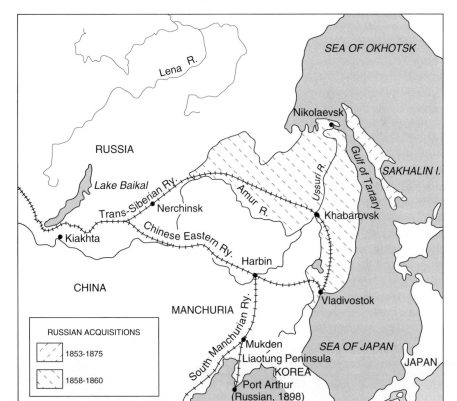

entire affair was concluded without the knowledge of the British. The treaty established virtually the present frontier between Russia and China. It recognized Russian rule not only over the Amur region but also over the entire area between the Ussuri River and the Gulf of Tartary with Vladivostok. Russia also obtained commercial privileges in Mongolia and Chinese Turkestan. Ignatiev departed Beijing in triumph and was carried like an emperor across Mongolia and Siberia. Concluded under the nose of Russia's chief rival, Great Britain, the Treaty of Beijing did much to compensate Russia for the Crimean debacle.

China lost further territory to Russia in central Asia a decade later. In 1871 a revolt against Chinese rule in Kashgar and Iarkand provoked a Russian occupation of Kuldja province. When the revolt was suppressed, Russian troops nonetheless remained. For a time it looked as if war might erupt between the two countries. Finally, under the Treaty of St. Petersburg (1881) Russia retained part of Kuldja, and received an indemnity and new commercial privileges. In its advance to the frontiers of China and Korea, imperial Russia was the beneficiary of Franco–British penetration of China and their victories over a disintegrating Manchu regime.

RUSSIA SELLS ALASKA, 1867

Alaska, or Russian America as it was sometimes known, was the easternmost of Russia's possessions and, following the Crimean War, the most vulnerable and least defensible. After the voyages (1728–1741) of Vitus Bering, a Danish captain in Russian service, Russian entrepreneurs and adventurers began settling first the offshore Aleutian Islands, then Alaska proper. They advanced southward along the coast of what is today the northwestern United States searching for furs as they had done during trans-Siberian expansion. Emperor Paul I's decree of 1799 created the Russian–American Company with a trading monopoly, control of the American coast north of 55° north latitude, and the right to occupy territory further south for the Russian crown. Designed on the model of the highly successful British East India Company, the Russian–American Company comprised part of an ambitious plan by the Russian imperial government to bring the entire northern Pacific Ocean under its control. This constituted, then, perhaps the most far-reaching of Russian imperial dreams in the nineteenth century. Affirmed a Russian scholar:

> This plan presupposed the further entrenchment of Russia along the west coast of North America, including California, the Hawaiian Islands, the southern part of Sakhalin, and the mouth of the Amur. These colonies, together with Kamchatka, Alaska and the Aleutians, which already belonged to Russia, were to make that country the all-powerful master of the whole northern Pacific.[4]

---

[4]S. B. Okun, *The Russian-American Company*. Trans. C. Ginsburg (Cambridge, MA, 1951), p. 50.

However, as we have seen, a Russo–American agreement in 1824, after the controversy surrounding the issuance of the Monroe Doctrine, set 54° 40′ north latitude as the southern limit of Russian claims. Signifying the end of Russian expansion in North America, it symbolized the abandonment of an impractical and exaggerated objective. With Russian foreign policy during much of the first half of the century in conservative hands, increasing friction developed between the St. Petersburg government and Russian leaders in Alaska.

The Russian decision to sell Alaska to the United States in 1867 is still somewhat shrouded in controversy, although the major elements seem clear. Economic factors were important: after 1824 the Russian–American Company fell deeply into debt, its fur trade with China was undermined by the opening of Chinese ports to Europeans in the 1840s. The company's inefficiency and mismanagement meant that Alaska, despite its evident potential, became of minor economic value to Russia and was viewed generally in St. Petersburg as a liability. Furthermore, Muraviov-Amurskii's penetration into the Amur region convinced some Russian leaders that the country's Pacific future lay in the fertile Amur valley, with its excellent harbors, rather than in an unproductive Alaska, rich only in potential. Politically, Russia and the United States found themselves drawn together during the 1860s by common hostility to Great Britain. Foreign Minister A. M. Gorchakov had assured the American federal government of Russia's sympathy with the North in the Civil War. The North hailed the coming of a Russian fleet to New York and San Francisco in the fall of 1863 as proof of Russian friendship and support; actually the Russians were anxious to get their ships out of harm's way in the face of a threatened British attack upon the Baltic ports over the Polish question. The realization grew in St. Petersburg that remote Alaska was indefensible. Growing Russo–British rivalry in central Asia likewise convinced the St. Petersburg government that it would be preferable for Alaska to pass to the United States rather than to Great Britain which at that time still ruled Canada.

One of the strongest advocates of selling Alaska to the United States was Grand Prince Konstantin Nikolaevich, the navy minister and liberal brother of Alexander II. After the Crimean War, in 1857, he declared that "in the event of war with a naval power [Britain] we are not in a position to defend our colony [Alaska]." In 1866 he reiterated his conviction that Russian America was very vulnerable:

> The condition of our colony worsens from day to day, and being so remote from the motherland, it is of no importance to Russia, whereas the necessity of defending it will continue to be as difficult and as expensive in the future as it has been in the past.[5]

---

[5] Quoted in Fred Starr, ed., *Russia's American Colony* (Durham, NC, 1987), p. 280, from U.S. National Archives, "Papers," annex no. 12.

However, several members of a Russian review committee argued that rivalry between the United States and Great Britain would protect Russian America which should be retained for political and strategic reasons. Stated Baron Theodor Osten-Saken, head of the Asiatic Department:

> ... The present generation has a sacred obligation to preserve for future generations every clod of earth along the coast of an ocean which has world-wide importance.[6]

But most high-ranking Russian officials concluded that there was no future for a Russian empire in North America in the face of increasing American political and naval power. Finance Minister Mikhail K. Reitern argued in 1866 that United States acquisition of Alaska would give it a common border with British Canada, thus increasing chances of Anglo–American rivalry and improving Russo–American relations.

Several of the more perceptive Russian statesmen of the time concluded that Russia's imperial destiny lay in Asia, not in North America. Thus Baron Edvard Stoeckl, Russian minister to Washington, advised Foreign Minister Gorchakov shortly before the sale of Alaska:

> It is in the lands of the Amur and especially in the territories to the south of that river that we must concentrate our resources and energies. These areas are fertile and will readily attract emigrants. They have magnificent harbors, and the vicinity of Japan and China assures them a profitable commerce. It is here that our power in the Pacific must be based.[7]

Sharing that view were Grand Prince Konstantin and Nicholas Muraviov.

Russo–American negotiations on the sale of Alaska, interrupted during the American Civil War, resumed in December 1866 and were conducted in greatest secrecy by Secretary of State William Seward and Baron Stoeckl. Seward's initial offer of $5 million was rejected by Stoeckl on instructions from home. Gradually Seward increased the amount offered until reaching the $7 million figure Stoeckl demanded, but the secretary refused to assume the debts of the moribund Russian–American Company. By the Treaty of March 29, 1867, all properties of that company were sold to the United States for $7.2 million, which was considerably more than the Russian envoy was authorized to accept. That amounts to roughly two cents per acre for Alaska. Because of the unpopularity of the deal in the United States, Stoeckl had to use almost $200,000 of the purchase price to bribe American congressmen into ratifying the treaty. This was the first territory of the Russian Empire to be surrendered voluntarily to a foreign power. Imagine the strategic picture in the northern Pacific today if Russia still held Alaska and the Aleutian Islands!

---

[6]Starr, p. 283.
[7]Starr, p. 288.

EXPANSION TOWARD JAPAN TO 1875

While Muraviov-Amurskii was leading the Russian penetration of the Amur region and establishing a Russian presence on Pacific shores, the island empire of Japan was emerging from two centuries of virtually complete isolation. From Japanese castaways discovered in Kamchatka and elsewhere in Siberia the Russians obtained exaggerated notions of the wealth of Japan. The prospect of discovering gold and silver there induced Russian adventurers to seek to enter Japan. Several Russian naval expeditions sent by Catherine the Great to the Kurile Islands and Japan failed to break the barriers erected by the Japanese Shogunate to prevent regular relations with Russia and other European powers. Japanese law prescribed that all vessels of countries with which Japan lacked diplomatic relations would be seized if they entered Japanese waters. In 1806–1807 two warships of the Russian–American Company marauded in Japan's northern possessions and spread a wave of Russophobia throughout Japan. Thus in 1811 when Captain V. M. Golovnin was dispatched by St. Petersburg to survey the southern Kuriles, he was seized with some of his men and imprisoned for two years then released. Repeated Russian efforts between 1814 and 1817 to maintain contact with Japanese authorities also failed.[8]

By 1850 as the United States and European countries sought to establish commercial and political ties with it, Japan began to emerge from its lengthy isolation. The expedition of Commodore Matthew Perry of the United States to Tokyo Bay in July 1853 first "opened" Japan, but only a few weeks later a Russian squadron commanded by Vice-Admiral E. V. Putiatin reached the Japanese port of Nagasaki. For awhile "Putiatin" became virtually synonymous with foreigner in Japan. His expedition had originally been slated to sail for Japan in 1843 but had been postponed for financial and diplomatic reasons until St. Petersburg learned that the United States was sending a similar expedition. Thus the "red devils," as the Japanese called Russians because of the red uniforms they wore, arrived soon after the Americans.[9]

Admiral Putiatin brought with him an official letter from Foreign Minister Nesselrode requesting Japan to open regular diplomatic relations and urging it to open its ports to trade with Russia and to Russian warships en route to Russian America. A month elapsed before this official Russian letter was accepted and another four months before there was any reply. Negotiations then dragged on for almost two years as the Japanese delayed their conclusion as long as possible. The Treaty of Shimoda (February 1855) provided for Russian consular representation in Japan, divided the Kurile Islands between the two countries, and provided for joint administration of the elongated and strategic island of Sakhalin off the Siberian coast. It also stipulated joint extraterritorial rights and opened three Japanese ports

---

[8]George A. Lensen, *Russia's Japan Expedition of 1852 to 1855* (Gainesville, FL, 1955), pp. xxi–xxii.

[9]Lensen, pp. 111 ff.

to Russian vessels.[10] By his tactful conduct Admiral Putiatin inspired the trust and respect of the Japanese. Thereby he contributed greatly to the supplementary Treaty of Nagasaki (1857) concluded between the two powers which confirmed the Shimoda agreements.[11]

Friction mounted in the following years between the Russians and Japan as Russian settlers continued to pour into Sakhalin Island and Governor General Muraviov sought to obtain that entire island for Russia. In 1862 Japan dispatched a delegation to St. Petersburg to negotiate an agreement over Sakhalin. It conferred with Count Ignatiev, then the director of the Asiatic Department, who declared flatly that all of Sakhalin belonged to Russia; later he proposed a partition. Subsequently, the Russians proposed an exchange of territories: Japan should abandon claims to Sakhalin in return for a Russian agreement to yield the remaining Kurile Islands to Japan.

Soon after the restoration in Japan of the rule of the emperor (1868), the Japanese government appealed to the United States as the "most impartial friend of both parties" to arbitrate the Sakhalin dispute. Therefore the American Secretary of State, Hamilton Fish, approached the Russian government in December 1870, but St. Petersburg declined the American offer of mediation. However, by 1874 Tokyo had decided to settle its dispute with Russia. Many of the Japanese colonists on Sakhalin were withdrawn, and the Japanese government decided to abandon the island to Russia. Under the subsequent Treaty of St. Petersburg (1875) Japan ceded all of Sakhalin Island to Russia in exchange for Russia's recognition of Japanese sovereignty over the northern Kurile Islands. The treaty also contained agreements on commerce and fisheries.[12] This established a sound basis for normal diplomatic relations between Russia and Japan.

CONCLUSION AND SUMMARY

Under Alexander II Russia underwent major reforms, notably the emancipation of the serfs, and confronted problems of defeat, loss of prestige, economic backwardness, and a chronically empty treasury. In European affairs, while pressing for revision of the Treaty of Paris, Russia acted officially as a peaceable, responsible member of the European community. By 1871 Foreign Minister Gorchakov had abrogated the onerous "Black Sea clauses" and restored Russia's prestige. In the Balkans Russian policy, dualistic and unclear, failed to achieve preeminence despite heavy expenditures in the Russo–Turkish War of 1877–1878. Instead, the Congress of Berlin enthroned Austria–Hungary as the dominant power in the western Balkans. Russia compensated itself for such setbacks in central Asia and the Far East by acquiring the Amur region and Vladivostok, entering Sakhalin, and by

---

[10]See Lensen, pp. 122–26, for the translated text of the Shimoda Treaty.

[11]Lensen, *The Russian Push Toward Japan: Russo–Japanese Relations, 1697–1875* (Princeton, NJ, 1959), pp. 425–36.

[12]Lensen, pp. 438–46. For the text of the treaty, see pp. 501–04.

conquering vast Turkestan. At times frontier generals, administrators, and Panslav diplomats escaped the control of the St. Petersburg government which worried about the danger to the Russian Empire should it again come into conflict with a European coalition.

Suggested Readings

Baddeley, J. F. *Russia, Mongolia, and China.* 2 vols. London, 1919.

Cahen, Gaston. *History of the Relations of Russia and China under Peter the Great, 1689–1730.* Trans. W. Ridge. Bangor, ME, 1967.

Dallin, David J. *The Rise of Russia in Asia.* New Haven, CT, 1949.

Foust, Clifford. *Muscovite and Mandarin: Russia's Trade with China and Its Setting, 1727–1805.* Chapel Hill, NC, 1969.

Golder, Frank A. *Russian Expansion on the Pacific, 1641–1850.* Cleveland, OH, 1914.

Harrison, John A. *Japan's Northern Frontier.* Gainesville, FL, 1953.

Lensen, George A., ed., *Russia's Eastward Expansion.* Englewood Cliffs, NJ, 1964.

Lensen, George A. *Russia's Japan Expedition of 1852 to 1855.* Gainesville, FL, 1955.

———. *The Russian Push Toward Japan: Russo–Japanese Relations, 1697–1875.* Princeton, NJ, 1959.

Mancall, Mark. *Russia and China: Their Diplomatic Relations to 1728.* Cambridge, MA, 1971.

Miller, D. H. *The Alaska Treaty.* Kingston, Canada, 1981.

Okun, S. B. *The Russian–American Company.* Cambridge, MA, 1951.

Quested, R. K. I. *The Expansion of Russia in East Asia, 1857–1860.* Kuala Lumpur, Malaysia, 1968.

Sladkovskii, M. I. *History of Economic Relations between Russia and China.* Trans. M. Roublev. Jerusalem, 1966.

Starr, Richard, ed., *Russia's American Colony.* Durham, NC, 1987.

THE REACTIONARY EMPIRE
FACES EUROPE, 1881–1904

The assassination of Alexander II in March 1881 by a terrorist belonging to the socialist People's Will organization ended an epoch that for the most part was one of liberal change. The People's Will aimed to overturn the tsarist autocracy and introduce a decentralized socialist order by striking down and thus disorganizing the leadership of the old regime. Instead their act brought to the imperial Russian throne Alexander III, the son of the murdered emperor and the last true Russian autocrat. This inaugurated a generation of reaction during which many of the "Great Reforms" were halted or reversed. The Russian Empire became truly "a prison of peoples" in which the numerous minority nationalities lost many of their remaining rights and became intensely dissatisfied with their subjugation to autocratic Russian rule.

THE RULERS, THEIR POLICIES
AND FOREIGN MINISTRY

Alexander III was a heavy, powerful, stubborn man of limited intelligence who reputedly could bend a horseshoe with his naked hands. Straightforward, fervently religious and nationalistic, Alexander Alexandrovich had supported some Panslav policies during the mid-1870s but had distanced himself from their more adventurous members subsequently. Alexander's chief tutor had been K. P. Pobedonostsev, a learned jurist, who became procurator of the Holy Synod of the Russian Orthodox Church; often he has justifiably been considered the evil genius of declining tsarism who helped to doom it to extinction. Pobedonostsev imbued his imperial pupil successfully with the traditional principles of Autocracy, Orthodoxy, and Nationalism—the official creed under Nicholas I—and with intense hatred for constitutions, liberal reform, and anything Western or European as being incompatible with basic Russian values. Within a year of Alexander III's accession the remaining liberal ministers of Alexander II—notably War Minister Dmitrii Miliutin—had been forced from office, all ideas of constitutional reform had been abandoned, and censorship and police controls were tightened.

T*SAR* A*LEXANDER* III *AND FAMILY; HE RULED* 1881–1894

Russification, or making everyone into Russians, became the official policy of the regime. Emperor Alexander III soon made his former tutor, K. P. Pobedonostsev, the most powerful man in Russia's domestic affairs. With Alexander's full support, he imposed rigid church-sponsored censorship upon the public media. His avowed aim was to forcibly convert national and religious minorities to the Russian language, customs, and Orthodoxy. Pobedonostsev believed that any liberal leader or publication he disapproved of must be Jewish or serving the Jews and that most Jews were foreign agents. His solution for the Jewish minority: one-third would be converted, one-third expelled, and one-third assimilated. Repression was directed especially against Jews and Catholic Poles, both more advanced culturally than the ruling Russians. Nor were the Finns, Baltic Germans, and Baltic peoples spared. Many of these minority elements, which had loyally served Russia in the past, were fatally alienated from the empire, driven into the revolutionary movement, and imbued with the determination to achieve autonomy or outright independence. By breeding intense discontent, Russification created a basis for an eventual explosion and the dissolution of the reactionary empire.

Alexander III's regime sought to reverse the erosion of the economic and political role of the nobility and clergy by granting them privileges and preferential treatment. The Land Captain Law of 1889 granted extensive rights to rural noblemen to supervise the peasantry and greatly restricted the district and provincial assemblies *(zemstva)* created by Alexander II and representing the principles of self-government and greater social equality. In the realm of education, rigid class barriers were restored in an attempt to reserve secondary schools and universities for the sons of noblemen and clergy. Restrictive quotas were imposed upon the Jews in order to hamper their chances of obtaining a higher education.

Despite these reactionary political and social trends, the industrialization of Russia spurted forward rapidly after 1892 following the appointment to the key post of finance minister of the extraordinarily able Sergei Iu. Witte, one of Russia's few successful private entrepreneurs. This drive had been preceded by large-scale railway construction, increasingly under state auspices, which created the communications network indispensable for industrial growth. Even Alexander III's conservative regime recognized the need for industrial development in order to maintain Russia's status as a great power. In a report submitted in February 1900 to Nicholas II, Count Witte emphasized the close relationship between economic development and imperial foreign policy:

> International competition does not wait. If we do not take energetic and decisive measures so that in the course of the next decades our industry will be able to satisfy the needs of Russia and Asian countries which are or should be under our influence, then the rapidly growing foreign industries . . . will establish themselves in our fatherland . . . . Our economic backwardness may lead to political and cultural backwardness as well.[1]

The "Witte System" thus was pervaded with a sense of urgency: Russia must catch up with the advanced West by pushing railway construction and heavy industry (especially iron and steel) financed largely by the state and foreign private investment. While high external tariffs would restrict

---

[1]Theodore von Laue, *Sergei Witte and the Industrialization of Russia* (New York, 1969), p. 3.

COUNT S. IU. WITTE, MINISTER OF FINANCE, *1892–1903; PREMIER, 1905–1906*

imports, the developing heavy industries would stimulate light consumer industry, and eventually agriculture would flourish as growing cities demanded more foodstuffs. Witte's experiment in state capitalism indicated a means by which a backward country might overtake the industrial frontrunners. Among Witte's major successes was attracting much foreign investment by placing Russia on the gold standard and making the ruble convertible into European currencies. Witte's most ambitious project was the Trans-Siberian Railroad across Siberia to the Pacific as a means to penetrate and even dominate Asian markets. Between 1893 and 1903 Russia's industrial growth rate compared favorably with those of the most advanced countries and a basis was laid for Russia to become a modern industrial country.

In 1894 Alexander III died suddenly of a stroke, bringing to the Russian throne his son, Nicholas II (ruled 1894–1917). Nicholas was more sensitive and intelligent than his formidable father, but was indecisive, easily influenced and dominated, and lacked Alexander's firmness and direction. As emperor Nicholas displayed inconsistent interest in political affairs and became absorbed increasingly in family matters. He was dominated from the start by his wife, "Alix," or Empress Alexandra. Of German origin, she was a fanatical convert to Orthodoxy, who at first did not interfere much in state affairs. Initially, Nicholas displayed reasonable judgment in selecting ministers of state, retaining the able Count Witte in office for almost a decade. However, he too remained under the tutelage of the reactionary Pobedonostsev and dedicated himself seemingly as firmly as his father to preserving the principles of a conservative autocracy. During the initial decade of Nicholas II's rule, 1894–1904, persisted the main trends of the era of Alexander III—Russification and rapid industrialization—but new and ominous for the monarchy was the rise of an increasingly potent liberal and revolutionary opposition that was not scared by the young emperor.

Under Alexander III persisted the custom of the immediately preceding reigns for consistent and cautious management of the Foreign Ministry by a single foreign minister. In April 1882 Nicholas K. Giers was named foreign minister, assuming the reins from the senile A. M. Gorchakov. The new minister served in that post until 1895. A Swedish Protestant lacking a private fortune, Giers was a highly trained, dedicated career diplomat with a long period of service under Gorchakov. During the latter's numerous declining years, Giers had done most of the real work at the Foreign Office. Count Witte described Giers as very prudent, of limited ability but wide experience. Alexander III, affirmed Witte, acted as his own foreign minister treating Giers as a mere secretary; nonetheless he frequently took Giers' sound advice. However, Boris Nolde, in his book on the Franco–Russian alliance, credited Giers with true statesmanship noting that he pursued with determination, consistency, and skill a policy of peace that was undeniably in Russia's best interests. The continuity represented by Giers' tenure of office throughout Alexander III's reign, like Gorchakov for Alexander II, enhanced the role of the Foreign Ministry. Giers did succeed in restraining nationalistic and militarist influences in Russia, especially at the imperial court, and contributed greatly to making Alexander III's reign a period of peace and relative tranquillity. Modest, realistic, and flexible, Giers was not wedded to any particular doctrine or ideology. Although he favored close ties with Germany, he later prepared the way for rapprochement with France and the Franco–Russian Alliance. Giers' role was particularly important since Alexander III was very limited intellectually, rather shy, and not given to dealing much directly with foreign diplomats. The only important instance of Alexander III's direct personal interference in the conduct of Russian foreign relations—seeking to maintain Russian predominance in Bulgaria in 1886—was a complete failure. Charles Jelavich, an American scholar, commented on Giers' crucial role: "In every crisis . . . he was ultimately able to win acceptance for his opinions. His position was consistently moderate and conciliatory." As to the relationship between Giers and Alexander III,

N. K. GIERS, FOREIGN MINISTER, 1882–1895

Jelavich claimed: "In major policy decisions the tsar eventually supported the position of the Foreign Office; in less important matters, however, he often acted impulsively and with violence."[2] Alexander III, and Russia, were fortunate to have a man of Giers' ability and good sense in the foreign office throughout the reign.

In contrast, Nicholas II, lacking real qualities of leadership himself, was served between 1894 and 1917 by eight different foreign ministers, none of whom possessed outstanding abilities. Giers at first retained office but died in 1895. His successor was A. B. Lobanov-Rostovskii, experienced and capable, but he died after about one year as foreign minister. Next came M. N. Muraviov, who was overshadowed by Count Witte, and served until 1900. Succeeding him was V. N. Lamzdorf, a fine administrator but without

---

[2]Charles Jelavich, *Tsarist Russia and Balkan Nationalism: Russian Influence in the Internal Affairs of Bulgaria and Serbia, 1879–1886* (Berkeley, CA, 1958), p. 281.

significant experience in foreign affairs, who served from 1900 to 1906. The frequent changes in chiefs helped undermine the Foreign Ministry's influence in determining external policy in a time of peril for Russia. It is no accident that this decline in the power of the foreign office coincided with an era of adventurism which brought Russia into the disastrous Russo–Japanese War.*

RUSSIA AND THE BISMARCKIAN SYSTEM, 1881–1890

During the 1880s Russia, seeking security and anxious to avoid conflict with a major European power, remained linked with varying degrees of closeness with Germany and Austria–Hungary, despite Alexander III's dislike for the latter.

Until his removal from office in 1890, German Chancellor Otto von Bismarck remained the dominant figure in European diplomacy. Following the Berlin Congress of 1878, Bismarck had chosen Austria–Hungary as Germany's chief ally. However, Alexander III, like his predecessor, fearing isolation and finding ideological differences with France insuperable, saw no alternative to reliance on the German powers. Thus, swallowing his pride, the new emperor sought admission to the German power club. Bismarck, to keep France isolated and thus insure Germany's security, obliged Alexander. In June 1881 Germany, Austria–Hungary, and Russia concluded the second League of Three Emperors. Shrouded in deep secrecy, this defensive alliance featured a binding treaty, not merely a personal understanding of sovereigns as in 1873. The three partners agreed that if one of them became involved in war with a fourth power, the others would remain benevolently neutral and seek to localize the conflict. Thus if Russia were drawn into war with Britain over the Turkish Straits or central Asia, the German powers would not join the conflict against her. This alliance, therefore, provided Russia with a measure of security lacking on the eve of the Crimean War. The three powers agreed to coordinate their policies in the Balkans, and pledged not to change the territorial status quo in the Ottoman Empire without mutual consent. Austria-Hungary, however, was authorized to annex the provinces of Bosnia and Hercegovina, which she had occupied in 1878, whenever she wished. Russia's signature of the Three Emperors' League of 1881 signified at least a temporary abandonment of the nationalist and Panslav program of 1876–1878. The treaty furthermore guaranteed the closure of the Turkish Straits which was significant for Russia since it reduced the chances of a British fleet coming into the Black Sea.

The conclusion of the Three Emperors' League in 1881 for a three-year term provoked a major controversy in Russia. It had been concluded largely because of the initiative of Giers while still Gorchakov's assistant. Alexander III for his part distrusted Austria–Hungary and believed that Constantinople and the Straits eventually must go to Russia. Therefore the

---

*See Chapter 10.

emperor was not wholly enthusiastic about cooperating with the German powers. Seeking to exploit this were leading Russian nationalists who considered such an understanding tantamount to betrayal of the Slavs and Russia's national cause. Ivan Aksakov, former chairman of the Moscow Slav Committee, denounced the treaty as treason to the Slav cause. General M. D. Skobelev, fresh from his victory over the Turcomans at Geok-Tepe and the darling of the superpatriots, in a St. Petersburg speech strongly supported insurgents in Hercegovina resisting the Austro–Hungarian occupation authorized by the Berlin Congress. In February 1882 Skobelev made a bellicose speech in Paris blaming "aliens" for Russia's recent departure from its Slav mission. Germany, declared Skobelev, was the mortal foe of Russia and Slavdom. In their imminent and inevitable struggle, he told Serbian students, the Slavs would triumph over the Germanic world. Meanwhile Count N. P. Ignatiev, very influential with Alexander III, was intriguing to replace the aged Gorchakov as foreign minister. However, in April 1882 the nationalists were rebuffed: Giers was appointed foreign minister, ending Ignatiev's political career, and Skobelev died suddenly after an all-night orgy.

Again in 1884, when the Three Emperors' League came up for renewal, Giers prevailed over aggressive, nationalist elements. P. A. Saburov, Russian ambassador to Berlin, urged that the treaty be sharpened to give Russia a free hand to act in Constantinople and the Straits in return for some compensation to the German powers. He was supported by A. I. Nelidov, Russian ambassador in Constantinople, a former colleague of Ignatiev who had consistently favored Russian control of the Turkish Straits. Saburov's amendment would have transformed the league from a treaty to preserve peace and the status quo into an instrument for territorial expansion and even war. Giers resisted such demands successfully: Saburov was recalled early in 1884 and the treaty was renewed without change for another three years. That September the three emperors met at Skiernewice, Poland, much to the dismay of French chauvinists and Russian Panslavs. At least for the time being Skiernewice precluded any Franco–Russian tie.

The apparent harmony between Russia and the German powers, however, was soon disrupted, as in 1875, by complications in the Balkans. The Bulgarian Crisis of 1885–1887 threatened to provoke war between Austria–Hungary and Russia over their conflicting Balkan interests. Again nationalist elements in Russia sought to exploit this crisis in order to remove the moderate, pro-German Giers from office. Thus on July 30, 1887, the prominent journalist M. N. Katkov, in an editorial in *Moskovskie Vedomosti*, denounced the Three Emperors' League as having led to Russia's total subservience to the German powers. Katkov called for the emancipation of Russia from that alliance:

> Only by virtue of that independence which is as necessary to the state as air is to the living being will we be able to distinguish enemies from friends and, in the context of moving events and changing circumstances, ascertain with

whom it is suitable for us, by the will of Providence, to go together and against
whom we should undertake preventative measures.[3]

Although Alexander III responded angrily to Katkov's disclosure of the secret
league, he appeared to sympathize secretly with the journalist's views. The
tsar's dislike of Austria and its role in the Serbo–Bulgarian War of 1885,*
made the continuation of the Three Emperors' League impossible.

Bismarck finally arranged a solution to the Bulgarian Crisis in 1887.
He managed to convince Alexander III that Germany supported him in
the Bulgarian affair by declaring publicly that Russia had every right to
dominate Bulgaria. This dissuaded the tsar from turning towards France,
as Katkov had suggested, which for Germany would create the danger of
a two-front war. However, Bismarck did not want Russia to seize control
of Bulgaria knowing that would provoke Austria–Hungary and probably lead
to an Austro–Russian war that would destroy his alliance system. Thus he
encouraged Italy to discuss the problem of Russian expansion in the Balkans
with Austria and Britain. The result was that those three concluded the
First Mediterranean Agreement to protect the status quo in the Balkans
and discourage any drastic Russian action. Then Bismarck encouraged the
Russian envoys, brothers Paul Shuvalov and Peter Shuvalov, to propose bases
for a new treaty to replace the shattered Three Emperors' League:

> Germany would recognize Russia's exclusive right to exercise her influence in
> Bulgaria and Rumelia. Russia furthermore could count on Germany's friendly
> neutrality if the Tsar found himself obliged to assure the closing of the Straits. . . .
> Germany, on the other hand, could count on the same friendly neutrality on
> Russia's part in the face of any conflict that might arise between Germany
> and France. Both powers recognized the existence of the Austro–Hungarian
> Empire as necessary to the maintenance of the European equilibrium and,
> except in the case of aggression on Austria's part, agreed not to take any action
> against that Empire's integrity. Both recognized the necessity of maintaining
> the independence of the Kingdom of Serbia.[4]

The result was the so-called secret Reinsurance Treaty, signed in June
1887. Russia and Germany pledged to remain neutral if either became
involved in war with a third power, except that Russia need not remain
neutral if Germany attacked France, nor did Germany have to stay neutral
if Russia attacked Austria. The purpose of those latter provisos was to make
the new treaty compatible with the secret Austro–German Alliance of 1879,
which Bismarck now showed to Alexander III. Nonetheless, the Bulgarian
Crisis that same year caused some cooling of Russo–German relations: the

---

[3]Quoted in George Kennan, *The Decline of Bismarck's European Order* (Princeton, NJ,
1979), p. 179.

*See Chapter 9.

[4]Quoted in Kennan, p. 257.

German grain tariff was raised, and with Bismarck's encouragement German bankers withdrew Russian bonds from the German money market. Furthermore, Bismarck had rumors circulated that Russia faced bankruptcy, thus making any Russian military action in the Balkans virtually impossible. Such moves were bound to arouse Russian suspicions about the sincerity of German friendship.

The European implications of the Bulgarian Crisis of 1887 were considerable. Revealed was the profound rivalry and hostility between Russia and Austria–Hungary over Balkan issues that Bismarck could merely paper over, not resolve. The crisis demonstrated that the three eastern European conservative empires were no longer truly united. Russia had already begun to drift away from its Germanic partners toward France. The European powers, as at the Berlin Congress, had not resolved Balkan problems but merely shoved them under the rug. Great Britain had reversed its policy from hostility toward Bulgarian nationalism to supporting it as the best barrier to Russian domination of the Balkans.

THE FRANCO–RUSSIAN ALLIANCE OF 1893

The death of ninety-one-year-old Emperor William I of Germany in 1888 and the accession that June of his grandson, the youthful William II, accelerated the deterioration of Russo–German relations. While the aged emperor lived, it appeared certain there would be no conflict between Germany and Russia. However, the tactless and impatient young emperor made a poor impression on Alexander III and grew very restive at the continued dominance of the elderly Prince Bismarck. Preparations for the renewal of the Reinsurance Treaty were proceeding normally when in March 1890 Emperor William II suddenly removed Bismarck from office and forced his retirement on grounds of health. German foreign office officials exerted strong pressure on the new chancellor, Leo von Caprivi, and on William II against renewal on the ground that the Reinsurance Treaty was incompatible with Germany's obligations under the Triple Alliance of 1882 (Germany, Austria, and Italy). They soon won over Emperor William to a simpler and more aggressive German policy known usually as *Weltpolitik* (world policy). German leaders now concluded mistakenly that Russia, France, and Great Britain were too deeply divided by colonial interests and rivalries ever to ally. They believed Germany could pursue an imperial drive for "a place in the sun" without the complicating link with Russia. Thus in March 1890 the German ambassador notified St. Petersburg that Germany, while desiring friendly relations with Russia, would not renew the Reinsurance Treaty. Leaving Russia in total diplomatic isolation, that German move led inexorably to the conclusion three years later of the Franco–Russian Alliance and therefore was fraught with fateful consequences. Under the frivolous William II the Germans lightheartedly destroyed the complex Bismarckian alliance system that had guaranteed Germany's security and European peace. They virtually drove France and Russia into each other's arms.

Former apparently insuperable obstacles to Franco–Russian rapprochement were now overcome swiftly. Once the Triple Alliance was renewed in May 1891, Alexander III faced a choice between diplomatic isolation before that hostile coalition or making an agreement with France; he chose the latter.[5] Nationalists in both France and Russia long had urged their alliance against the German powers, but mutual suspicion, and the profound ideological differences between Alexander III's reactionary autocracy and the radical Third French Republic had seemed to preclude an understanding between them. But now that William II had "dropped the pilot"— Chancellor Bismarck—and blown his bridges with St. Petersburg, Russia stood vulnerable and alone. Giers' foreign policy, which had rested solely on the German alliance, lay in ruins. Meanwhile Franco–Russian economic ties were multiplying: in 1888 Russia had ordered a large number of French rifles to reequip its army. After the Berlin money market had been closed to Russian bonds, Russia obtained major loans from France. German overtures to London at this time sparked Franco–Russian concern that Britain might eventually join the Triple Alliance. Alexander III felt increasingly worried about a possible allied attack on Russia. In July 1891 a visit of the French battlefleet to the Russian naval base of Kronstadt, headquarters of the Baltic Fleet, provoked an enthusiastic Russian reception. Alexander III stood bareheaded as the anthem of revolution, the Marseillaise, was played. That almost incredible scene revealed that ideological hostilities tended to yield to the imperatives of power politics.

In August 1891 an exchange of notes between the French and Russian governments established a Franco–Russian entente (understanding) as the predecessor to an alliance. If a threat to European peace were to arise, the two governments would concert countermeasures immediately. On the Russian side, however, both Foreign Minister Giers and Count Lamzdorf had the gravest reservations about committing Russia to French intrigues to recover the lost provinces of Alsace and Lorraine. "The commitment they [the French] are demanding of us," noted Lamzdorf in his diary on March 17, 1892, "would give the French a carte blanche for adventures and for the provocation of conflicts . . . and then we would be obliged to support them with an army of 800,000 men!" Both French and Russian leaders, except for Giers and Lamzdorf, aimed to undo Bismarck's work. When Giers took the French military proposal to Alexander III without comment, the Russian emperor responded:

> We really do have to come to an agreement with the French. We must be prepared to attack the Germans at once, in order not to give them time to defeat France first and then to turn upon us . . . We must correct the mistakes of the past and destroy Germany at the first possible moment.

---

[5]William L. Langer, *The Diplomacy of Imperialism* 2nd ed. (New York, 1960), p. 20.

Once Germany had been broken up, argued Alexander, Austria–Hungary would not dare to act. Queried Giers: "But what would we gain by helping the French to destroy Germany?" Responded Alexander III: " . . . Germany as such would disappear. It would break up into a number of small, weak states, the way it used to be." Giers later confided to Lamzdorf:

> Our monarch thinks that when he has taken care of the great Germany, he will be the master of the world. He spoke such nonsense and revealed such savage instincts that nothing was left for me but to hear him patiently out.[6]

The tsar's views apparently reflected the influence of military circles close to General N. N. Obruchev, Russia's chief of staff. For his part Giers hesitated to make binding commitments to France, remaining an obstacle to the conclusion of the alliance.

A military agreement, however, was concluded at the insistence of Alexander III and General Obruchev over the persistent opposition of the Russian war and foreign ministers. It provided that if France were attacked by Germany or by Italy supported by Germany, or if Russia were attacked by Germany or by Austria–Hungary backed by Germany, the other party to the alliance would employ all available forces to fight Germany. France would employ 1.3 million men, and Russia 800,000. The general staffs of France and Russia were to draw up detailed military plans, and both partners pledged not to conclude a separate peace. The military convention would last as long as the Triple Alliance which it was designed to oppose. The Franco–Russian Alliance was finally ratified by the respective governments only in December 1893 and January 1894 respectively; Giers never did support it openly. The alliance reflected the political effects of Russia's great dependence on foreign capital. French high finance was the main creditor in the expansion of Russian industry and railroads under the Witte System.[7]

Of the four powers affected directly by the Franco–Russian Alliance (France, Russia, Germany, and Austria–Hungary), affirms the American scholar, George Kennan, only the two partners of the new alliance had clearly expansionist motives. France definitely aimed to regain Alsace–Lorraine. On the Russian side different goals were envisioned by military men such as Obruchev, civilian chauvinists, and Alexander III, including taking Austrian portions of divided Poland and barring foreign warships from the Turkish Straits. Alexander wished to convert Bulgaria into a Russian satellite state. However, Giers and Lamzdorf opposed any expansionist aim.[8]

Although defensive in origin, like the Triple Alliance it was designed to combat, the Franco–Russian Alliance of 1894 in its military provisions

---

[6]George Kennan, *The Fateful Alliance* (New York, 1984), pp. 153–54, quoting V. N. Lamzdorf, *Dnevnik, 1891–1892*.

[7]D. Geyer, *Russian Imperialism: The Interaction of Domestic and Foreign Policy, 1860–1914*. Trans. B. Little (New Haven, CT, 1987) pp. 136 ff.

[8]Kennan, *The Fateful Alliance*, pp. 249 ff.

contained the seeds of World War I. Thus if any member of the Triple Alliance should mobilize its forces, even partially, the Franco–Russian response was to be the immediate launching of war against all its parties. One can argue that the Franco–Russian Alliance created a rough power equilibrium on the European continent in place of threatened German hegemony from 1894 to 1914, but it ensured that once war came—and most statesmen considered that virtually inevitable—it would necessarily be an all-European conflict.

However, when a Near Eastern crisis threatened late in 1896, Russian leaders discovered that the alliance with France was of no help there. After renewed Turkish massacres of Armenians sparked talk of international action, a Russian crown council in December 1896 approved a plan by Ambassador A. I. Nelidov in Constantinople to seize control of the Turkish Straits. Concluded this secret council: "We need the Bosphorus and the entrance to the Black Sea. The rest, i.e., free passage through the Dardanelles, must be secured later by diplomatic means."[9] Nelidov urged prompt action, but when St. Petersburg approached the French for support in case Russia had to act militarily, they refused any military backing and interpreted their military convention very narrowly. The Russians backed away, and some of the gloss was removed from the Franco–Russian Alliance.[10]

Nonetheless, Russia derived indirect benefits from that Near Eastern crisis. The failure of Austria–Hungary late in 1896 to forge an anti-Russian coalition in that region virtually compelled Vienna to seek an accord with Russia on the best terms it could. Engaged already in a highly adventurous policy in the Far East, Russia required peace on its Balkan flank. Thus when Emperor Franz Josef and Foreign Minister Agenor Goluchowsky visited St. Petersburg in April 1897, they were surprised to discover that the Russians were anxious to protect the status quo in the Balkans and keep foreign warships out of the Straits. The Austro–Russian agreement of May 1897 thus virtually placed the Balkans "on ice" for the next decade: both powers pledged to preserve existing Balkan boundaries, or if any changes were contemplated, to consult with each other on any territorial alterations. That agreement was renewed by the Russian and Austrian emperors in 1903 when they met at Mürzsteg. These accords gave Russia considerable latitude to pursue an expansionist course in the Far East.

Suggested Readings

Brennan, W. H. "The Russian Foreign Ministry and the Alliance with Germany," *Russian History.* vol. I (1974), pp. 18–30.

Byrnes, Robert F. *Pobedonostsev: His Life and Thought.* Bloomington, IN, 1968.

Feis, Herbert. *Europe, the World's Banker, 1870–1914.* New Haven, CT, 1930.

---

[9]V. Khvostov article, quoted by Langer, p. 206.

[10]Khvostov, in Langer, pp. 207–08; A.J.P. Taylor, *The Struggle for Mastery in Europe, 1848–1918* (Oxford, England, 1954), pp. 368–69.

Geyer, Dietrich. *Russian Imperialism: The Interaction of Domestic and Foreign Policy, 1860–1914*. New Haven, CT, 1987.

Grüning, Irene. *Die russische öffentliche Meinung und ihre Stellung zu den Grossmächten, 1878–1894*. Berlin, 1929.

Holborn, Hajo. "Russia and the European Political System," in Ivo Lederer, ed., *Russian Foreign Policy: Essays in Historical Perspective*. New Haven, CT, 1962, pp. 377–416.

Kennan, George F. *The Decline of Bismarck's European Order: Franco-Russian Relations, 1875–1890*. Princeton, NJ, 1979.

_____. *The Fateful Alliance: France, Russia and the Coming of the First World War*. New York, 1984.

Langer, William L. *The Franco–Russian Alliance*. Cambridge, MA, 1929.

_____. *European Alliances and Alignments, 1871–1890*. 2nd ed. New York, 1950.

_____. *The Diplomacy of Imperialism*. 2nd ed. New York, 1951.

Mansergh, Nicholas. *The Coming of the First World War: A Study in the European Balance, 1878–1914*. New York, 1949.

Michon, Georges. *L'Alliance Franco–Russe, 1891–1917*. Paris, 1927.

Rogger, Hans. *Russia in the Age of Modernization and Revolution, 1881–1917*. New York, 1983.

Taylor, A.J.P. *The Struggle for Mastery in Europe, 1848–1918*. Oxford, England, 1954.

Von Laue, Theodor. *Sergei Witte and the Industrialization of Russia*. New York, 1963.

Zaionchkovskii, P. A. *The Russian Autocracy Under Alexander III*. Trans. D. D. Jones. Gulf Breeze, FL, 1976.

RUSSIA IN THE NEAR
AND MIDDLE EAST, 1881–1904

During the reigns of Alexander III and the first decade of rule by Nicholas II, Russia pursued cautious, defensive foreign policies toward Europe while continuing to chase imperial dreams in the Balkans, central Asia, and the Far East. In the Balkans, having surrendered its former client, Serbia, to the stifling embraces of Austria–Hungary at the Congress of Berlin, Russia in the 1880s attempted to convert Bulgaria into an obedient satellite and military base in order to exert predominant influence in the area of the Turkish Straits only to be frustrated once again by Austro–British opposition. After the scheme of A. I. Nelidov, Russian ambassador in Constantinople, to seize the Straits had been blocked, Russia reached accords with Austria–Hungary to guarantee the status quo in the Balkans. Meanwhile in central Asia, until the Pendjeh crisis of 1885 over Afghanistan threatened to provoke war with Britain, Russian southward expansion into the Hindu-Kush Mountains continued. Once frontier settlements with Great Britain were reached in 1885 and 1895, ending that expansion, the focus of Anglo–Russian rivalry shifted to Persia. Russian encroachments on Persia's independence persisted until the Russo–Japanese War. During St. Petersburg's reckless pursuit of expansionism in the Far East, 1895–1904, Russian Balkan policies reverted to cautious avoidance of conflict with a major European power.

RUSSIA, SERBIA, AND BULGARIA, 1878–1903

During the Russo–Turkish War of 1877–1878 advancing Russian armies freeing Bulgaria from direct Turkish rule had been greeted enthusiastically by the Bulgarian people as liberators. The Treaty of San Stefano of March 1878, proposing to create a greater Bulgaria as a Russian satellite, had to be abandoned under Austro–British pressure because those powers assumed that a Big Bulgaria would necessarily be Russian-dominated. The Berlin Treaty (July 1878) had fragmented Greater Bulgaria. Macedonia was restored to direct Turkish rule while the rest was divided between an autonomous principality of Bulgaria north of the Balkan Mountains and a semi-autonomous Eastern Rumelia with its own Christian governor. At the insistence of Tsar Alexander II, Alexander of Battenberg, a youthful Prussian cavalry officer, became prince of the autonomous portion of Bulgaria where Russian occupation troops remained until 1879. Soon the prince, detesting the liberal Russian-sponsored Tyrnovo Constitution, sought to govern through the minority Conservative Party. Supporting the more popular Liberals, the St. Petersburg government became alienated from Battenberg. Meanwhile the Bulgarian army and administration were dominated by Russians who comported themselves often like little Caesars and alienated the Bulgarian people with their high-handed policies.

After Alexander III assumed power in Russia in March 1881, Russian policy in the Balkans began to drift without clear purpose or direction. Between 1879 and 1885 the Russian imperial court, War Ministry, Foreign Ministry, and Panslav elements implemented contradictory policies, quarreled among themselves, and frequently reversed course until they had alienated Bulgarians and Serbs who in 1877–1878 had been overwhelmingly devoted to Russia. In May 1881 Prince Alexander of Battenberg carried out a coup d'état that abrogated the Tyrnovo Constitution and made himself dictator with the support of Russian officers. However, that system proved a failure, and the Tyrnovo Constitution had to be restored and the Russian generals withdrawn. Russia's prestige in the Balkans and especially in Bulgaria was gravely undermined. Meanwhile Prince Alexander turned more and more to Austria–Hungary for economic assistance.

Russia's weakened Balkan position after 1878 was revealed in the affair of constructing Serbia's railroads. At the Berlin Congress Serbia had found itself compelled to promise to conclude a railway convention with Austria–Hungary but remained free theoretically to grant anyone the concession to build the lines. Some Serbian leaders wished to give this to a Russian group headed by the banker S. S. Poliakov, represented in Serbia by the ex-lion of Tashkent, General M. G. Cherniaev. However, late in 1880 Foreign Minister Jovan Ristić, who favored retaining Serbia's links with Russia, fell from power under Austrian pressure, and his successor concluded a railway agreement with the Austrian-backed and well-financed Union Générale of Paris. In disgust Cherniaev wrote fellow Panslav, Ivan Aksakov:

> Amazing things are happening in little Serbia with her strawlike independence. She has turned literally into an Austrian province and [Prince] Milan into an Austrian official straining to display devotion to the House of Habsburg . . .[1]

Indeed, confirming Cherniaev's verdict, the conservative and Austrophile Prince Milan, promised a kingly title by Vienna, surrendered meekly to European capital and Austrian power.

---

[1]Cherniaev to Aksakov, letter dated January 19, 1881; quoted in David MacKenzie, *The Lion of Tashkent* (Athens, GA, 1974), p. 205.

Further complicating Russian and Balkan relations, an unfortunate personal feud developed between Tsar Alexander III and Alexander of Battenberg during which the Russian ruler foolishly severed their personal relations. In 1885 Bulgarian nationalists overthrew the Turkish governor of Eastern Rumelia and proclaimed the union of the two Bulgarian states under the rule of Prince Alexander in violation of the Treaty of Berlin. Alexander III, who desired the unification of Bulgaria to occur only under Russian auspices, not at Bulgarian initiative, refused petulantly to recognize this union. This alienated Bulgarian nationalist opinion which gave increasing support to Battenberg. In September 1885 the tsar wrote his chief of staff, General N. N. Obruchev: "We have had enough of doing popular things to the detriment of Russia's true interests. The Slavs must now serve Russia, and not we them."[2]

This triggered a strange reversal of positions by the leading powers on the Bulgarian question. Russia, the champion of Bulgarian unification since the Treaty of San Stefano, now protested its unification as a violation of the Berlin Treaty. Great Britain under the government of Lord Salisbury defended the Bulgarian action. The British government was beginning to view Bulgarian nationalism as worthy of support as an obstacle to Russian domination of the eastern Balkans. Opposing Bulgarian unification, the Russian government ordered the withdrawal of all Russian officers from Bulgaria on the ground that Bulgaria had revealed gross "ingratitude" toward a benevolent Russia. Alexander III apparently believed that the Russians' departure would render the Bulgarian army impotent. King Milan of Serbia, Bulgaria's chief Balkan rival, reached the same conclusion and responded to a clamor at home to secure compensation for Bulgarian unification. In November 1885 King Milan took a reluctant army and people into an aggressive war with Bulgaria, but only two weeks later the Serbian forces were decisively beaten at Slivnica. Only the diplomatic intervention of Austria–Hungary prevented a Bulgarian occupation of Belgrade, the Serbian capital. Peace was restored at Austrian insistence on the basis of the territorial *status quo ante bellum*, but Bulgaria's victory saved unified Bulgaria. Thereafter Prince Alexander of Battenberg achieved a peaceful settlement of the unification dispute with the Porte. The sultan recognized Battenberg as governor-general of Eastern Rumelia, which remained theoretically Turkish but de facto was an integral part of a unified Bulgaria. Despite this major success, the Bulgarian prince had still to face the hostility of the stubborn Alexander III.

The Russian emperor acted highhandedly to remove Prince Alexander from the Bulgarian throne. In August 1886 pro-Russian Bulgarian officers, with the knowledge of Alexander III and Foreign Minister N. K. Giers, arrested Alexander of Battenberg, forced him to abdicate the throne, and

---

[2]Ivo Lederer, "Russia and the Balkans," in I. Lederer, ed., *Russian Foreign Policy* (New Haven, CT, 1962), p. 437.

abducted him to Russia. Sent in from Russia, Baron A. V. Kaulbars, named Bulgarian war minister under pressure from St. Petersburg, sought to dominate Bulgaria with the use of violence, but his efforts failed in the face of aroused Bulgarian national feeling. When the Bulgarian assembly, contrary to Russian wishes, elected a new ruler, Prince Ferdinand of Saxe-Coburg, all Russian officers were withdrawn from Bulgaria, resulting in a complete breach of diplomatic relations. These unwise measures effectively undermined what formerly had seemed unassailable Russian predominance in the country.

Such arbitrary Russian actions, sponsored personally by the shortsighted Alexander III with the apparent aim to assume direct control over Bulgaria, aroused the European powers to protest. The Austrian foreign minister declared that if Russia sought to annex Bulgaria or turn it into a Russian protectorate, Austria–Hungary would go to war. That provoked an angry counterexplosion from Russian nationalists and Panslavs. One Russian statesman went so far as to affirm undiplomatically that Austria should be expunged from the map of Europe. All this plunged Europe into a severe crisis from which German Chancellor Otto von Bismarck finally rescued it. By encouraging an alignment of the Mediterranean powers (Italy, Britain, and Austria–Hungary), Bismarck induced Alexander III to back away from war. As Baron R. R. Rosen, Russia's ambassador to Japan, commented later:

> Pan-Slavism under the headship of Russia never could have become a reality for the simple reason that Slavdom, divided itself against itself by more than one deadly feud, was united only in its reluctance to submit to the supremacy, let alone domination, of Russia in any shape or form. Of this we had an enlightening experience when we tried our domineering policies on the Bulgarians we had just liberated from the Turkish yoke.[3]

However, in Serbia there remained strong public support for renewed ties with Russia. After the abdication of unpopular King Milan in 1889 brought his young son, Alexander Obrenović, to the Serbian throne under a regency led by Jovan Ristić, the new broadly popular Radical Party headed by Nikola Pašić, a Russophile, sought to restore Serbia's traditional pro-Russian orientation. Already in close touch with Russian Panslav leaders, in 1890 Pašić was received and decorated in St. Petersburg by Alexander III, returning home with a Russian loan and a present of 75,000 rifles for the Serbian army. As Serbia's premier, Pašić returned to St. Petersburg the following year with young King Alexander. Serbia veered toward Russia which indicated its sympathy for Serbian activities in disputed Macedonia.[4] And in 1893 as Serbian ambassador in Russia, Pašić made solid friendships and contacts there which would prove very valuable subsequently during

---

[3]Baron R. R. Rosen, *Forty Years of Diplomacy*, vol. 2 (New York, 1922), p. 100.

[4]Slobodan Jovanović, *Vlada Aleksandra Obrenovića*, vol. 1 (Belgrade, 1929–1931), p. 88 ff.; William L. Langer, *The Diplomacy of Imperialism*, 2nd ed. (New York, 1960), pp. 307–11.

Serbia's drive to unify the South Slavs.[5] However, King Alexander Obrenović, after removing the regency in 1893 by coup d'état, zigzagged inconsistently between Russia and Austria–Hungary until neither power trusted or supported him. As long as the Obrenović dynasty ruled Serbia, however, it remained apparently in the Austrian camp.

CENTRAL ASIA: RUSSIAN ADVANCES AND FRONTIER DELIMITATION, 1881–1904

The threat of a possible Russian advance across the Himalayas into British India reemerged during the 1880s. General M. D. Skobelev's capture of Geok-Tepe in 1881 and the occupation of Akhal oasis in Turkmenia brought Russia close to Persia and Afghanistan. In response to a query by British journalist Charles Marvin about a possible Russian invasion of India, Skobelev replied: "I would not like to command such an expedition. The difficulties would be enormous." And General L. N. Sobolev, chief of the Asian section of the Russian General Staff, declared: "We could invade India, but we do not wish to."[6] In May 1882 General Cherniaev, the conqueror of Tashkent, replaced the deceased General K. P. fon-Kaufman as governor general of Turkestan, reawakening London's fears. Before assuming his post in Tashkent, Cherniaev, at a special conference in St. Petersburg, argued that Russia's existing frontiers in Turkestan were unfavorable and urged the immediate annexation of the central Asian khanates. Bukhara's "pro-Russian party," affirmed Cherniaev, would welcome annexation which would bring to Russia a thickly populated region more fertile and wealthy than all of its previous acquisitions in central Asia.

During his brief tenure as Turkestan governor-general (1882–1884), Cherniaev proposed to the War Ministry that Russian troops aid the emir of Bukhara against the Afghans. Simultaneously, the Russians moved into Merv oasis in Turkmenia provoking intense "nervousness" in London. This annexation, noted the military historian M. A. Terentiev, aroused Cherniaev's aggressive proclivities. Bypassing the war minister, Cherniaev sent telegrams to St. Petersburg advocating a Russian invasion of Afghanistan. Ambassador Edward Thornton of Britain heard that Cherniaev had even submitted a plan for an invasion of India should Anglo–Russian relations rupture over Afghanistan. With the British growing more and more alarmed, Foreign Minister Giers persuaded Alexander III to recall the perennially reckless Cherniaev from Tashkent. Cherniaev's successor, confirmed Giers, would avoid conflicts with neighboring states and execute his orders precisely.[7]

Great Britain had long desired a permanent settlement of central Asian issues through the establishment of some sort of natural boundary between

---

[5]Lazar Marcovitch, "Nikolas Pachitch: Histoire d'un Olympien serbe," (Geneva-Lausanne, 1955, unpublished manuscript), pp. 13–22.

[6]Charles Marvin, *The Russian Advance Towards India* (London, 1882), pp. 5 ff.

[7]MacKenzie, *The Lion of Tashkent*, pp. 223–26.

M. G. Cherniaev, governor–general of Turkestan, 1882–1884

the British and Russian spheres of interest in the region. However, Russian military leaders wished to continue their favorite game of making additional advances screened by pacific assurances from the Foreign Ministry. Under constant prodding from London, the Russian government agreed in July 1884 to establish a boundary commission, but its work soon bogged down. Clearly Russia was in no hurry to reach agreement and kept procrastinating, feigning the sickness of its commission members while its troops continued to advance southward. Meanwhile the struggle within the St. Petersburg leadership over imperial expansion in central Asia resumed. Heading the moderates, Foreign Minister Giers desired peace and a definitive settlement with Great Britain in Turkestan. However, generals such as Leonid N. Sobolev, chief of the Asiatic section of the War Ministry, looking for conflict with the British, argued that war with them in India would allow Russia to seize Constantinople and the Straits.[8]

---

[8]Firuz Kazemzadeh, "Russia and the Middle East," in Lederer, p. 506.

Russia and Great Britain appeared headed for war in March 1885 during the Pendjeh Crisis over Afghanistan. London's deep involvement in the Sudan encouraged Russian nationalists and militarists. When news arrived of the massacre of General Charles George Gordon at Khartoum, Panslav elements in Russia rejoiced at London's discomfiture and urged immediate military action to exploit it. Indicating that support for such views existed within the Russian government, Russian troops advanced close to the Afghan frontiers, even entering areas formerly considered to be part of Afghanistan. Danger of war escalated between Russia and an Afghanistan backed by Great Britain. As British troops prepared to march on Herat, Queen Victoria issued a personal appeal to Alexander III to prevent war. But on March 30 Russian troops attacked an Afghan force at Pendjeh and drove it away killing several hundred Afghans. War between Russia and Britain then seemed probable. Even Prime Minister William Gladstone, previously conciliatory toward Russia, requested Parliament for money to prepare for war. The powerful British reaction convinced Russian leaders that they faced war unless a compromise settlement were reached promptly. In September 1885 Anglo–Russian negotiations on delimiting the Russo–Afghan frontier produced a final agreement. Pendjeh district went to Russia but the strategic Zulfikar Pass, which Russia had long coveted, reverted to Afghanistan. During 1886–1887 other segments of the disputed frontier were settled by negotiation.

The events of 1885 proved highly significant for Russian policy in central Asia. Having filled the power vacuum there, Russia had advanced southward as far as it could without provoking war with Britain. The steady Russian expansion of the previous twenty years now was halted by firm British resistance and the natural barrier represented by the Hindu Kush and Himalaya Mountains. The acute phase of Anglo–Russian rivalry in central Asia ended as Russian attention shifted to Persia.

In the early 1890s, when small Russian forces moved into the mountainous Pamir region near Afghanistan, Anglo–Russian negotiations were resumed. In the Pamir Agreement of 1895 Russia received part of that region as Russian and British spheres of influence were more precisely defined. A narrow strip of Afghan territory lay between them as neutral ground. A Captain Skerskii of the Russian General Staff pointed out that possession of the Pamir Mountains would give Russia important advantages in any conflict with Afghanistan or India. The General Staff investigated routes through the mountains, and although Russia apparently never planned to attack British India, it utilized the threat of one. Thus in 1899 Nicholas II boasted that he could decide the outcome of the Boer War in South Africa by instructing his Turkestan army to march to the Indian frontier, but that he would not do so because Turkestan was not yet linked by railway with Russia proper. Instructions in 1900 from the Russian Foreign Ministry to its consul in Bombay stated:

> The fundamental meaning of India to us is that she represents Great Britain's most vulnerable point, a sensitive nerve on which one touch may perhaps easily

induce Her Majesty's Government to alter its hostile policy to us and to show the desired compliance on all those questions where . . . our interests collide.[9]

Meanwhile Russia's position in central Asia was being enhanced by railway construction. The Transcaspian Railroad (later called the Central Asian Railroad), begun in 1880 eastward from the Caspian Sea in support of General M. D. Skobelev's campaign in Turkmenia, soon altered the entire strategic situation in the region. Noted a German observer:

> The railroad . . . has cut through the desert belt which England regarded as a protection for India . . . , has made possible the simultaneous reinforcement of large masses of troops from Turkestan, the Caucasus and Volga regions to Ashkhabad and Merv, and has firmly connected the province of Transcaspia with . . . Turkestan; Russia's prestige in Central Asia has been consolidated. . . .[10]

Despite the doubts of influential generals such as Skobelev and Cherniaev, the War Ministry continued the railway, which by 1898 had reached Samarkand and Tashkent. In 1889 Lord George Curzon, British viceroy of India, stressed the Central Asian Railroad's vast significance for Russia's position because of her enhanced ability to threaten India. By unifying Russian central Asia, formerly split by an impassable desert, the railway had reduced Bukhara to complete dependence on Russia.[11] The Orenburg-Tashkent Railway, completed in 1905, further reinforced central Asia's links with European Russia. Built at the urging of War Minister A. N. Kuropatkin for strategic reasons, it was soon carrying large amounts of freight. These railway lines made Turkestan vitally important to the imperial Russian economy, especially since they provided quantities of raw cotton for Russia's growing textile industries.

ANGLO–RUSSIAN RIVALRY IN PERSIA

After 1885 the imperial rivalry of Russia and Britain in Asia, known popularly as "the Great Game," shifted mostly from Turkestan and Afghanistan to Persia (now Iran), a large Middle Eastern empire with a weak and ineffective government. Whereas in central Asia the army had been the chief instrument of Russian penetration, in Persia subtler means had to be employed to advance Russian influence. Viewing it similarly to far smaller Khiva and Bukhara, Russian leaders believed that Persia was destined eventually to be incorporated into the Russian Empire. Declared Count S. Iu. Witte, Russia's finance minister, 1892–1903, who was also highly influential in determining Russian foreign policy:

---

[9] Quoted in D. MacKenzie, "Turkestan's Significance to Russia, 1850–1917," *The Russian Review*, vol. 33, no. 2 (April 1974), p. 178.

[10] MacKenzie, "Turkestan's Significance," p. 179.

[11] George Curzon, *Russia in Central Asia in 1889* (New York, 1967, reprint), pp. 44, 276.

The entire northern part of Persia was intended, as if by nature, to turn in the future if not into a part of the great Russian Empire, then in any case, into a country under our complete protectorate.[12]

A leading designer of Russia's imperial policies towards Persia, I. A. Zinoviev, who served as minister to Persia then as director of the Asiatic Department, advocated bringing Persia gradually under complete Russian control. Nicholas II also believed that the continued existence of an independent Persia was undesirable.[13]

Officials of various Russian ministries and military men operating inside Persia were even more openly imperialistic than their superiors back in St. Petersburg. They pushed for the rapid extension of Russian influence there through the construction of strategic railroads, commercial ports, and naval bases. Prior to 1905 they rejected any notion of dividing Persia with Great Britain into spheres of influence since they believed that the entire country should belong to Russia. They were supported strongly by the nationalist Russian press which exerted pressure on the Russian government to act decisively. Even moderate statesmen such as Foreign Minister Count V. N. Lamzdorf believed Persia should become a Russian protectorate. The Shah's territories should be preserved, wrote Lamzdorf, while Russia gradually subjected Persia to its dominant influence. "Our task is to make Persia politically an obedient . . . instrument in our hands."[14]

After 1880 the Cossack Brigade served as an effective Russian tool inside Persia. Organized in 1879 at the Shah's request by Russian officers, its Persian Cossack rank and file became intensely loyal to their Russian commanders who viewed the brigade as Russia's spearhead in a worldwide struggle against British imperialism. As the Persian state disintegrated increasingly, the Cossack Brigade gave Russia important leverage over Persia's domestic affairs.

Russian leaders realized that Great Britain stood as the only significant obstacle to complete Russian domination over Persia. All Russian agencies in Persia considered themselves involved in commercial and political competition with the British. Wrote the semi-official Russian newspaper *Novoe Vremia* in May 1889:

Two forces alone are struggling for supremacy on the vast expanse of Asia—Russia and England. . . . An understanding with England would be possible only if the two powers had common aims.[15]

And *Novoe Vremia* doubted that the British fleet could maintain Britain's supremacy in southern Persia and the Persian Gulf.

---

[12]Sergei Iu. Witte, *Vospominaniia*, vol. II (Berlin, 1922), pp. 407–08.

[13]F. Kazemzadeh, "Russia and the Middle East," in Lederer, p. 508.

[14]Kazemzadeh, pp. 508–09.

[15]Kazemzadeh, pp. 509–10.

Anglo–Russian commercial and railway building rivalry in Persia grew more intense in the final years of the nineteenth century. Foreign Minister Mikhail Muraviov's memorandum of January 1900 called the Russian position in north Persia unassailable but doubted Russia could advance into the center and the south without large troop concentrations and possible war with Britain. Indeed, in a September 1899 memorandum Lord Curzon, British viceroy of India, had urged London to adopt well-defined, decisive policies of either opposing Russian expansion in Persia or reaching agreement with St. Petersburg. In any case, argued Curzon, Russia must be prevented from reaching the Persian Gulf.[16] As the British gradually lost ground in the Persian competition, they sought repeatedly to reach agreement with Russia to divide it into spheres of interest. By 1900 a British diplomat reported pessimistically to London that Russian troops under Russian officers were keeping order in Persia, its finances were supported with Russian loans, while its goods were moving along Russian roads and railways. The threatened creation of a Russian naval base on the Persian Gulf finally induced London to issue a sharp warning to St. Petersburg. In May 1903 Lord Lansdowne, the foreign secretary, clearly pointing his finger at Russia, declared in the House of Lords that Great Britain did not seek to exclude other nations from trading in the Persian Gulf, but:

> We should regard the establishment of a naval base, or of a fortified port, in the Persian Gulf by any other Power as a very grave menace to British interests, and we should certainly resist it with all the means at our disposal.[17]

This unequivocal British statement helped induce the Russian government to restrain the actions of its personnel in Persia, especially since the Boer War had now ended and Great Britain was allied with Japan, with which Russia was embroiled in dangerous rivalry in the Far East. In Persia Russian leaders once again recoiled before the prospect of a war with Great Britain. However, such sensible restraint was conspicuously absent from Nicholas II's policies in the Far East toward the island empire of Japan.

Suggested Readings

Black, Cyril E. *The Establishment of Constitutional Government in Bulgaria.* Princeton, NJ, 1943.

Cecil, Lady Gwendolyn. *Life of Robert Marquis of Salisbury,* vols. 3–4. London, 1931–1932.

Curzon, Lord George. *Russia in Central Asia in 1889.* New York, 1967, reprint.

Huhn, Avon. *The Kidnapping of Prince Alexander of Battenberg.* London, 1887.

Hyam, Ronald. *Britain's Imperial Century, 1815–1914: A Study of Empire and Expansion.* London, 1976.

---

[16]Langer, pp. 666–68.

[17]Kazemzadeh, p. 517.

Jelavich, Barbara. *The Ottoman Empire, the Great Powers and the Straits Question, 1870–1887.* Bloomington, IN, 1973.

Jelavich, Charles. *Tsarist Russia and Balkan Nationalism: Russian Influence in the Internal Affairs of Bulgaria and Serbia, 1879–1886.* Berkeley, CA, 1958.

Kazemzadeh, Firuz. *Russia and Britain in Persia, 1864–1914.* New Haven, CT, 1968.

Langer, William L. *The Diplomacy of Imperialism.* 2nd ed. New York, 1960.

MacKenzie, David. *The Lion of Tashkent: The Career of General M. G. Cherniaev.* Athens, GA, 1974.

———. "Turkestan's Significance to Russia (1850–1917)," *The Russian Review,* vol. 33, no. 2 (April 1974), pp. 167–88.

Marvin, Charles. *The Russian Advance Toward India.* London, 1882.

Medlicott, W. N. *The Congress of Berlin and After: A Diplomatic History of the Near Eastern Settlement, 1878–1880.* London, 1938, 1963.

Mijatovich, Chedomille. *The Memoirs of a Balkan Diplomat.* London, 1917.

Morgan, G. *Anglo–Russian Rivalry in Central Asia, 1810–1895.* London, 1981.

Porter, B. *The Lion's Share: A Short History of British Imperialism, 1850–1983.* London, 1983.

Pribram, Alfred. *The Secret Treaties of Austria–Hungary, 1879–1914.* 2 vols. Cambridge, MA, 1920–1921.

Sumner, B. H. *Tsardom and Imperialism in the Far East and Middle East, 1880–1914.* London, 1940.

Terenzio, Pio. *La rivalité anglo–russe en Perse et en Afghanistan jusqu'aux accords de 1907.* Paris, 1947.

Wilson, Arnold T. *The Persian Gulf.* Oxford, England, 1928.

Witte, Sergei Iu. *The Memoirs of Count Witte.* New York, 1921, 1990.

10

EXPANSION IN
THE FAR EAST, 1881–1904

Russian actions in the Far East between 1894 and 1904 constitute the exception to generally prudent external policies in the post-Crimean era. Russian expansionism in the Orient, which the German scholar, Dietrich Geyer appropriately designates "borrowed imperialism," was unlike that of the great industrial powers of Europe, an expression of economic weakness, underdevelopment, and a compensatory effort to appear to be a great power.[1] With the influence of the Foreign Ministry undermined by frequent changes in its leadership, and the tendency of Nicholas II to follow the imprudent counsel of shallow adventurers, Russia launched on a course of reckless advances which led a decade later to a disastrous and humiliating defeat by Japan.

RUSSIA'S INTERESTS AND
IMPERIALIST IDEOLOGY, 1880s

With Siberia in a process of growth and development, after 1850 Russian leaders grew more interested in establishing a powerful presence on the shores of the Pacific Ocean. The Treaty of Beijing of 1860 had confirmed Russian control over the Amur Valley, the Ussuri, and Vladivostok, while the Treaty of St. Petersburg (1875) gave Russia control over Sakhalin Island and favorable commercial agreements with Japan. Meanwhile the European powers continued to penetrate a decaying Manchu China. The British were firmly established in Shanghai and the Yangtse Valley of central China. The French became dominant in south China and Indochina. Japan became engaged in a deepening rivalry with China over Korea, a dependency of the Celestial Empire. Russia wisely refused to become involved directly in that dispute. In 1886 an oral agreement between the Russian envoy and the Chinese foreign minister, Li Hung-chang, provided for preserving the status quo in Korea and protecting its territorial integrity.

---

[1]Dietrich Geyer, *Russian Imperialism: The Interaction of Domestic and Foreign Policy, 1860–1914* (New Haven, CT, 1987), p. 205.

Nonetheless, in the 1880s Russia's position in the Far East remained rather vulnerable. As Great Britain and Russia competed over influence in Afghanistan and as the Japanese interest in the Asian mainland grew, Russia lacked modern overland communications with its Pacific holdings, few Russian troops were stationed in the Far East, and there was no sizable fleet or convenient naval bases. Also, Russia remained a backward agrarian power lagging ever further behind western Europe.

Russian interests in the Far East in the late nineteenth century appear inadequate to explain St. Petersburg's extreme imperialist policies adopted in the mid-1890s. Russia lacked sufficient capital to develop the Amur region or Sakhalin, to say nothing of any major economic penetration of Manchuria. However, since its products remained mostly uncompetitive in Europe, Russia did desire to gain firmer access to Chinese markets. Russian leaders aimed to secure ice-free ports on the Pacific, helping to account for the drive to penetrate Manchuria. The prestige factor also bulked large in Russia's Far Eastern policies. St. Petersburg aimed to prove Russia's equality with the European imperialist powers by securing special rights and spheres of interest in a weakening China. Among Russians prevailed the widespread belief in their superiority over the Japanese and Chinese.

During the 1880s in Russia developed an imperialist ideology based on current theories of manifest destiny and the "white man's burden" promoted by a group of publicists and scholars known as the *Vostochniki* (Easterners). Their views stemmed from the Slavophile tenet that Russian culture, wholly distinct from the European, was destined to develop along its own unique lines. From there it was but a short step to assert that Russia, with traditions derived from both Europe and Asia, had a great mission to spread European and Russian values to the Orient. Extreme Vostochniki, arguing that Russia was more closely affiliated culturally with the Orient than with Europe, advocated a merging of Russia and the Orient by the incorporation of large portions of Asia into the Russian Empire on the grounds that Russia's future lay primarily in Asia.

Thus during the late 1880s the great Russian explorer and zoologist, Nicholas M. Przhevalskii, propagated the view that the inhabitants of Mongolia and Sinkiang, which belonged to the Chinese Empire, longed to become Russian citizens:

These poor Asiatics look to the advance of Russian power with the firm conviction that its advent is synonomous with the beginning of a happier era, a life of greater security for themselves.[2]

---

[2]A. Malozemoff, *Russian Far Eastern Policy, 1881–1904* (Berkeley, CA, 1958), p. 42; Donald Rayfield, *The Dream of Lhasa: The Life of Nikolay Przhevalsky (1839–1888)* (Athens, OH, 1976), p. 185.

Such attitudes, claimed Przhevalskii, had spread among the nomadic Dungans and Mongols of Sinkiang because of maladministration by Chinese officials and the severity of their rule unlike the relatively just, benevolent Russian regime in Russian Turkestan.

A leading Russian scholar of international law, F. F. Martens, provided legal arguments to support a Russian expansionist policy in the Orient. "International rights cannot be taken into account when dealing with semi-barbarous peoples," proclaimed Martens, essentially the same assertion Foreign Minister A. M. Gorchakov had employed in his circular of 1864 in regard to central Asia. And V. P. Vasiliev, Russia's leading Sinologist, in 1883 put forward the concept of Russia as cultural missionary in the Orient. Unlike Europeans, argued Vasiliev, Russians came to the Orient with a sacred duty as "liberators" of peoples "oppressed by the tyranny of internecine strife and impotency." An outstanding Russian philosopher, Vladimir Soloviev, proclaimed that Russia must advance in Asia in order to protect European civilization from the "yellow peril." Oriental races, asserted Soloviev in a typical misuse of social Darwinism, must either submit to the superior white races of Europe or disappear.[3]

Prince E. E. Ukhtomskii, a journalist and student of Oriental philosophy, became an enthusiastic spokesman for the Vostochniki and for Russia's manifest destiny in Asia. Once opened up by modern communications, Siberia was destined to become Russia's treasurehouse and land of the future. Whereas Europeans invaded Asia with foreign standards and ways of life in order to make money, any Asiatic borderland soon became a home for Russians. Asserted Ukhtomskii: "The more actively Europe presses against Asia, the brighter becomes the name of the White Tsar." Returning from a trip to the Far East in 1890–1891 as tutor to the future Nicholas II, Ukhtomskii stated: "We have nothing to conquer. All these peoples of various races feel themselves drawn to us, and are ours, by blood, by tradition, and by ideas. . . . The great and mysterious Orient is ready to become ours."[4] These views of the Vostochniki were accepted and developed further during the 1890s by Finance Minister Sergei Iu. Witte into a theory of economic imperialism based on Russian domination of Manchuria and north China through the Trans-Siberian Railroad.

Although Alexander III revealed little enthusiasm for these Asiatic dreams, by the time of Nicholas II's accession in 1894 the Vostochniki had laid ideological bases for Russian expansion in the Far East at the expense of China and possibly Japan, much as the Panslavs had done in the Balkans. Nicholas, who as a highly impressionable heir to the throne had visited Japan, was deeply influenced by arguments of the Vostochniki and dreamed of realizing them at the first opportunity. Thus in 1895 Nicholas II penned this comment on a report of his foreign minister:

---

[3]Malozemoff, p. 43.
[4]Malozemoff, pp. 43–44.

It is absolutely necessary that Russia should have a port [on the Pacific Ocean] open all year. This port must be on the littoral [of southeast Korea] and must be connected by a stretch of land with our possessions.[5]

THE TRANS-SIBERIAN AND CHINESE EASTERN RAILWAYS, 1891–1896

During the 1890s state-directed economic expansion under the leadership of the Ministry of Finance penetrated the entire Russian Empire, but especially in the Far East where Finance Minister Witte, after 1895, became the dominant Russian figure with the railroad as his primary instrument.[6] The construction during the 1890s of the transcontinental railway known as the Trans-Siberian altered fundamentally the entire balance of forces in the northern Pacific and greatly stimulated Russia's imperialist surge there. The idea of building such a line had been broached originally by the farsighted Governor General N. N. Muraviov-Amurskii in the 1840s, but the Russian government then lacked funds, imagination, and interest in railways. After a favorable report in 1887 about the military benefits of such a railway, the imperial government decided in February 1891 to proceed with its construction. Soon after becoming minister of finance in August 1892, Count Witte, who had been a successful private railway entrepreneur, submitted a report to Alexander III outlining his grandiose dream of Russian domination of Eurasia through the Trans-Siberian Railroad. It would establish, claimed Witte, "uninterrupted European rail communication with the Great Ocean and the Asiatic East" thus breaking a "new path and opening new horizons not only for Russia but for world trade." By opening the Siberian treasure house of natural resources for the Russian economy, it would fuel a great economic boom. This would "rank it as one of those world events that usher in new epochs in the history of nations. . . ."[7] The Trans-Siberian, predicted Witte, would deflect freight from the Suez Canal and become the bearer of Russian manufactures to the vast Chinese market. By guaranteeing the essentials for a Russian Far Eastern fleet, the railroad when completed would enable that fleet to be greatly strengthened. In case of a crisis either in Europe or Asia, the Russian Far Eastern flotilla would become highly significant "controlling the whole movement of international commerce in Pacific waters."[8] Witte's lengthy memorandum was the first statement of a new imperialistic Russian Far Eastern program.

Under Witte's energetic direction, construction of the Trans-Siberian Railroad was pushed throughout the 1890s at an unprecedented pace,

---

[5]Boris A. Romanov, *Russia in Manchuria (1892–1906)*. Trans. Susan Jones (New York, 1974), p. 53.

[6]Geyer, p. 186.

[7]Romanov, p. 42.

[8]Romanov, p. 45.

although costs far exceeded expectations, placing a terrible strain on Russian finances. By the eve of the Russo–Japanese War (1904), the single-tracked railroad was nearly completed except around mountain-rimmed Lake Baikal where hundreds of tunnels had to be constructed. Although begun largely for military reasons, the railway opened up vast Siberia to more rapid colonization which the government encouraged in order to drain excess peasant populations from the Black Soil region of southern European Russia.

In February 1893, P. A. Badmaev—an Orientalist, adventurer, and entrepreneur—submitted to Witte an extensive memorandum concerning Russia's urgent historic mission in the Far East, requesting that it be transmitted immediately to Alexander III. Badmaev urged the extension of the Trans-Siberian from Lake Baikal to Vladivostok and also southward 1,200 miles into China as a prelude to the bloodless annexation "of the whole Mongol-Tibetan-Chinese east" by thousands of frontiersmen whom he proposed to send out in all directions. Should Badmaev's scheme succeed, commented Witte approvingly, then "from the shores of the Pacific and the heights of the Himalalyas Russia would dominate not only the affairs of Asia but those of Europe as well." Here Witte revealed his sponsorship of the most extreme and enthusiastic Vostochnik views. This was an imperial dream far beyond the capacities of a still backward Russia. Alexander III, although pleased, reacted realistically: "This is all so new, unusual and fantastic that it is hard to believe in the possibility of success."[9]

The accession of the naive and unrealistic Nicholas II in 1894 coincided with the Sino–Japanese War, which followed an uprising in Chinese-ruled Korea. In that conflict China was defeated on land and sea by a despised Japan which over the previous twenty-five years had modernized its government, army, and navy while corrupt Manchu China had stood still. As Japanese victories mounted, Russian leaders discussed what to do, especially when the Treaty of Shimonoseki of March 1895 stipulated the independence of Korea and Japanese possession of Port Arthur and the Liaotung Peninsula. Russian nationalists clamored for annexing to Russia an ice-free port in Korea and part of northern Manchuria so that the Trans-Siberian Railway could be "straightened out" and shortened. They favored a deal with Japan which would cede parts of China to both powers. The Japanese attack on China, argued Witte, had represented a concealed offensive against Russia. Under the Shimonoseki Treaty Russia would have to commit large military forces to protect the Trans-Siberian Railroad. Thus Witte advocated maintaining north China's territorial integrity in order to prevent a Japanese seizure of southern Manchuria with strategic Port Arthur. Russia's interest dictated, continued Witte, preserving a relatively strong though passive China in order to guarantee Russia's security in the East. Opposing any partition of Chinese territory, he advocated turning China instead into the obedient ally of Russia. Supported by War Minister P. S.

---

[9]Romanov, pp. 46–47.

Vannovskii, the energetic Witte obtained the backing of both Germany and France. The three European powers thereupon issued a virtual ultimatum to victorious Japan, undercutting the Treaty of Shimonoseki and compelling the Japanese to return strategic Liaotung Peninsula to China. The Japanese yielded reluctantly, accepting instead a sizable war indemnity and the island of Taiwan (Formosa). Thus Japan was denied a foothold on the Asian mainland and China became Russia's subservient partner.

By now Count Witte, the dominant figure in Russia's great industrial surge of the 1890s, had virtually taken over the conduct of Russian foreign policy in the Far East from the Foreign Ministry. He argued that Foreign Minister A. B. Lobanov-Rostovskii was ignorant of Oriental problems, but the true reason was the crucial role of economic and financial matters in Russia's Far Eastern policies. Nicholas II allowed Witte to lead. Thus Witte began immediate negotiations with the Chinese government offering to secure for China a large foreign loan with which it could pay off the indemnity to Japan. Witte had the Russian Treasury negotiate a loan to China from France; the loan contract stipulated Russia's participation in any future international supervision of Chinese finances. In September 1895 Witte organized the founding of a Russo–Chinese Bank which would operate in China with broad powers over tax collection. The French were the chief shareholders, but the bank's patron was the Russian government. This was the first step in Witte's planned program of economic imperialism in China.

When the Chinese statesman Li Hung-chang came to Russia early in 1896, ostensibly to attend Nicholas II's coronation, Witte conducted the actual negotiations with him about constructing the Trans-Siberian Railway through northern Manchuria to Vladivostok, thus shortening that line by some 300 miles and greatly facilitating its construction. This so-called Li-Lobanov Agreement, negotiated entirely by Witte, prescribed that China would grant permission for the Chinese Eastern Railroad Corporation to build a railway from China through Harbin to Vladivostok to be called the Chinese Eastern Railroad. The corporation was to be organized by the Russo–Chinese Bank and be mostly controlled by St. Petersburg. China was to cede to this corporation sufficient land for the railroad and to allow it to exercise full authority and provide its own police. China was granted permission to purchase the railroad for 700 million rubles after thirty-six years, but that price was so high that it was very unlikely that China could ever pay it. A defensive alliance was also concluded between Russia and China obligating them to defend one another against any Japanese attack. That accord confirmed Russia's economic domination over northern Manchuria.

The Treaty of Shimonoseki, stipulating Korea's independence, had been designed to prepare the way for Japanese domination. However, brutal Japanese actions in Korea, including the murder of the queen, caused the king of Korea in January 1896 to seek refuge in the Russian diplomatic mission. Exploiting this opening, in June 1896 the Russians reached an agreement with Japan by which both sides pledged to respect Korean independence, to cooperate in assisting its administration, and to carry out financial reform. Thereby, Russia obtained the opportunity to penetrate Korea economically along with Japan. Thus, in September 1897, Witte arranged the creation of a Russo–Korean Bank, modelled after the Russo–Chinese Bank and sought to bring Korean tariff administration under Russian control and to open gold and copper mines on the Yalu River.[10] During 1896–1897, thanks largely to Witte, Russia emerged as a principal beneficiary of the Sino–Japanese War, greatly strengthening her influence in both China and Korea.

PORT ARTHUR AND THE YALU CONCESSION

In 1897–1898 the European imperialist powers completed their division of a helpless China into spheres of influence. Their drive was triggered by Germany's sudden seizure in October 1897 of the port of Kiaochow on the Kwangtung Peninsula. The Germans had been seeking a Chinese treaty port ever since their participation in the 1895 European ultimatum to Japan and that question had been discussed between William II and Nicholas II then. Since the Russian ruler had raised no objections, William assumed that Russia would support German claims. But to William's embarrassment, Russia protested Germany's move and threatened to send its Far Eastern fleet to Kiaochow. Foreign Minister M. N. Muraviov, taken aback by the German move, recommended that Russia exploit the situation and demand from China a treaty port of its own in compensation. At a conference in November 1897 Muraviov advocated seizing the naval base of Port Arthur on Liaotung Peninsula in southern Manchuria because of its great strategic importance as an ice-free port on the Yellow Sea. Witte claims that he protested such a scheme indignantly, reminding Muraviov of Russia's pledge under the Li-Lobanov Treaty to protect China's territorial integrity. Seizing Port Arthur, Witte warned, would constitute treachery and faithlessness toward an ally, would rouse Chinese hostility and endanger the Chinese Eastern Railway. The war and foreign ministers urged taking over Port Arthur whereas the navy minister wished to obtain a port on the east coast of Korea closer to the open ocean. However, Nicholas II had already decided in favor of taking Port Arthur and in December 1897 a Russian squadron occupied it and the neighboring commercial port of Talienwan (named Dalny by the Russians) after Foreign Minister Muraviov warned that otherwise the British would seize them.

Simultaneously, Witte, urged by Li Hung-Chang to guarantee a new loan in order to pay the war indemnity to Japan, demanded that China grant Russia railway and industrial monopolies throughout Manchuria and Mongolia, and the right to build a branch railway line running southward from the Chinese Eastern to a port on the Yellow Sea. Knowing that Port Arthur's occupation had already been decided on, Witte sought at a

---

[10]Romanov, pp. 109 ff.

single stroke to complete Russian domination of both Manchuria and Mongolia.[11] All this made Witte's pose as a pacifist and his pious objections against violating China's territorial integrity appear rather transparent.

By April 1898 the entire sordid imperialist seizure had been completed. General A. N. Kuropatkin had just been named Russian war minister. He was a conservative opposed to Witte's peaceful economic penetration of China. Kuropatkin argued that China should be compelled to grant Russia not just two treaty ports but most of the Liaotung Peninsula. Soon thereafter Russia obtained from China a twenty-five-year lease of the entire peninsula, authorization to build a naval base at Port Arthur and a commercial port at neighboring Dalny. Furthermore, Russia could construct a railroad from Port Arthur northward to Harbin where it would intersect the Chinese Eastern line. Criticizing that arrangement, Witte called it a violation of Russia's traditional relations with China and designated it as "child's play which will end disastrously." Great Britain and France both exploited China's pitiful weakness to seize additional ports. Japanese resentment of Russian moves in southern Manchuria were assuaged by St. Petersburg's pledge to recognize Japan's special economic interests in Korea. From the events of 1898 Russia emerged dominant in all of Manchuria. However, it was becoming evident that Russian financial resources were inadequate to finance such major imperial expansion. With economic recession gathering force in Europe and Russia, Witte opposed the increased military budget, which War Minister Kuropatkin claimed was required to protect Russia's Far Eastern positions. Consequently, Kuropatkin urged "extreme caution in our foreign relations," especially in Korea, in order to avoid any conflict with Japan.[12]

These ruthless actions by the European imperialist powers provoked a powerful nationalist reaction in China where there had long been sporadic agitation against the "foreign devils" (sometimes called "the big noses"). Serious disturbances were begun by the nationalist secret society of Harmonious Fists, popularly known as the Boxers, protected by the Manchu imperial court. In May 1900 erupted the "Boxer Rebellion," during which Boxers besieged the foreign legations in Beijing. The siege was broken by an international army led by a German general. Russia took the lead in having a European army march on Beijing despite Witte's plea to let other powers act and thus take the blame. The Boxer Rebellion threatened Witte's entire imperial plan based on the Chinese Eastern and South Manchurian Railroads.

War Minister Kuropatkin reacted joyfully to news of the Boxer uprising, declaring, "This will give us an excuse to seize Manchuria." Queried Witte: "What will we do with it?" Responded Kuropatkin: "Turn it into another

---

[11]Romanov, pp. 140–41.
[12]Geyer, pp. 202–03.

Bukhara."[13] Indeed, Boxer attacks on the Chinese Eastern Railroad brought Kuropatkin to order the occupation of Manchuria by 170,000 men, the largest European military force sent to Asia during the age of imperialism. The troops acted as if they were in a conquered country causing Witte to oppose the occupation vigorously. But the war minister insisted on maintaining the military occupation for almost three years. While the Russians pillaged Manchuria's resources, Nicholas II vacillated and made inconsistent decisions. After a series of foreign protests and lengthy negotiations, Russia by an April 1902 treaty recognized China's sovereignty over Manchuria and promised to evacuate its troops within eighteen months. However, Kuropatkin still regarded at least northern Manchuria as destined in the future to belong to Russia. Witte depicted Kuropatkin's policies there as unduly aggressive, although the war minister wished by all means to avoid conflict with Japan.

Meanwhile the division and confusion within the Russian government over Far Eastern policies grew ever deeper. The Foreign Ministry, headed from June 1900 by Count V. N. Lamzdorf, a competent but uninspiring official, gradually lost control over events; often Nicholas II did not even inform Lamzdorf of his decisions. Lamzdorf and Witte continued to favor peaceful diplomatic and economic penetration of China while avoiding any collision with Japan. However, the successful suppression of the Boxer Rebellion gave military elements in Russia predominant influence over policy-making as Nicholas II came more and more under the influence of irresponsible, adventurist elements.

Late in 1897 two influential ex-Guards officers, A. N. Bezobrazov and V. M. Vonliarliarskii, became interested in a huge timber concession on the Yalu and Tumen rivers on the Manchurian–Korean frontier. Under cover of this private economic concession, Bezobrazov sought to regain Russian influence in Korea, winning to his view Count Vorontsov-Dashkov and Grand Prince Alexander Mikhailovich who introduced Bezobrazov to Nicholas II. They all envisioned the Yalu Concession as a means to penetrate and eventually control Korea which Japan for years had considered its rightful sphere of interest. Supported by conservatives and some military and naval leaders, Bezobrazov converted the poorly informed tsar to a policy of reckless advance.

Opposing Bezobrazov's schemes vigorously, Witte wrote Lamzdorf in November 1901 warning that unless Russia removed misunderstandings over Korea with Japan, war with her was likely. An armed clash with Japan in the near future, affirmed Witte, would be disastrous for Russia. Instead, it would be preferable, he believed, to abandon any Russian involvement in Korea.

Emperor William II of Germany, anxious to distract Russia's attention from Europe, encouraged Nicholas II consistently in his "great task" in Asia.

---

[13]S. Iu. Witte, *Vospominaniia*, vol. 1 (Moscow, 1923), p. 142.

Russia's destiny, wrote William in 1895, was "to cultivate the Asian continent and to defend Europe against the inroads of the Great Yellow Race. In this you will always find me on your side ready to help you as best I can . . . ." Later, William stated: "It is evident to every unbiased mind that Korea must and will be Russian."[14]

By 1903 Bezobrazov and his cousin, Admiral A. M. Abaza, had reached the peak of their influence. Bezobrazov was named secretary of state in charge of all matters relating to the Far East. The peaceful approach of Witte and Lamzdorf of compromising differences with Japan was repudiated; their defeat was fostered by the support given to adventurous elements by Interior Minister, V. K. Pleve. At an imperial conference in May 1903 when Foreign Minister Lamzdorf argued that the diplomats should have full charge of Far Eastern problems, Pleve objected:

> Russia has been made by bayonets, not diplomacy . . . and we must decide the issue with China and Japan with bayonets and not with diplomatic pens.[15]

"A little victorious war" with Japan, Pleve was convinced, would do much to clear the air by calming revolutionary agitation inside Russia. The final blow for Witte was the appointment of Admiral E. I. Alekseev as imperial viceroy over the entire region east of Lake Baikal, entrusted with handling diplomatic relations with China, Japan, and Korea. Alekseev soon went over to the extremist Bezobrazov camp. In August 1903, considering his cause lost and war with Japan inevitable, Count Witte resigned as finance minister.

Negotiations between Japan and Russia failed to discover a diplomatic solution to their differences. Already in 1901 Tokyo had dispatched a high-powered mission under Viscount Hirobumi Ito to Russia to settle outstanding issues; it failed partly because of Bezobrazov's growing influence. Ito had offered a Japanese pledge to guarantee the Russian sphere of interest in all Manchuria in return for a Russian guarantee of a Japanese sphere in Korea, but Russian leaders prevaricated and avoided a direct response. Rebuffed in Russia, except by Count Witte, the Japanese turned to Great Britain, just emerging from "splendid isolation" after the Boer War and desirous of obtaining an ally in the Far East in order to safeguard its positions against possible Russian expansion. A defensive Anglo–Japanese alliance was concluded in 1902, obligating each to remain neutral in a war against a third power but to join its partner if another power entered the conflict.

---

[14]William II, *Letters from the Kaiser to the Czar*, Isaac D. Levine, ed. (New York, 1920), pp. 10–13.

[15]B. H. Sumner, *Tsardom and Imperialism in the Far East and Middle East, 1880–1914* (London, 1940), p. 14.

The alliance protected Great Britain against further Russian advances in China while Japan obtained support for its asserted predominance in Korea. Russia was left diplomatically isolated since France refused to support its anti-Japanese course.

In July 1903 Tokyo made a final attempt to reach accord with St. Petersburg on terms similar to those of 1901: Manchuria for Korea. But the naming of Admiral Alekseev as viceroy of Kwangtung and Amur provinces suggested that the extremists were dominant. Russian moderates and realists, including Witte, Lamzdorf, and even Kuropatkin, favored accepting the Japanese proposals. In December 1903 Kuropatkin proposed to Nicholas II that Russia "restore Port Arthur and Kwangtung province to China and sell the southern branch of the Chinese Eastern Railroad" in return for guaranteed special rights in northern Manchuria.[16] Such a solution would surely have satisfied the Japanese.

All such proposals, however, fell on deaf ears. Nicholas II continued blissfully ignorant and overconfident replying to Emperor William of Germany: "There will be no war because I do not wish it." Russia would not declare war, and Japan would surely not dare to do so! Nicholas told a meeting of top advisors in December 1903 that the situation reminded him of that after the Sino–Japanese War in 1895 when Russia had told Japan: "Go back!", and it had obeyed. "Now the Japanese are becoming ever more demanding. It is a barbarous country." Lamzdorf urged continued negotiations and the need to determine what Russia really wanted in Manchuria. Declared Nicholas: "War is absolutely impossible. Time is the best ally of Russia. Each year strengthens us."[17]

Early in January 1904 Japanese ambassador Shinichiro Kurino warned Witte that Foreign Minister Lamzdorf should make an immediate and satisfactory reply to Japan's offer. If no reply were received, cautioned Kurino, war would break out within a few days. Soon thereafter Japan broke off negotiations, and, in February 1904 without warning or a formal declaration of war, launched a surprise attack on the Russian naval base at Port Arthur, launching the Russo–Japanese War. Thus Russian leaders had blundered into another wholly unnecessary, unpopular conflict largely because policy-making and the conduct of negotiations had been removed arbitrarily from the Foreign Ministry and given to military extremists and political adventurers. Such confusion prevailed within the Russian government prior to the outbreak of war that no proper negotiations could even be conducted. Russia would pay a high price for Nicholas II's overconfidence, indecisiveness, and irresponsibility.

---

[16]Noel F. Jones, "The Far Eastern Crisis and the Career of General Kuropatkin, 1895–1905," Master's Thesis (UNC–Greensboro, 1991), pp. 64–65.

[17]"Dnevnik Kuropatkina," No. 19, entry of December 15, 1903, in *Krasnyi Arkhiv* vol. II (Moscow, 1922), p. 95.

Suggested Readings

Conroy, H. *The Japanese Seizure of Korea, 1869–1910.* Philadelphia, 1960.

Dallin, D. J. *The Rise of Russia in Asia.* New Haven, CT, 1949.

Hsü, I. C. *The Rise of Modern China.* Oxford, England, 1975.

Lensen, George A. *Korea and Manchuria Between Russia and Japan, 1897–1904.* Tallahassee, FL, 1966.

———. *Balance of Intrigue: International Rivalry in Korea and Manchuria, 1884–1899.* Tallahassee, FL, 1982.

Malozemoff, Andrew. *Russian Far Eastern Policy, 1881–1904.* Berkeley, CA, 1958.

McDonald, David M. *United Government and Foreign Policy in Russia, 1900–1914.* Cambridge, MA, 1992.

Morley, J.W., ed., *Japan's Foreign Policy: A Research Guide.* New York, 1974.

Nish, Ian H. *The Anglo–Japanese Alliance: The Diplomacy of Two Island Empires, 1894–1907.* London, 1966.

———. *Japanese Foreign Policy, 1869–1942.* London, 1977.

———. *The Origins of the Russo–Japanese War.* London, 1985.

Price, D. C. *Russia and the Roots of the Chinese Revolution, 1896–1911.* Cambridge, MA, 1974.

Purcell, V. C. *The Boxer Uprising.* Cambridge, England, 1963.

Riasanovsky, Nicholas. "Asia through Russian Eyes," in W. Vucinich, ed., *Russia and Asia.* Stanford, CA, 1972, pp. 3–29.

Romanov, Boris A. *Russia in Manchuria (1892–1906).* Trans. Susan W. Jones, New York, 1974.

Rosen, Baron R. R. *Forty Years of Diplomacy.* 2 vols. New York, 1922.

Sumner, B. H. *Tsardom and Imperialism in the Far East and Middle East, 1880–1914.* London, 1940.

Treadgold, Donald. *The Great Siberian Migration.* Princeton, NJ, 1957.

Tupper, H. *To the Great Ocean: Siberia and the Trans-Siberian Railway.* London, 1965.

Valliant, R. B. "Japan and the Trans-Siberian Railroad, 1885–1905," Ph.D. Thesis, University of Hawaii, Honolulu, 1974.

Young, L. K. *British Policy in China, 1895–1902.* Oxford, England, 1969.

Zabriskie, E. H. *American–Russian Rivalry in the Far East: A Study in Diplomacy and Power Politics, 1895–1914.* Philadelphia, 1946.

THE RUSSO–JAPANESE WAR, REVOLUTION, AND REFORM

In the Russo–Japanese War of 1904–1905, which few Russians had believed the Japanese would launch, St. Petersburg found itself, as in the Crimean conflict, unprepared—virtually isolated diplomatically and greatly over-confident. Japan was in a far stronger diplomatic position because of its alliance with Britain and near unanimous support from British and American public opinion. The Franco–Russian Alliance, on the other hand, was of no real help to Russia in the Far East. And at home the war was unpopular. In Russia only a few nationalists and adventurers really wanted war or believed it was necessary. The Russian public, revealing increasing dissatisfaction over economic and political conditions, failed to rally around the throne. In fact growing unrest and agitation on the home front and a worsening financial situation, more than defeats in the field, eventually forced Russian leaders to seek peace. In the aftermath of war came a revolution that nearly toppled the imperial regime, compelled it to make significant concessions both to Russians and minority groups, and left Russia weakened internationally.

THE RUSSO–JAPANESE WAR

The ineptness and confusion within the Russian command in the Far East in 1904–1905 reflected the incompetence and divided counsels in St. Petersburg on the eve of the war. The indecisive and passive Admiral E. I. Alekseev was named supreme commander. Overconfident and ignorant about land warfare, he opposed withdrawals in Manchuria as unnecessary and urged dispatching the Baltic Fleet to the Orient. General A. N. Kuropatkin, the former war minister, commanded Russia's land forces in Manchuria. With little battlefield experience, Kuropatkin advocated the "Kutuzov strategy" of fighting delaying actions and gradually retreating until reinforced from European Russia. The two commanders were as personally incompatible as were their strategies, and they often issued conflicting orders to their subordinates. Only after the incompetent Alekseev was recalled late in 1904 could Kuropatkin implement what was probably a sound policy of trading space for time in Manchuria.

After their initial surprise attacks in February 1904 at Port Arthur and Chemulpo had neutralized Russia's Far Eastern squadron, the Japanese landed in Korea, and defeated a Russian force on the Yalu River dividing Korea from Manchuria in April, the first Oriental army to defeat a European one in centuries. The Japanese then cut the South Manchurian Railroad north of Port Arthur. During the initial land fighting the Japanese considerably outnumbered Kuropatkin's forces and were fighting close to their home bases whereas Russian reinforcements had to travel 5,500 miles from Moscow. In May the Japanese occupied Dalny and besieged Port Arthur, Russia's main naval base. After a five-month siege, Port Arthur's commander surrendered the fortress, although adequate stocks of food and munitions remained. This dealt a major blow to Russian imperial pretensions in the Orient and gave Japan revenge for its evacuation of Port Arthur in 1895.*

In August 1904, with Russian reinforcements arriving over the single-tracked and overburdened Trans-Siberian Railroad, began a second and deadlier phase of the land war in Manchuria. Despite slight numerical superiority, Kuropatkin's army met defeat in two great battles at Liaoyang and in a cautious Shaho River offensive. In February 1905, at Mukden, the greatest battle in history up to that point in number of men engaged—some 300,000 on each side—was fought. A Japanese pincer move forced Kuropatkin to retreat ingloriously northward. Both sides suffered heavy casualties, but the Russians, with far greater manpower, could tolerate them better than the Japanese. As his forces retired northward toward Harbin and the Chinese Eastern Railway, Kuropatkin requested transfer. The front then stabilized south of Harbin remaining basically unchanged until war's end. Although Kuropatkin won no victories, his army avoided decisive defeat and remained in the field. Later, in his memoirs, Kuropatkin asserted that his undefeated army had been stabbed in the back by the politicians.

Russia also suffered a series of disastrous naval defeats. In August 1904, while trying to break through to Vladivostok, the Port Arthur squadron was destroyed by Japan's Admiral Heichahiro Togo. In October the Baltic Fleet was dispatched from St. Petersburg, but while crossing the Dogger Bank in a fog Russian ships fired at each other in the belief they had been attacked by Japanese torpedo boats. In the confusion they sank several British fishing boats causing such anger in Great Britain that war almost resulted. After sailing halfway around the globe, in May 1905 the Baltic Fleet of Admiral Z. P. Rozhdestvenskii, featuring eight elderly battleships, entered incautiously the straits between Japan and Korea. There, near Tsushima Island, Admiral Togo's superior and modern battlefleet in a few hours virtually annihilated the Russian fleet. This shattering and humiliating defeat at the hands of "the little yellow dwarfs," plus the rising tide of revolution in Russia and an increasingly perilous financial situation, finally induced Nicholas II to

---

*For a sound and readable account of the war see David Walder, *The Short Victorious War: The Russo–Japanese Conflict 1904–5*. London, 1973.

seek peace. Even then hardliners such as Admiral F. V. Dubasov insisted unrealistically that the war must be continued until final victory: "Our eastward expansion is an elemental drive, a movement to natural borders. We cannot retreat here."[1]

St. Petersburg found the Japanese equally anxious for peace. Indeed, right after the Tsushima Strait victory, Japan requested President Theodore Roosevelt of the United States to act as mediator. Although the Japanese had won all the victories, their finances were exhausted, their armies had suffered grievous losses, and the Russians in Manchuria were being reinforced steadily. William II of Germany, fearing that the Russian monarchy would succumb to revolution, now urged his cousin, Nicholas II, to accept Roosevelt's good offices. During the summer of 1905 little fighting occurred, although the Japanese did occupy the offshore island of Sakhalin and expelled the Russians from Korea.

The peace conference to end the war began in Portsmouth, New Hampshire, in August 1905 after Russia also accepted Roosevelt's mediation. Foreign Minister V. N. Lamzdorf persuaded the reluctant Nicholas II to name Sergei Iu. Witte as Russia's chief delegate after assuring the tsar that he would not be given much freedom of action. Thus Witte was instructed neither to yield any Russian territory, agree to payment of a war indemnity, nor yield the Chinese Eastern Railroad.[2] Nevertheless, the able Witte managed to skirt these limitations and through tact and hard work salvaged much for Russia, partly by winning over much of American public opinion.

By the terms of the Treaty of Portsmouth Japan received from Russia—with China's reluctant consent—the Liaotung leased territory with Port Arthur and the South Manchurian Railroad, thus giving Japan predominance in southern Manchuria. Both sides agreed to evacuate their troops from Manchuria within eighteen months, except for guards to protect their respective railway properties. Russia had to accept Japan's predominance politically, militarily, and economically in a nominally-independent Korea. Instead of paying an indemnity, which St. Petersburg considered too humiliating, Russia ceded the southern half of Sakhalin Island to Japan (soon renamed Karafuto), and the Japanese received fishing rights in Siberian territorial waters.

The futile Russo–Japanese War, costing each side almost half a million casualties, deprived Russia of most of its gains during the previous decade of reckless expansion in the Far East. Russian opinion accepted the territorial losses with complete indifference. Manchuria became divided into a Russian sphere in the north and a Japanese one in the south. Later, Witte wrote in his memoirs: "The treaty, when all is said, was a heavy blow to our amour-propre." When he arrived home, Witte was greeted warmly by

---

[1]Dietrich Geyer, *Russian Imperialism: The Interaction of Domestic and Foreign Policy, 1860–1914* (New Haven, CT, 1987), pp. 235–36.

[2]A. V. Ignatiev, *S. Iu. Vitte—Diplomat* (Moscow, 1989), pp. 205 ff.

Nicholas II, who granted him the title of count for "having brilliantly carried out the mission of first class importance."[3] The new count failed to receive similar accolades from the Russian public.

The Russian defeat by Japan, the first major victory by an Asian power over a European imperialist power, began to undermine the prestige of European imperialism. If little Japan could humiliate vast Russia, why could not other Asian countries expel the Europeans? Russia's defeat weakened severely the Franco–Russian Alliance, tempting imperial Germany to seek to detach France while its ally was helpless. The Tsushima debacle ended British fears of Russian naval prowess and expansionism and paved the way for the subsequent Anglo–Russian rapprochement of 1907. More immediately, defeat in the Far East seriously discredited the tsarist regime at home, and contributed greatly to the Revolution of 1905 by encouraging liberal and radical opponents to strike against a vulnerable government. Military defeat, as in the Crimean case, again led to major domestic reforms in Russia.

Finally, the Treaty of Portsmouth served as a basis for subsequent Russo–Japanese cooperation in the Far East, notably in the partition of northern China into spheres of interest and in opposition to the economic schemes of other powers. Thus in July 1907 a Russo–Japanese convention, reaffirming the Treaty of Portsmouth, committed them publicly to respect each other's spheres of interest and respective railway properties in Manchuria and to preserve the "open door" principle in China. Secret provisions drew a line of demarcation between their respective spheres: Russia gave Japan a free hand to act in Korea (which Japan annexed in 1910), southern Manchuria, and Inner Mongolia; Japan reciprocated by confirming that northern Manchuria and Outer Mongolia lay in Russia's sphere. These arrangements were reaffirmed by a second Russo–Japanese treaty of July 1910, worked out between the Japanese ambassador, Ichiro Motono, and Russian Foreign Minister Alexander P. Izvolskii. That accord had been sparked by a plan proposed by American railway tycoon, Edward Harriman, and accepted by the United States Secretary of State Philander Knox to neutralize the Manchurian railways and place them under joint Japanese–American control. The Russo–Japanese Treaty of 1910 confirmed that the two powers held identical views on protecting their interests and privileges in Manchuria against efforts of the United States or European powers to interfere there.

The overthrow and dissolution of the Chinese Manchu Empire in 1911 by the revolutionary forces of Sun Yat-sen reaffirmed the similarity of Russian and Japanese interests in China. Both powers sought to profit from China's turmoil in order to strengthen their influence and prevent its resurgence; they were seconded generally by Russia's ally, France. On the other hand, the leading capitalist powers—Germany, Great Britain, and the United States—aimed to restore order in China and foster its recovery. After

---

[3]Raymond Esthus, *Double Eagle and Rising Sun* (Durham, NC, 1988), pp. 181, 191.

Outer Mongolia proclaimed its "independence" from China in 1912 and became de facto a Russian protectorate, a third Russo–Japanese secret treaty of July 1912 extended the demarcation line they had agreed to in 1907 by confirming Russia's predominance in Outer Mongolia and Japan's preeminence in Inner Mongolia, and pledging to respect each other's interest sphere. They were aided by Anglo–German naval tensions, which helped block a united front in China by the leading capitalist powers. These Russo–Japanese imperialist bargains, accepted by France and Great Britain, to which both parties were tied by alliances or ententes, consolidated Russia's shrunken Far Eastern position and enabled St. Petersburg to place that region "on ice" in order to pursue its Balkan interests.

REVOLUTION AND REFORM, 1905–1914

Interior Minister V. K. Pleve had favored a brief, successful little war against the "yellow dwarfs" of Japan to "clear the air" in Russia by destroying the growing opposition movement. Instead, a lengthy, costly, and disastrous Russo–Japanese War focused opposition to the imperial regime and nearly overthrew it. There was a close correlation between defeats in the Far East and demonstrations and strikes at home. Thus the fall of Port Arthur in December 1904 was followed swiftly by "Bloody Sunday" in St. Petersburg. Scattered mutinies in the armed forces, such as that on the battlecruiser *Potiomkin*, gave dramatic warning that unless the war were ended speedily the military forces would dissolve and the state might go bankrupt.

In Russia in 1905 the first general revolutionary movement against the autocracy in which industrial workers participated erupted, a type of dress rehearsal for the March Revolution of 1917, which would destroy tsarism. Most Western scholars view 1905 as chiefly a liberal-democratic movement—much like the European Revolutions of 1848 and bringing similar results. Causes of the 1905 Revolution include the failure of Nicholas II's regime to respond to rising demands for change by liberals, workers, peasants, and nationalities and a lack of governmental leadership. The opposition, growing more cohesive and articulate, needed only the opportunity provided by a distant, unsuccessful war to break loose. Military defeat, revealing incompetence, confusion, and mismanagement in the armed forces and regime, supplied the catalyst for revolution.

Liberal professional elements, aiming at a constitutional monarchy or a republic by universal and direct suffrage, led the Revolution of 1905. A crucial early event was "Bloody Sunday" on January 9, 1905. A huge, peaceful demonstration of industrial workers in St. Petersburg, seeking redress of its grievances from the tsar, was fired upon by palace guards. The workers demanded a constitutional convention, free universal education, and the right to strike. Reinforcing liberal political demands with rapidly spreading strikes, the workers by that fall had tied up the entire country in history's first successful general strike. Major peasant revolts against the landowners, combined with worker strikes and agitation by national minorities for autonomy brought the imperial regime to bay that fall. In desperation Nicholas II again approached Count Witte who insisted that the tsar issue a manifesto to split the opposition by satisfying moderate and legitimate demands. Thus the October Manifesto promised a State Duma, or parliament, elected by universal male suffrage, to grant civil liberties, legalize trade unions and most strikes, eliminate peasant redemption payments, and make concessions to national minorities.

Named premier, Count Witte helped save the imperial regime. His skillful diplomacy had extricated Russia relatively painlessly from the conflict with Japan; now he applied those skills to Russia's internal problems. The October Manifesto did indeed split the opposition, isolating the extreme revolutionaries. Through his international banking connections Witte arranged a large foreign loan by French bankers in April 1906, which propped up the country's shaken finances and cemented Russia's ties with France. His able political leadership steered the imperial government through the crisis of 1905–1906. The economy proved remarkably resilient—again due largely to Witte's economic policies—and rebounded after the French loan. Finally, the revolutionaries were neither as influential nor as well-organized as they would be in 1917.

In 1906 a new semi-constitutional regime was created in Russia under Nicholas II. A national parliament—Duma—with limited powers, was elected by broad suffrage. The emperor controlled foreign policy and the armed forces, the Duma's financial authority was restricted, and ministers of state remained responsible to the tsar alone. The executive branch could rule by decree when the Duma was not in session, and the tsar could dismiss it at will. In the first two Dumas deadlock developed between the parliament on the one hand and the emperor and conservative bureaucrats on the other who refused essential concessions. Once the revolutionary crisis passed, Nicholas II sacked Count Witte.

The revolutionary wave of 1905–1906 yielded to political reaction combined with efforts at economic reform and attempts to restore the state's finances under Peter A. Stolypin, premier from 1906 to 1911 and tsarism's last strong and effective leader. As premier and interior minister Stolypin utilized police powers to crush revolutionary terror. Then he instituted electoral reforms that produced conservative Dumas dominated by landowners. Stolypin sought to break up the village community *(mir)* and repartitional system, which he believed retarded agricultural progress and turned peasants into revolutionaries. His purpose was to promote individual farmers in the belief they would support the imperial regime. Stolypin's was "a wager on the sturdy and the strong" individual farmer. He stressed that twenty years of peace would be needed to complete this transformation. When his agrarian reforms halted in 1915 only about 10 percent of Russia's farms were fully consolidated under private ownership. Tiring of the self-confident Stolypin's tutelage, Nicholas II eventually withdrew his support. In 1911 Stolypin was assassinated by a Socialist Revolutionary doubling as a police agent. Subsequent premiers were less dynamic and successful.

Russia had emerged from the expensive Russo–Japanese War financially weakened and with its gold standard undermined. Faced with large budget deficits in 1905 and 1906, Finance Minister V. N. Kokovstov was the chief figure in the Stolypin cabinet to oppose extravagant requests for funds by military leaders. Until its financial crisis had been overcome, insisted Kokovtsov in 1906, the empire had to be protected primarily by able diplomacy and an appropriate orientation in its foreign policy. Even after 1908, when Russia entered a period of rapid economic expansion, Kokovtsov sought to adhere to his tight money policies only to be forced to yield by an influential military. During 1907–1913 regular military expenditures rose steadily but the military's share in an expanding budget increased by only 3 percent to 26.7 percent in 1913.[4]

Russian leaders realized that the country's military and naval power had to be rebuilt swiftly if the empire was to play a major international role. The foreign and finance ministers argued that Russia would have to share Manchuria with Japan and Persia with Great Britain indefinitely, but found it hard to convince the military that Russian power was now very limited. In 1906 Russian naval leaders, influenced by their counterparts in Germany and Great Britain, insisted that a new fleet must be built around the most modern battleships, known as dreadnoughts. The following year four of these were authorized for the Baltic Fleet and three had been completed by 1914. During this period Admiral I. K. Grigorevich, on intimate terms with the tsar, persuaded him that naval rearmament should become Russia's top priority. Naval building programs, consuming an undue share of the military budget, proved largely useless militarily. At first reforming and rebuilding the army proceeded more slowly under a hesitant war minister, A. F. Rediger. Then the Bosnian Crisis* sparked a faster pace after War Minister V. A. Sukhomlinov warned in March 1909 that the Russian army was unprepared for war and could not even defend Russian soil. Thereafter more balanced appropriations between army and navy enabled Sukhomlinov to modernize by 1914 what had been a rather decrepit army.[5]

Where was imperial Russia headed and what were its prospects in 1914 on the eve of World War I? By then Russia was the world's fifth greatest industrial producer, but most of the population remained peasant and was two-thirds illiterate. With west European economies generally growing faster, Russia remained a relatively backward country heavily dependent upon European, especially French, investment. Education advanced at all levels and plans for universal compulsory primary schooling had been approved by the Duma. A less onerous censorship permitted the press to carry Duma debates and to exert increasing influence over both domestic and foreign

---

[4]Geyer, pp. 255–61.
*See Chapter 12.
[5]Geyer, pp. 278–89.

policy. Optimists viewed Russia advancing steadily along the road taken earlier by west European countries toward industrialization, constitutionalism, and political freedom. Pessimists objected that tsarist autocracy was hopelessly rigid and incompetent and the economy unbalanced and structurally unsound. Rising social contradictions, they added, sooner or later would produce revolution. In 1914 Russia unquestionably was undergoing rapid and profound changes but was burdened by an incompetent leadership.

Suggested Readings

Charques, Richard. *The Twilight of Imperial Russia*. London, 1958, 1974.

Conroy, Hilary. *The Japanese Seizure of Korea, 1868–1910*. Philadelphia, 1960.

Esthus, Raymond A. *Double Eagle and Rising Sun: The Russians and Japanese at Portsmouth in 1905*. Durham, NC, 1988.

Galai, S. *The Liberation Movement in Russia, 1900–1905*. Cambridge, England, 1973.

Hamadi, Kengi. *Prince Ito*. Tokyo, 1936.

Harcave, Sidney. *The Russian Revolution of 1905*. London, 1970.

McDonald, David M. *United Government and Foreign Policy in Russia 1900–1914*. Cambridge, MA, 1992.

Mehlinger, Howard and John Thompson. *Count Witte and the Tsarist Government in the 1905 Revolution*. Bloomington, IN, 1972.

Mossolov, A. A. *At the Court of the Last Tsar, 1900–1916*. A. Pilenco, ed., Trans. E. W. Dickes. London, 1935.

Okamoto, Shumpei. *The Japanese Oligarchy and the Russo–Japanese War*. New York, 1970.

Price, Ernest. *The Russo–Japanese Treaties of 1907–1916: Concerning Manchuria and Mongolia*. Baltimore, MD, 1933.

Rosen, Baron R. R. *Forty Years of Diplomacy*. 2 vols. New York, 1922.

Sablinsky, Walter. *The Road to Bloody Sunday*. Princeton, NJ, 1976.

Schwartz, S. M. *The Russian Revolution of 1905*. Chicago, 1967.

Stavrou, T. G., ed., *Russia Under the Last Tsar*. Minneapolis, MN, 1969.

Trotsky, L. D. *1905*. Trans. A. Bostock. New York, 1972.

Walder, David. *The Short Victorious War: The Russo–Japanese Conflict, 1904–5*. London, 1973.

Warner, Denis and Peggy Warner. *The Tide at Sunrise: A History of the Russo–Japanese War*. New York, 1974.

White, John A. *The Diplomacy of the Russo–Japanese War*. Princeton, NJ, 1964.

Wilson, Thomas and D. Vaughan. *The Peace of Portsmouth*. Portsmouth, NH, 1957.

Zenkovsky, A. V. *Stolypin: Russia's Last Great Reformer*. Trans. M. Patoski. Princeton, NJ, 1986.

RUSSIA AND THE ROAD
TO WORLD WAR I, 1905–1914

The defeat of tsarist Russia in the war with Japan seriously weakened its position in world politics for some years. As in the case of the Crimean War, the Russo–Japanese War revealed grave inadequacies in the leadership, tactics, and armament of the Russian army and navy necessitating major reorganizations of both forces. Shaken by defeat and revolution, Russia at least temporarily could not back up its policies with force, yet its leaders recognized the need to restore its prestige. Placing the Far Eastern theater on hold, tsarist statesmen concentrated their attention once again on the Balkans and the Turkish Straits. Eventually, this would help cause the disaster of World War I.

RELATIONS WITH EUROPEAN POWERS, 1904–1907

The Dogger Bank incident of October 1904 had temporarily raised German hopes of a conflict between Russia and Britain that would weaken both powers. Then the very anti-English Emperor William II promptly suggested a German–Russian defensive alliance that France also should join as a continental alliance against Britain. To William's initial overture, Nicholas II wired the Kaiser on October 28:

> The only way, as you say, [to make England behave] would be that Germany, Russia and France should at once unite upon arrangements to abolish English and Japanese arrogance and insolence. Would you like to lay down and frame the outlines of such a treaty?[1]

Emperor William complied happily and with Chancellor Bernhard von Bülow drafted a defensive Russo–German alliance. German leaders saw a golden opportunity to end the danger of war on two fronts posed by the Franco–Russian Alliance of 1893 either by compelling France to abandon its hostility to Germany by adhering to this Russo–German alliance or by

---

[1]Wilhelm II, *The Kaiser's Letters to the Tsar*, N. F. Grant, ed. (London, 1920), p. 139.

undermining the Franco–Russian Alliance. Tsar Nicholas approved the Russo–German treaty proposed by William, then suddenly realized the necessity to consult Russia's ally, France, especially since St. Petersburg then was seeking a major loan in Paris. When Nicholas insisted that France be consulted, and Great Britain acted in conciliatory fashion over Dogger Bank, the "Willy-Nicky" treaty project was dropped.

However, William II was not ready to give up on this idea. During the summer of 1905 while the Treaty of Portsmouth was being negotiated, William arranged a private meeting with Nicholas as their imperial yachts were cruising in Finnish waters. The kaiser employed his persuasive powers to induce the gullible Nicholas to sign the so-called Björkö Treaty of July 24, 1905. It was countersigned by a Russian admiral, who was not allowed to read its text. Thus according to Russian law, the treaty became binding at that point. Not until almost two months later did Nicholas II, rather embarrassed, show the secret Treaty of Björkö to Foreign Minister V. N. Lamzdorf. Amazed and shocked, the usually obedient Lamzdorf demanded that it be cancelled immediately as being incompatible with the Franco–Russian Alliance. Count S. Iu. Witte, then premier, agreed and subsequently affirmed incorrectly that Björkö constituted a treasonable act by the tsar against France.[2] Nicholas then pleaded in vain with William to revise the treaty; neither he nor Lamzdorf and Witte would yield. Björkö was not formally abrogated but Germany was informed by St. Petersburg that Russia's obligation to aid Germany in case of a war with France did not apply and that the Franco–Russian Alliance remained in full force.

Here is the text of the controversial Björkö Treaty, which was published by the Provisional Government in August 1917 partly to discredit its imperial predecessor:

Their Imperial Majesties, the Emperor of all the Russias, of the one part, and the Emperor of Germany, of the other part, with the object of assuring the peace of Europe, have agreed upon . . . the following . . . defensive alliance:

Article I: If any European State shall attack either of the two Empires, the allied party engages to aid his co-contractor with all his forces on land and sea.

Article II. The high contracting parties agree not to conclude a separate peace with any enemy whatsoever.

Article III. The present treaty shall be in force from the moment of the conclusion of peace between Russia and Japan, and may only be cancelled by a year's previous notice.

---

[2]For details see Charles Seeger, ed., *The Memoirs of Alexander Iswolsky* (London, 1920; reprint, 1974 Gulf Breeze, FL), pp. 40 ff.

Article IV. When this treaty goes into effect, Russia will take the necessary steps to make its terms known to France and invite her to subscribe to it as an ally.

(Signed) Nicholas William.[3]

This reveals that this secret treaty was not directed against France which was to be informed of its terms. However, Björkö was a rather typical example of Nicholas' shortsightedness and disastrous interference in matters of foreign policy.

Russia's defeat by Japan largely ended persistent British fears about Russian imperial pretensions. Meanwhile Franco–British concern over expansionist German policies and growing German military and naval power was increasing. In the years after 1904 these and other factors gradually brought France, Britain and Russia closer together, something that German leaders after Otto von Bismarck believed could never happen. Thus in forming their Entente Cordiale (friendly understanding) of 1904 France and Britain settled their outstanding colonial disputes in north Africa and the Far East. Their entente was strengthened by German efforts to break it up over Morocco. The First Moroccan Crisis (1905–1906) resulted from Germany's attempt to humiliate France while its ally, Russia, lay prostrate in defeat. But at the Algeciras Conference (January 1906) Germany found itself isolated diplomatically except for its ally, Austria–Hungary. The crisis sounded a vague warning of a potential European war of France, Russian and Great Britain against the German powers.

Hostility between Russia and Great Britain reached a peak during the Dogger Bank incident of 1904; once that was settled amicably their relations began to improve. The fact that both Russia and Great Britain were linked with France eased this process of reconciliation. Indeed, the idea of a triple entente had already occurred to the British foreign secretary, Lord Edward Grey, at Algeciras: "An entente between Russia, France and ourselves would be absolutely secure. If it is necessary to check Germany, it could then be done."[4] Actually, the entente initially had little to do with Germany, claims A.J.P. Taylor, a leading British scholar. The British had sought a compromise settlement with Russia for years, especially to halt Russian inroads in Persia, and now the Russians, humbled by defeat, also were willing. Anglo–Russian negotiations were limited to the Middle East since Russia's defeat by Japan had already eliminated any rivalry between them in the Far East. Official talks dragged on for fifteen months, beginning in June 1906, between Alexander P. Izvolskii, the new Russian foreign minister, and Sir Arthur Nicolson, the British ambassador in Russia.

---

[3]Seeger, p. 54.

[4]Grey's Memorandum of February 20, 1906, cited in A.J.P. Taylor, *The Struggle for Mastery in Europe 1848–1918* (Oxford, England, 1954), pp. 441–42.

Becoming Russia's foreign minister in May 1906 after serving as Russian minister in Tokyo (1899–1902) and in Denmark, Izvolskii had been a consistent advocate of a pacific settlement with Japan. As foreign minister designate, Izvolskii had conferred in March 1905 in Paris with Russia's ambassadors in England, France and Italy on Russia's future course in foreign policy. Later he wrote:

> We came unanimously to the conclusion that Russia's foreign policy must continue to rest on the indestructible basis of her alliance with France, but that this alliance should be reinforced by agreements with Great Britain and Japan.[5]

As the new foreign minister, Izvolskii's immediate aim was to disentangle Russia from unwanted Asian complications and achieve secure eastern frontiers by agreement with Japan. Once that had been achieved, Izvolskii believed that Russia could focus once again on accomplishing its "historic" goals in the Balkans. Thus in 1906 he inaugurated discussions with London and Tokyo in order to settle disputes with them in Asia. Izvolskii's proposal that spring to partition Persia into British and Russian interest zones at first inspired strong resistance from General F. F. Palitsyn of the General Staff to ending Russian expansionism along its Asian borders. Izvolskii assiduously built support for his new policy until a conference of Russian leaders in February 1907 endorsed his idea of reaching an entente with the British. Presiding at the conference of August 11, 1907, Premier Peter A. Stolypin expressed St. Petersburg's view on the imminent Anglo–Russian accord, which remained his approach until his assassination:

> The successful conclusion of the agreement with England represents a truly great matter of state. Our internal situation does not allow us to conduct an aggressive foreign policy.... (This) will give us the opportunity to dedicate with full tranquillity our strength to the repair of matters within the country.[6]

The Convention of August 31, 1907, confirmed Anglo–Russian accord on Middle Eastern matters. Tibet became a neutral buffer state. Russia abandoned any direct contact with British-protected Afghanistan thus providing India security on its northwest frontier. But the major bargain was over Persia (Iran). The north, including Tehran and the area bordering the Caspian Sea, was confirmed as Russia's sphere of interest. Southeastern Persia, next to India, became a British zone. The center and area along the Persian Gulf was established as a neutral zone. The whole arrangement was purely strategic. No consideration was given to Persian oil, which accidentally

---

[5]David MacKenzie, "Aleksandr P. Izvol'skii," in *Modern Encyclopedia of Russian and Soviet History*, vol. 9 (Gulf Breeze, FL, 1978), p. 98.

[6]David M. McDonald, *United Government and Foreign Policy in Russia 1900–1914* (Cambridge, MA, 1992), pp. 108–10.

A. P. Izvolskii, foreign minister, 1906–1910; ambassador to France, 1910–1917

turned out to be mainly in the neutral zone. For the next three years the Russians were restrained by this agreement, but then they resumed their usual freewheeling actions in Persia with their civil officials and military running the north. By 1914 Persia had virtually ceased to exist as a country; its government was virtually run by Russia.

Supposedly this convention constituted only an Asian settlement, but by removing Anglo–Russian frictions it had important effects on the European scene. During the negotiations Izvolskii had raised the issue of allowing Russian warships to pass through the Turkish Straits. Since Russia had virtually no Black Sea fleet, he did so for prestige reasons; actually closure of the Straits suited her. Grey responded that Russia might be accommodated if the entente proved its worth elsewhere, noting:

MAP 12-1   Anglo–Russian agreement on Persia of 1907

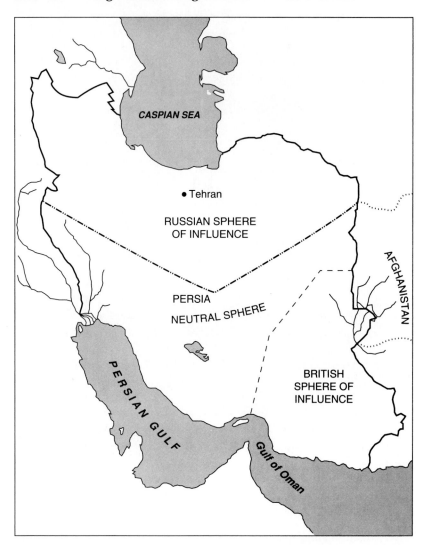

Good relations with Russia meant that our old policy of closing the Straits against her and throwing our weight against her at any conference of the Powers must be abandoned.[7]

Whether this constituted a British pledge of support for Russia on the Straits question, however, remained unclear. The Anglo–Russian convention was not regarded then as a basis for their cooperation against Germany and

---

[7]Grey's Memorandum of March 15, 1907, cited in Taylor, p. 443.

did not prove popular in either Great Britain or Russia. It was chiefly aggressive German policies that transformed it eventually into an alliance.

RUSSIA AND THE BALKANS, 1903–1914

Defeat in the Far East induced the Russian government to undertake a more active Balkan and Near Eastern policy in order to recoup prestige. An initial opportunity appeared in June 1903, when the last of the Obrenović rulers of Serbia was overthrown and murdered by a popularly backed military coup led by Colonel Dragutin Dimitrijević-Apis. Assuming the throne was the pretender, Peter Karadjordjević, a liberal, pro-Russian constitutional monarch whose sons were educated in Russia. Under King Peter I and the Radical Party of Nikola Pašić Serbia flourished economically and politically becoming the South Slav Piedmont and soon Russia's strong ally. Serbia reformed and reequipped its army and forged better relations with its neighbor, Bulgaria, creating the potential for a Balkan league. Nikola Pašić, Serbia's outstanding statesman, relied heavily on Russia's friendship and protection, was ardently Russophile, and had served as Serbian ambassador in Russia.*

After Izvolskii became Russian foreign minister in 1906, Russia's Balkan policies were reactivated and the ministry regained much of its former control over affairs. However, Izvolskii tended to become involved in rash projects without thinking through their consequences. His search for success and prestige in the Balkans was complicated by Russia's persisting military weakness and the growing danger of clashes with the German powers. Simultaneously, in 1906 General Conrad von Hötzendorf became chief of the Austro–Hungarian General Staff. He advocated preventive war against a dynamic Serbia in order to halt the disintegration of the Dual Monarchy. In the same year the able and forceful Alois von Aehrenthal became Austro–Hungarian foreign minister. He was determined to annex the provinces of Bosnia and Hercegovina to demonstrate that the Dual Monarchy was not declining as a great power. Those provinces remained legally Turkish possessions but had been occupied by Austria–Hungary ever since 1878. With their large Serbian population, they were regarded by Pašić and other Serbian leaders as the key to a Greater Serbia.

Visiting Vienna in September 1907 and impatient for a major success in foreign policy, Izvolskii broached to Aehrenthal his aim of obtaining the Powers' consent to opening the Turkish Straits to warships of Russia and other Black Sea states. In February 1908 Izvolskii proposed to a meeting of the Russian Council of Ministers Anglo–Russian military action against the Ottoman Empire "which might bring dazzling results and the realization

---

*On events in Serbia from 1903 see Wayne Vucinich, *Serbia Between East and West: The Events of 1903–1908* (Stanford, CA, 1954); David MacKenzie, *Apis: The Congenial Conspirator* (Boulder, CO, 1989), chapters 5 and 6; and Barbara Jelavich, *Russia's Balkan Entanglements, 1806–1914* (Cambridge, England, 1991), pp. 210 ff.

of Russia's historic mission in the Near East." Premier Stolypin objected that Russia lacked money and an adequate navy, adding: "Only after some years of complete quiet can Russia speak again as in the past."[8] However, Izvolskii ignored his well-founded warning.

Izvolskii and Aehrenthal met at Buchlau (Buchlov) in Bohemia in September 1908 to concoct an Austro–Russian bargain over the Near East. Considering eventual Austrian annexation of Bosnia–Hercegovina to be inevitable, Izvolskii consented to support such an annexation of the province *(sanjak)* of Novi Pazar in return for Austro–Hungarian backing for his scheme to reopen the Straits to Russian warships. There was no written accord at the secret Buchlau meeting, but Izvolskii apparently assumed that Vienna would take no action without a European conference and consent to revise the Berlin Treaty of 1878. Proceeding to Paris, Izvolskii learned with dismay from Aehrenthal that the Dual Monarchy would proclaim the annexation of the two provinces on October 7 without any gain for Russia. Premier Stolypin and Finance Minister V. N. Kokovtsov waxed indignant at Izvolskii's unauthorized surrender of two Slav provinces.[9] St. Petersburg promptly repudiated Izvolskii's rash action, and he failed to win either British or Ottoman support to change the restrictive Straits convention.[10]

Soon the Bosnian annexation blew into a full-fledged European crisis which threatened a general European war. The Serbian government angrily demanded an autonomous status for Bosnia–Hercegovina and territorial compensation. Germany hastened to support its Austrian ally with a virtual ultimatum to Russia. Because war seemed likely between Serbia and Austria–Hungary, Russian leaders at an imperial conference agreed that Russia could not fight in any case because of financial and military weakness. St. Petersburg advised Serbia to yield to Austrian terms, and a German ultimatum forced her and Russia to accept the annexation. Thus the Bosnian crisis ended in a complete diplomatic victory for Austria–Hungary, humiliation for Izvolskii, and left the Serbs infuriated. The crisis caused much anti-German and anti-Austrian feeling in Russia, gave the Austrians exaggerated confidence in German support no matter what they did, and further inflamed Serbian nationalism against the Dual Monarchy.

Izvolskii's defeat in the Bosnian affair contributed soon to his replacement as Russian foreign minister by Sergei D. Sazonov, who was conscientious and mildly Slavophile, but ineffective. Sazonov lacked real control over his subordinates in the Foreign Ministry or over Russian envoys abroad. At the end of 1911 Sazonov fell ill and went off to Switzerland for a six months' cure, handing over direction of his ministry to his assistant, A. A. Neratov. Previously, Sazonov had submitted his resignation to Nicholas

---

[8]Taylor, p. 449.

[9]V. N. Kokovstov, *Out of My Past* (Stanford, CA, 1935), pp. 214–18.

[10]B. Jelavich, *Russia's Balkan Entanglements, 1806–1914* (Cambridge, England, 1991), pp. 219–22.

S. D. SAZONOV, FOREIGN MINISTER, 1910–1916

II, but the emperor had refused it "using expressions which showed his great kindness of heart." Nicholas had declared that he and Neratov would perform the work of the Foreign Ministry until Sazonov had recovered.[11] However, Tsar Nicholas, while kind, was also quite ignorant, and there occurred in Sazonov's absence some revival of Panslav tendencies and an independent role for Russia's Balkan representatives as in 1875–1877, notably by Russian envoys N. G. Hartvig in Belgrade and A. Nekliudov in Sofia, Bulgaria. Seeking to become a second Count Ignatiev, Hartvig displayed great sympathy for the Balkan Slavs (unless this conflicted with direct Russian interests) and became immensely popular in Serbia. In November 1911 Hartvig informed Neratov that Russian policy in the Balkans

> pursues two clear and quite definite aims: 1) to help the Slav nations, which are assisted by Russia . . . , to attain their cherished ideal—the amicable division

---

[11]Serge Sazonov, *Fateful Years, 1909–1916* (New York, 1928), pp. 35–36.

among them of all the Turkish possessions in the Balkan peninsula, and 2) to fulfill its own age-old historical mission which is to obtain a firm foothold on the shores of the Bosphorus . . . at the Straits.[12]

With the warm encouragement of the Russian Panslav envoys Hartvig and Nekliudov, and with St. Petersburg's apparent blessing, Serbia and Bulgaria achieved full rapprochement and concluded a military alliance in March 1912. Seeking to maintain stability in the Balkans, the Russian government agreed to mediate any quarrels between them, notably over the division of disputed Macedonia, and reserved the right to decide the question of war or peace. Greece and Bulgaria reached a similar accord also directed against the Ottoman Empire. In vain Sazonov and Neratov sought to prevent aggressive use of this Balkan League only to find that they could not control Hartvig and Nekliudov who urged the Balkan states to act forcefully. In October 1912 the Balkan League (Serbia, Bulgaria, Greece, and Montenegro) attacked the Turks despite an Austro–Russian warning that the Powers could not allow them to seize Ottoman territory. To the surprise of Europeans, the Balkan allies swiftly defeated the Turks and virtually drove them out of Europe. When they quarreled over their respective shares of Macedonia, Foreign Minister Sazonov agreed to act as arbiter, but their territorial settlement was altered by Austria's support for creation of an independent Albania dominated by Austria in order to block Serbia's access to the Adriatic Sea. A second Balkan war erupted when Bulgaria under its pro-German King Ferdinand suddenly attacked the Serbian army. When Serbia was joined by Greece and Turkey, Bulgaria was decisively defeated. The subsequent Treaty of Bucharest (August 1913) awarded most of Macedonia to Serbia and Greece. The Balkan League dissolved, Bulgaria became embittered, and Russian prestige suffered another severe blow when St. Petersburg again had to back down in the face of Austro–German pressure. As Serbia and Bulgaria resumed their enmity, prospects for Russian hegemony in the Balkans disappeared.

Russia's interest in the fate of Constantinople and the Straits was reawakened by the Italo–Turkish War of 1911–1912 since the Turks closed the Straits to all vessels thus damaging Russia's grain export trade. Late in 1911 Russia made another attempt to reopen the Straits to its warships. N. V. Charykov, Russian ambassador to Constantinople, presented a plan by which the Turks would open the Straits to Russian warships in return for permission for Russia to build railways in eastern Anatolia. However, the Turks delayed, the Germans were hostile, and when Sazonov resumed his post as foreign minister, the idea was dropped and Charykov was recalled. Since commercial use of the Straits was vital for Russia, Sazonov sought to prevent any power other than the Ottoman Empire from controlling

---

[12]*Krasnyi Arkhiv*, vol. 8 (Moscow, 1925), p. 46.

MAP 12-2   **Russia and the Balkans, 1912–1914**

them. Therefore Sazonov was profoundly worried by the appointment in
November 1913 of a German general, Liman von Sanders, as commander
of an instructional army corps in Constantinople. Sazonov protested strongly
that this threatened to place the Straits under German control. As if on

cue, the Russian press reinforced this protest.[13] Finally, in January 1914 Berlin responded by promoting von Sanders so that he could no longer command a Turkish army corps. Sazonov remained suspicious of German intentions in the Ottoman Empire and the Straits, but he and the St. Petersburg cabinet were primarily concerned to preserve the existing situation in the Near East.

AIMS AND RESULTS OF TSARIST FOREIGN POLICY, 1815–1914

In the century after the Vienna Congress of 1815 imperial Russia remained generally a satiated power vis-à-vis Europe, except from 1856 to 1878 when it aimed to revise the unfavorable Treaty of Paris. At most Russia sought limited gains within the European balance of power. In eastern Europe (Baltic region, Poland) Russia aimed merely to preserve its predominance. Nineteenth-century tsars attempted to maintain conservative institutions in Russia and Europe, and therefore usually preferred to cooperate with conservative monarchies such as Prussia–Germany and Austria against the perceived dangers of liberalism, nationalism, and socialism. Russia was virtually forced into the open arms of republican France by Emperor William II's expansionist *Weltpolitik* (world policy), although the initially defensive Franco–Russian Alliance later developed certain aspirations to undo the unification of Germany.

In the Balkan region, until 1856, Russian rulers preferred, usually, to support legitimacy and the Ottoman sultan over backing the national aspirations of South Slav and Orthodox peoples, although sporadically they assisted the Serbs and Greeks against their Turkish overlords. However, under Alexander II both St. Petersburg and the Panslavs fostered the Serbian and Bulgarian struggles against Ottoman rule and promoted Romanian unification. Balkan peoples then generally regarded a liberalized Russia as their ally and protector. However, at the Congress of Berlin (1878) and on numerous other occasions it became evident that Russia's interests as a great power and its relations with other powers invariably took precedence over support for a Balkan nationalism which Russian leaders often alienated. In the Balkans, Russian policy, often gravely divided and dualistic, frequently played a revisionist and expansionist role, sporadically seeking control of the Turkish Straits, and working through a client state such as Serbia or Bulgaria. In 1914 Russia, partly because of dualistic policies, was no closer to dominating the Balkans or uniting its peoples than in 1854.

Meanwhile, in Asia, Russia acted as a typical European imperialist power. The conquest of the Kazakh steppe and oasis region of south-central Asia filled a power vacuum, gave her leverage against British India, and catered to her prestige and need for victories. Expansion there brought valuable resources into the Empire including the cotton of Turkestan and the oil

---

[13]McDonald, pp. 190–94.

fields of the Caucasus. Furthermore, in central Asia stable, natural frontiers were achieved that ended previously damaging native raids. In Asia, too, Russia when challenged invariably backed away from conflict with Great Britain. In the Far East, except for the decade 1894–1904, Russian aims and gains were modest. Carried away in the 1890s by imperial fever when foreign policy came under the control of irresponsible elements, Russia paid an exorbitant price for this aberration in the Russo–Japanese War.

All in all, tsarist Russia between 1815 and 1914 did well to defend and expand the frontiers acquired at the Vienna Congress. This was accomplished despite numerous cases of diplomatic envoys, frontier generals, and administrators making policy on their own hook and of foolish tsars undertaking risky, ill-conceived personal policies. Nevertheless, repeatedly— in the Crimean, Russo–Turkish, and Russo–Japanese wars—the St. Petersburg government blundered into unnecessary and costly conflicts that wrecked Russia's finances and held back its economic development only to be saved from absolute disaster by compromise and retreat.

RUSSIA AND THE OUTBREAK OF WORLD WAR I IN 1914

On June 28, 1914, in Sarajevo—then the capital of Bosnia–Hercegovina, which had been annexed to Austria–Hungary in 1908—Archduke Franz Ferdinand, heir to the Austrian throne, was assassinated by Gavrilo Princip, a Bosnian student linked with Serbian nationalist organizations. That grave incident was the spark that touched off a European conflict that subsequently grew into World War I, a war which in turn would bring about the collapse of the Russian, German, Austro–Hungarian, and Ottoman empires. How important was Russia's role in the coming of World War I?

Sarajevo was merely the trigger that set off the war. It occurred against the background of increasingly rigid systems of secret alliances that divided Europe into hostile camps and made it virtually inevitable that a conflict involving two countries would draw in all the powers. Europe after 1890 saw a steady growth of armies and armaments as the powers sought security in maintaining armed forces of unprecedented size. This was accompanied by the great influence exercised in some countries by military and naval leaders. Probably the most potent single cause of war was an intense and intolerant nationalism expressed in preaching hatred for one's neighbors in the schoolrooms and newspapers of Europe. Nowhere was this extreme nationalism stronger than in France, aggrieved over the loss of Alsace–Lorraine in 1871 and determined upon revenge, and in Serbia, where the long-standing goal of unifying all Serbs and South Slavs under the aegis of Belgrade conflicted fatally with the determination of the leaders of Austria–Hungary to preserve a multinational empire that held millions of these same South Slavs in subjugation. In such a charged atmosphere European diplomats were fatally hampered in their attempts to work out reasonable, compromise solutions to complex problems, especially since there was no international organization to help them keep the peace.

After the Sarajevo assassination, the question arose as to what actions Austria–Hungary would take to restore its prestige and gain satisfaction. Austrian leaders Count Leopold Berchtold and Conrad von Hötzendorf both considered "Greater Serbism" a deadly threat to the monarchy's existence that needed to be scotched by force. Germany's response to the Austrian request for support urged immediate strong action against Serbia and promised full backing to its ally (July 5). Later, German leaders would regret issuing this famous "blank check." A pause ensued while Austro–Hungarian leaders debated their course of action and prepared an ultimatum to be presented to Serbia, although they could not prove any direct Serbian complicity in the murder.

The mood in St. Petersburg in early July was calm. The Russian capital was virtually empty of top officials, who were off on vacation. Foreign Minister Sazonov, absent from town, clearly did not anticipate that war would break out. The Russian press and public, much more influential than before the Revolution of 1905, were generally anti-Austrian and pro-Serbian, as they had been for a long time, but not violently so. There is no clear indication that Russian diplomacy bore any direct responsibility for the outbreak of war until after the Austrian ultimatum was delivered in Belgrade, although there are indications that Izvolskii, then Russian ambassador in Paris, had been advocating a strong, even bellicose, Russian policy. The danger of war seemed so remote, noted the quartermaster of the Russian army, General G. A. Danilov, that he was dispatched in mid-July on a routine mission to the Caucasus.

Russian leaders returned to St. Petersburg by July 20 mainly because of the upcoming state visit by French President Raymond Poincaré, planned much earlier. He spent July 20–23 in the Russian capital. Austria's brutal ultimatum to Serbia was ready for delivery by July 19, but Vienna deliberately delayed sending it until the afternoon of July 23 so that word of it could not reach St. Petersburg prior to Poincaré's departure for France in order to make Franco–Russian coordination of their response harder.

The Austrian ultimatum to Serbia was deliberately framed so as to be unacceptable by an independent state. It demanded suppression of all anti-Austrian publications and organizations and asked that Austrian officials be admitted to Serbia to eliminate anti-Austrian agitation there, provisions incompatible with Serbian laws. Foreign Minister Sazonov's reaction to the ultimatum was: "That means European war." Nonetheless, he urged the Serbs to exercise extreme moderation in their reply, which they did. He also urged the Serbs not to resist militarily but to appeal to the powers, and requested Vienna to extend its twenty-four-hour time limit. The Russian Council of Ministers convened July 24 and empowered the war and navy ministers to undertake partial mobilization. War Minister V. A. Sukhomlinov and Chief of Staff General N. N. Ianushkevich did not oppose the decision for partial mobilization only opposite the frontiers of Austria–Hungary, although their subordinates realized that such a measure was virtually impossible given the nature of Russian military organization and inadequate railroad communications.

Serbia's reply, conciliatory and carefully crafted, accepted all Austrian demands compatible with Serbian law and offered to submit the others to impartial adjudication by the international court of justice in the Hague. However, Vienna interpreted that reply as a rejection, immediately mobilized and on July 28 declared war on Serbia and bombarded Belgrade.

Russian leaders realized that Russia could not afford to back down again in this crisis. St. Petersburg had yielded repeatedly to the German powers previously: in 1878, 1909, and 1913. On each occasion Russia had played an important role in preserving European peace. To back down once more might well prove fatal for Russia's prestige and credibility in Europe and among the Balkan Slavs. With its military reorganization well advanced though incomplete, Russian leaders, while opposing war in 1914, believed that if necessary Russia could fight to preserve its great power role. Thus Nicholas II had assured Serbia's visiting Premier Pašić in January 1914 that in case of an Austrian attack, Serbia could count on Russia. On July 27 Nicholas II, replying to Prince Regent Alexander's appeal for aid, admonished the Serbian government to avoid war if at all possible:

> As long as there is the least hope of avoiding an effusion of blood, all our efforts should be turned toward that aim. If, in spite of our most sincere desire, we do not succeed in this, His Highness can be assured that in any case Russia is not disinterested in the fate of Serbia.[14]

Similarly, Russia's military attaché in Belgrade, Colonel Viktor Artamonov, apparently reiterated assurances of Russian military support to Colonel Dimitrijević-Apis, Serbia's chief of intelligence, shortly before the Sarajevo assassination.*

In view of Austria–Hungary's declaration of war on Serbia, on July 28 Sazonov announced to European capitals that Russia had decided on partial mobilization against Austria as a diplomatic move in support of its Serbian ally. However, subordinate General Staff officers warned their superiors and Sazonov that plans for partial mobilization were lacking and might delay a subsequent total mobilization.[15] Under heavy pressure from top Russian generals Sazonov on July 30 convinced Nicholas II, who was strongly opposed to war, that only a full mobilization was practicable. By then Sazonov realized that Berlin would not prevent an Austrian invasion of Serbia and believed that Russia could not abandon its small ally. Finally, Russian military leaders feared that they could not counter rapid German

---

[14]Jelavich, p. 261.

*About the role of Dimitrijević-Apis in preparing the Sarajevo assassination see David MacKenzie, *Apis: The Congenial Conspirator* (Boulder, CO, 1989), pp. 123 ff.

[15]M. T. Florinsky, *Russia: A History and an Interpretation*, vol. 2 (New York, 1953), p. 1317.

mobilization with anything but full-scale Russian mobilization.[16] Russia's general mobilization of July 30 doomed belated British and German efforts to arrange a diplomatic solution to the crisis. It forced Germany's hand, since having to fight on two fronts German strategy under its Schlieffen Plan was to strike swiftly at France before a more slow-moving Russia was ready. Thus Germany declared war on Russia and France; Great Britain entered the war on their side when the Germans in their haste to invade France violated Belgian neutrality.

At the end of World War I the victorious Allied powers (Russia earlier had concluded a separate peace with Germany) placed all the blame on Germany and Austria–Hungary for planning and launching an aggressive war. Later, German and other revisionist historians rejected this assertion arguing that Russia, France, and Serbia had been equally responsible for the outbreak of the war.

Baron Max von Montgelas, for instance, argued that Russia's total mobilization had derailed agreements nearly reached between Russia and Austria–Hungary. Erich Brandenburg, a German scholar, noted that Russian leaders in July 1914 had been sharply divided, and that most military men and Panslavs had urged war. Izvolskii, he affirmed, became a tool of the belligerent Delcassé-Poincaré faction in France and sought Russian control of the Straits and Slav liberation which could only be achieved by war. Brandenburg blamed them for the hasty Russian mobilization. Sidney Fay, an American moderate revisionist, concluded Russia had been partly responsible for the Austro–Serbian conflict because of its frequent encouragement to Belgrade through Hartvig. However, in the 1960s German scholars Fritz Fischer and Imanuel Geiss argued that German aggression and "a grab for world power" had sparked World War I. Berlin had sought to make Russia appear the aggressor by forcing her to undertake general mobilization first.*

The revisionists have shown that Russia and France bore a measure of responsibility for the war's outbreak. Russian hesitation over mobilization and the final decision for full mobilization contributed to that result but seemingly less than did Austria–Hungary, Germany, or Serbia. All the European great powers and nationalistic Serbia shared in responsibility for the terrible tragedy which overtook Europe in 1914.

Suggested Readings

Albertini, Luigi. *The Origins of the War of 1914.* 3 vols. London, 1952–1957.
Charques, Richard. *The Twilight of Imperial Russia.* London, 1958, 1974.

---

[16]Dietrich Geyer, *Russian Imperialism: The Interaction of Domestic and Foreign Policy, 1860–1914* (New Haven, CT, 1987) , pp. 312–13.

*From the very extensive literature on the debate over the causes of World War I see especially Luigi Albertini, *The Origins of the War of 1914* 3 vols. (London, 1952–1957); Count Max von Montgelas, *The Case for the Central Powers* (New York, 1925); Fritz Fischer, *Germany's Aims in the First World War* (London, 1967); and Imanuel Geiss, ed., *July 1914* (London, 1967).

Dedijer, Vladimir. *The Road to Sarajevo.* New York, 1966.

Evans, R.J.W. and H. von Strandman, eds., *The Coming of the First World War.* Oxford, England, 1988.

Fay, Sidney B. *The Origins of the World War.* 2 vols. New York, 1966.

Helmreich, E.C. *The Diplomacy of the Balkan Wars.* Cambridge, MA, 1938.

Izvolsky, A.P. *Recollections of a Foreign Minister.* New York, 1921.

Jelavich, Barbara. *Russia's Balkan Entanglements, 1806–1914.* Cambridge, England, 1991.

Kokovtsov, V.N. *Out of My Past.* Stanford, CA, 1935.

Lieven, D.C.B. *Russia and the Origins of the First World War.* London, 1983.

Lincoln, W. Bruce. *In War's Dark Shadow: The Russians Before the Great War.* New York, 1983.

MacKenzie, David. *Apis: The Congenial Conspirator.* Boulder, CO, 1989.

McNeal, Robert, ed., *Russia in Transition, 1905–1914.* New York, 1970.

Remak, Joachim. *Sarajevo: The Origins of a Political Murder.* New York, 1959.

Rossos, Andrew. *Russia and the Balkans: Inter-Balkan Rivalries and Russian Foreign Policy, 1908–1914.* Toronto, Canada, 1981.

Sazonov, Serge. *Fateful Years, 1909–1916.* New York, 1928.

Spring, D.W. "Russia and the Coming of the War," in R.J.W. Evans and H. von Strandman, eds., *The Coming of the First World War.* Oxford, England, 1988, pp. 57–86.

Taylor, A.J.P. *The Struggle for Mastery in Europe: 1848–1918.* Oxford, England, 1954.

Thaden, Edward. *Russia and the Balkan Alliance of 1912.* University Park, PA, 1965.

Vucinich, Wayne. *Serbia Between East and West, 1903–1908.* Stanford, CA, 1954.

Zenkovsky, A.V. *Stolypin: Russia's Last Great Reformer.* Trans. M. Patoski. Princeton, NJ, 1986.

13

RUSSIA IN WORLD WAR I, 1914–1917

As Russia was drawn into World War I in August 1914, in sharp contrast to the mood at the outbreak of the Russo–Japanese War came an outburst of nationalistic fervor and loyalty to the Crown. The strike movement ended abruptly and virtually the entire Duma pledged its support of the war. This patriotism was largely defensive: the belief was prevalent that Russia was fighting a just war of self-defense and to protect its brother Serbs from a brutal invasion. This apparent devotion to "faith, tsar, and country" was fueled by unreasoned optimism, a belief in a speedy and inexpensive victory as the Russian "steamroller" advanced inexorably to Berlin. Initial defeats, and the poor performance of the high command and government, soon revealed the falsity of these assumptions and punctured the mood of optimism and unity.

RUSSIAN WAR AIMS

Imperial Russia had stumbled into war without defined objectives except to defend itself and its Serbian ally. St. Petersburg, soon to be renamed Petrograd for patriotic reasons, had no real quarrel with Germany, and Russian military leaders wished to leave her alone while seeking to destroy Austria–Hungary. However, from the start Foreign Minister Sergei D. Sazonov realized that a new Polish settlement would be indispensable since Russia was fighting the German powers—with which Catherine II had partitioned Poland—and was allied with France, the leading traditional European champion of Polish freedom. Sazonov succeeded in persuading Nicholas II that he should proclaim as an official Russian war aim the reunification of Poland as an autonomous part of the Russian Empire. Furthermore, Ukrainian territories belonging to Austria–Hungary were likewise to be annexed. The proclamation of August 16, 1914, pledged that Poland would be reunited under the Russian tsar and "come together free in faith, in language, and in self-government." The French ambassador, Maurice Paléologue, assured Sazonov that this would create a most favorable impression in France.[1]

---

[1] C. Jay Smith, *The Russian Struggle for Power, 1914–1917* (New York, 1956), pp. 8–10.

Initial Russian victories over the Austrians and agitation by numerous Czech colonists living around Russia's chief cities triggered the creation of a special Czech army detachment, later composed of Austro–Hungarian prisoners. Foreign Minister Sazonov at an audience granted to members of a Czech National Committee, declared, according to notes kept by the Czechs:

> Should God grant decisive victory to Russian arms, the reestablishment of an entirely independent Czech Kingdom would be in accordance with the intentions of the Russian Government.

Then Sazonov issued in the name of Russia's commander-in-chief, Grand Prince Nicholas Nikolaevich, a proclamation to the "Peoples of Austria–Hungary" stating that Russia sought only right and justice and would bring them "freedom and the realization of your national strivings." However, Russian leaders remained vague about the boundaries of the proposed new Czech state.[2]

Sazonov's initial program of war aims announced to the French and British ambassadors in September 1914 included reorganization of Austria–Hungary as a triple monarchy with the Czechs as its third element. In November, in a private conversation with French Ambassador Paléologue, Nicholas declared:

> . . . We must *dictate* the peace and I am determined to continue the war until the Central Powers are destroyed. . . . The terms of peace should be discussed by us three, France, England, and Russia. No Congress or mediation for me! So when the time comes we shall *impose* our will upon Germany and Austria.

Asked by Paléologue about his general views about peace terms, the Russian emperor declared: "Our first object is the destruction of German militarism. . . . We must make it impossible for the German people even to think of revenge." As to peace terms, added Nicholas: "I accept here and now any conditions France and England think it is their duty to put forward in their own interest." Specifically, from Germany Nicholas claimed parts of East Prussia, Posen, and perhaps part of Silesia. From Austria, "Galicia and the western half of the Bukovina will enable Russia to obtain her natural frontier, the Carpathians." Finally, he said, "I shall be compelled to secure my Empire a free passage through the Straits." The Turks would be expelled from Europe with Constantinople under a neutral, international regime. In the Balkans Serbia should receive Bosnia, Hercegovina, Dalmatia, and northern Albania; Greece should have southern Albania except Valona, which would go to Italy. "If Bulgaria behaves properly," Nicholas promised, "she should receive compensation in Macedonia from Serbia." Indulging his imperial dreams, Nicholas envisioned the destruction of the German,

---

[2]Smith, pp. 16–19.

MAP 13-1   War aims of the Entente, 1914–1917

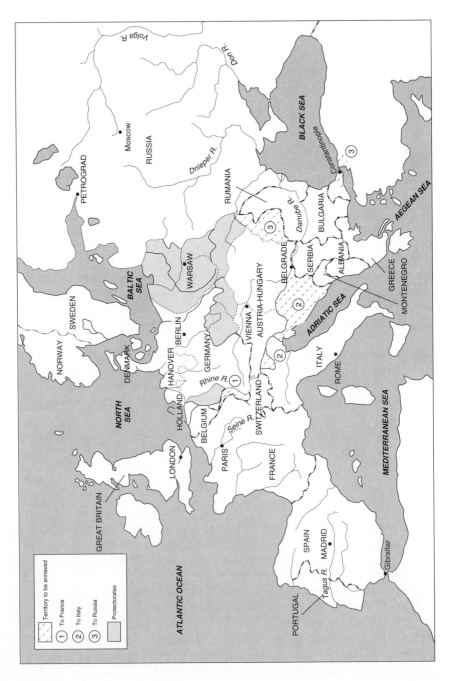

Austro–Hungarian, and Ottoman empires, with the victorious allies taking for themselves whatever they wished. Concluded Nicholas: "What glorious memories we shall share, my dear Ambassador!"[3] All that remained to be done was to defeat the enemy.

Amidst the general euphoria that prevailed within the Russian leadership, a significant exception was the retired Count Sergei Iu. Witte who told Ambassador Paléologue in September 1914:

> This war's madness. It has been forced on the Tsar's prudence by stupid and short-sighted politicians. It can only have disastrous results for Russia. France and England alone can hope to derive any benefit from victory . . . and, anyhow, a victory for us seems to me highly questionable.

Witte rejected the popular view that Russia had gone to war to protect its blood brothers and its historic and sacred mission in the Balkans:

> Why, that's a romantic, old-fashioned chimera. No one here . . . now cares a fig for these turbulent and vain Balkan folk. . . . We ought to have let the Serbs suffer the chastisement they deserved.

And what could Russia hope to gain from the war? The Russian Empire was big enough already, affirmed Witte. Even if the German powers were wholly defeated, it would mean the proclamation of republics throughout Central Europe. "That," claimed Witte, "means the simultaneous end of Tsarism!" Witte's conclusion was that the war should be ended as soon as possible.[4] Dismissing Nicholas' imperial dreams, Witte discerned only harsh realities.

Once the Ottoman Empire had been dragged into World War I by German actions, the Straits issue figured very large in Russian and allied calculations. Turkey's entry caused Russian war aims to become much more ambitious. An imperial manifesto by Nicholas spoke of solving "the historic task bequeathed to us by our forefathers on the shores of the Black Sea." That hint was swiftly taken up by the Russian press and in the Duma. The liberal G. N. Trubetskoi declared that Russia must acquire Constantinople; this was soon echoed by Paul N. Miliukov, leader of the Constitutional Democrats, who advocated having both Constantinople and the Straits go to Russia. Henceforth the Turkish Straits became the cornerstone of all Russian war aims. A memorandum of March 4, 1915, stated that in the event of victory, Russia should annex Constantinople, the western shore of the Bosphorus, the Dardanelles, southern Thrace up to the Enos-Midia line, and a strip of the southern coast of the Black Sea. Sazonov's demands were accepted by Russia's western allies, anxious to keep

---

[3]Maurice Paléologue, *An Ambassador's Memoirs* vol. I (London, 1923), pp. 190–96.
[4]Paléologue, pp. 122–23.

Russia in the war. Lord Edward Grey of Great Britain approved Russian claims to the Straits provided that the neutral zone in Persia should become British. The French, still reluctant, finally yielded to Sazonov in April 1915. Finally, the Crimean powers had sanctioned Russian claims at the Straits. However, the British-led Dardanelles campaign proved a miserable failure, the Turkish Straits remained closed, and this meant Russia could not be supplied with railway or military equipment by its allies. Russia's subsequent defeat in World War I meant that she would not obtain the Straits after all.

Other allied secret agreements also involved or affected Russia. The French gave in on the Straits question after Nicholas II had told Paléologue, "Take the left bank of the Rhine; take Mainz; go further if you like."[5] Under the secret Treaty of London (April 1915), which brought Italy into the war on the side of the Allies, she was promised most of Dalmatia, which was inhabited primarily by Yugoslavs; Russia made major concessions to Italy at the expense of its Serbian ally. Once again Russian interests were allowed to supersede those of its "little Slav brothers." As a result of Anglo–French agreements to partition the Ottoman Empire, Russia would receive part of eastern Anatolia contiguous to the Caucasus. These sections of Armenia and Kurdistan were promised by the Allies to Russia in September 1916. Naturally, these prospective Russian gains, which would have made the Russian Empire dominant in eastern Europe and the Black Sea, depended wholly on its military performance. Anglo–French concessions to Russia were prompted by the realization that without Russia fighting on the eastern front, they would lose the war.

Meanwhile during the summer of 1915 German armies conquered most of Russian Poland. French pressure and Russian fears that the Central Powers would reconstitute Poland under their control induced Foreign Minister Sazonov to press the imperial government to fulfill the promises it had made on Polish autonomy in August 1914. Sazonov's efforts to have issued an imperial proclamation on an autonomous postwar Poland within the Russian Empire triggered his forced "retirement" at the insistence of Empress Alexandra and Rasputin, the empress' influential confidant, in July 1916. His replacement by the ignorant and incompetent Boris V. Stürmer confirmed Russia's coming eclipse as a major world power.

THE WAR AND IMPERIAL COLLAPSE, 1914–1917

The Russian "steamroller," supposed to advance irresistibly to Berlin, proved to be an antiquated, rickety machine. Inadequately prepared for war, imperial Russia pursued faulty strategy and tactics under generally incompetent leadership. The Russian armies, although the largest in the world, were

---

[5] A.J.P. Taylor, *The Struggle for Mastery in Europe, 1848–1918* (Oxford, England, 1954), p. 542.

defeated consistently by the Germans, who were better trained, equipped, and led. On the other hand, the Russians usually defeated the even more disorganized forces of Austria–Hungary. Appointed commander-in-chief with semi-dictatorial powers in 1914 was Grand Prince Nicholas Nikolaevich, the tsar's uncle, who was poorly prepared for his thankless task although popular with his subordinates. Just as he began to master his responsibilities, the Grand Prince was replaced by Nicholas II, who knew far less and by coming to military headquarters lost control over the imperial regime back in Petrograd. This represented a carry-over of a disastrous old Romanov habit of placing members of the imperial family in top military posts when most of them were prepared only to review troops on the paradeground. Russia's chiefs of staff and War Minister V. A. Sukhomlinov were undistinguished or incompetent.

Russia's original strategic plan in 1914 called for purely defensive operations against Germany while launching a powerful offense against weaker Austria–Hungary in Galicia. However, desperate French appeals to Petrograd to relieve the German pressure against Paris brought an improvised Russian offensive into East Prussia. With numerical superiority, but without coordination or proper maps, two Russian armies were trapped near Tannenberg. At the end of August 1914 two entire army corps surrendered and their commander, General A. V. Samsonov, shot himself. Heavy losses of equipment and officers could not be replaced, and the Russians grew convinced of German military superiority. A better planned Russian offensive in Galicia cost Austria–Hungary heavily.

A war of maneuver persisted on the eastern front. The German offensive of 1915 overran Russian Poland, part of the Baltic provinces, and regained Galicia. Severe shortages of war supplies and even food demoralized the Russian forces. Morale plummeted as rumors spread: "Britain will fight to the last drop of Russian blood." Only swampy terrain, overextended German supply lines, and the heroism of Russian soldiers prevented a complete collapse. However, during 1916 occurred a temporary Russian recovery highlighted by General A. A. Brusilov's June offensive in Galicia, a success that induced Romania to join the Allies. The Russian army, while unable to defeat the Germans, tied down much of the Central Powers' manpower and saved the western allies from defeat. Nonetheless, by early 1917 Russia's army was again deteriorating with low morale and high desertion rates.*

A protracted total war with two great powers proved too much for Russia's semi-developed, poorly organized economy. The war deprived Russia of its grain exports and their revenues. There was enough to eat in the countryside, but the peasantry had few incentives to produce food for the cities. The railway system, short of imported spare parts and rolling

---

*See Norman Stone, *The Eastern Front* (New York, 1975).

stock, broke down increasingly. Industry was dislocated by mobilization of many skilled workers, shortages of raw materials, isolation from European suppliers, and the loss of industrialized Russian Poland. Grave financial-mismanagement by the imperial government magnified these economic problems. Compulsory prohibition of alcohol cost the treasury almost one-third its revenue. Since war expenditures were not met out of taxation, uncontrolled inflation raged. By 1917 the Russian economy was near collapse.

The tsarist government and bureaucracy, too, were disintegrating for lack of leadership. The imperial family isolated itself from Russian realities. When Nicholas II became commander-in-chief at the front, the empress and the sinister monk Rasputin dominated the Petrograd regime and removed most of the more competent ministers. An open struggle raged between liberal Duma leaders, the executive, and its ineffective bureaucracy. The murder of Rasputin, organized by members of the imperial family in December 1916, failed to arrest the regime's inexorable decay. As the year 1917 began, growing hunger, strikes, and demonstrations prevailed in Petrograd. Allied insistence that Russia remain in the war, and the disintegration of the army, economy, and government heralded the spontaneous overthrow of the imperial regime in March 1917.

NICHOLAS II, HIS WIFE ALEXANDRA, AND THEIR CHILDREN; HE RULED *1894–1917*

THE MARCH REVOLUTION, THE PROVISIONAL GOVERNMENT, AND THE SOVIET

A popular revolt began in hungry Petrograd on March 8, 1917 ("New Style").* Placards appeared among disgruntled women and workers: "Down with the autocracy!", "Down with the war!", and "Give us bread!" The next day, noted the moderate socialist, N. N. Sukhanov: "The movement swept over Petersburg like a great flood. The Nevsky and many squares in the center were crowded with workers."[6] Nicholas II was off at military headquarters, oblivious of events in the capital. When the regime sought to suppress the movement with mounted Cossacks and the 150,000-man garrison, the troops began to mutiny and go over to the insurgents. After the last government troops refused to fight, the tsarist ministers were arrested on March 12. Three days later Nicholas II abdicated the throne. The 300-year-old dynasty fell almost without resistance, having been almost wholly discredited.

Succeeding tsarism was a democratic Provisional Government derived from liberal members of the Fourth Duma. Of the new ministers, most representing the well-born and the well-heeled, only Alexander Kerenskii, a mild socialist, represented even vaguely the workers, women, and soldiers who had made the March Revolution. Issuing an amnesty to all political prisoners and proclaiming civil liberties, the Provisional Government helped make Russia one of the freest countries in the world for the following months but had little actual authority. Much more was possessed by the other element of the "dual power," the Petrograd Soviet of Workers' and Soldiers' Deputies. Hastily formed and ill-defined in membership, that body took charge in Petrograd and coordinated other soviets (councils), which sprang up like mushrooms throughout Russia. Clashes developed between the Provisional Government and Petrograd Soviet over foreign policy and control of the armed forces with the latter tending to prevail.

Allied reactions to the March Revolution were mixed. Their ambassadors in Petrograd had known something was gravely wrong in Russia, but their warnings to Nicholas II and their own governments of probable revolution had been disregarded. The British and French governments believed that the weakening of Russia had been due to German influence and intrigue, not Russian domestic conditions. Actually, German efforts to subvert the tsarist court were not very successful; contrary to widespread rumors, Empress Alexandra was not involved with the Germans. Despite their misgivings, the Allied governments soon recognized the Provisional Government and sought to persuade it to remain in World War I to final

---

*Early in 1918 the Soviet regime adopted the Gregorian calendar used in the West. "Old Style" dates of the Julian calendar lagged thirteen days behind those of the Gregorian calendar by 1917. Here "New Style" dates have been used beginning in March 1917.

[6]N.N. Sukhanov, *The Russian Revolution of 1917*, J. Carmichael, ed. (New York, 1962), pp. 6 ff.

victory. To the United States the overthrow of tsarism seemed the answer to prayer. About to enter the conflict, American leaders had no wish to fight alongside tsarist autocracy. President Woodrow Wilson revealed his ignorance of Russia's past by asserting that Russia had always been democratic at heart. Now, he predicted, the great Russian people would join the struggle for freedom and democracy. The United States promptly recognized the Provisional Government, extended it credits, and in April 1917 entered the war on the Allied side.

During 1917 the war became a major and emotional issue among contending Russian groups. Initially, most members of the Provisional Government favored remaining in the war to the bitter end. The Constitutional Democrats and Octobrists in the cabinet adhered to the territorial aims described in wartime secret treaties concluded with the Allies. The strongest spokesman for this position was Foreign Minister Paul N. Miliukov, who assured the Allies that the entry of the United States had reinforced the Provisional Government's resolve to fight on. In his May 1, 1917, note to the Allies, Miliukov rejected as unfounded rumors that Russia might conclude a separate peace and he insisted that she would remain in the war until victory. However, with discipline vanishing in the Russian army, opposition to the war grew rapidly within the Petrograd Soviet. Its more moderate members were willing to continue a defensive war but not one for imperial gains. The Provisional Government found itself caught between Allied insistence on a maximum war effort and increasing pressure from the Soviet for a democratic separate peace. Thus Miliukov's note of May 1, insisting that Russia would fight on, provoked massive demonstrations in Petrograd. Most demonstrators carried banners demanding "peace without annexations and indemnities." Miliukov and the conservative War Minister A. I. Guchkov were forced to resign.

In the reorganized Provisional Government, representing a coalition between moderates and democratic socialists, M. I. Tereshchenko, a millionaire, became foreign minister on May 18. Whereas the new cabinet reflected the Soviet formula of "peace without annexations and indemnities," Tereshchenko right up to the November Revolution remained basically loyal to Miliukov's program. The higher personnel of the Foreign Ministry continued on with few changes or departures from traditional diplomacy. Exchanges of views between Russia and the Allied powers during the following months achieved little since they insisted on adhering to their imperialistic war aims even if Russia renounced all annexations. In late October 1917 Tereshchenko declared that Russia would not yield any territory which might block her access to the Baltic Sea. "No Russian," declared Tereshchenko, "would agree to a peace that would humiliate Russia and infringe upon her national interests."[7]

---

[7]M.T. Florinsky, *Russia: A History and an Interpretation*, vol. II (New York, 1953), pp. 1426–27.

However, from May until November 1917 the dominant figure in the Provisional Government was the youthful and dynamic Alexander F. Kerenskii, who continued the thankless task of attempting to satisfy both the Allies and the restless Petrograd Soviet. Then and later Kerenskii emphasized that the Provisional Government had to remain in World War I, not for imperial conquests, which he opposed, but to destroy German militarism, to achieve the democratic aims shared by the Allied powers, and to secure Allied financial and political support. As war minister, Kerenskii in June decided to launch a major offensive on the Galician front against Austria–Hungary—partly in response to French pleas—in order to prevent the Germans from shifting forces to the western front. Kerenskii also aimed to revive sagging Russian morale and to impress the Allies with Russia's determination to continue fighting.

When the Germans reinforced the faltering Austrians, Kerenskii's June offensive turned into a disastrous Russian retreat, which triggered the major disorders of the "July Days" in Petrograd. On July 3 the All-Russian Congress of Soviets endorsed self-determination for all peoples of the Russian Empire, "including the right of secession," and the soviets adhered to that position right to November. The Soviet delegate to a proposed Paris conference was instructed in mid-October to advocate "the full right of self-determination for Poland, Latvia and Lithuania."[8] Meanwhile V. I. Lenin, who had returned to Russia from Swiss exile in April, had won over the Bolshevik Party in his "April Theses" to uncompromising opposition to "the imperialist war" and put forward a program of "Bread, Land, and Peace," and eventually all power to the soviets. Insisting that the Bolshevik Party oppose both the feeble Provisional Government and Russia's continuance in World War I, Lenin called on the Bolsheviks to help turn "the imperialist war into a civil war." By November 7, 1917, when the Bolsheviks—led capably by Lenin and L. N. Trotskii—seized power in Petrograd, the Russian army was dissolving and had virtually ceased to fight. The Russian Empire then disintegrated swiftly as its non-Russian elements sought to form independent countries.

Despite severe local defeats in the Crimea and the Far East, Imperial Russia, from the Congress of Vienna in 1815 until the outbreak of World War I, had preserved successfully its favorable boundaries of 1815, adding to them the upland Caucasus region, central Asia, and strategic territories in the Far East. Russia's chief unrealized foreign policy objective in Europe remained to acquire the Turkish Straits and Constantinople. That goal seemed readily achievable in 1915 when the Allies gave their consent, and until May 1917 Foreign Minister Miliukov was still pursuing the dream of the Straits. However, Russia's general defeat at the hands of Germany helped trigger the Revolutions of 1917 and doomed the Russian Empire to dissolution. Russia's imperial dreams, already severely shaken by the fiasco

---

[8]Florinsky, pp. 1427–28.

of the Russo–Japanese War, were dissipated in 1917 by the harsh realities of total collapse and Bolshevik dictatorship.

Suggested Readings

Benjamin, Alfred. "The Great Dilemma: The Foreign Policy of the Provisional Government, March–May 1917." Ph.D. thesis, Columbia University, New York, 1950.

Buchanan, George W. *My Mission to Russia*. 2 vols. New York, 1923.

Chernov, Victor. *The Great Russian Revolution*. New Haven, CT, 1936.

Dallin, Alexander, ed., *Russian Diplomacy and Eastern Europe, 1914–1917*. New York, 1963.

Florinsky, Michael T. *The End of the Russian Empire*. New Haven, CT, 1931.

Gankin, O. H. and H. H. Fisher. *The Bolsheviks and the World War*. Stanford, CA, 1940.

Golder, F. A. *Documents of Russian History, 1914–1917*. New York, 1927.

Golovin, N. N. *The Russian Army in the World War*. New Haven, CT, 1931.

Joll, James. *The Origins of the First World War*. London, 1984.

Kettle, Michael. *The Allies and the Russian Collapse (March 1917–March 1918)*. Minneapolis, MN, 1981.

Lieven, D. C. B. *Russia and the Origins of the First World War*. New York, 1983.

Massie, R. *Nicholas and Alexandra*. New York, 1967.

Paléologue, Maurice. *An Ambassador's Memoirs*. 3 vols. London, 1923; New York, 1972, reprint.

Pares, Sir Bernard. *The Fall of the Russian Monarchy; A Study of the Evidence*. New York, 1961, reprint.

Pipes, Richard. *The Russian Revolution*. New York, 1990.

Smith, C. Jay. *The Russian Struggle for Power, 1914–1917*. New York, 1956.

Solzhenitsyn, Alexander. *August 1914*. New York, 1972.

Stone, Norman. *The Eastern Front*. New York, 1975.

Sukhanov, N. N. *The Russian Revolution of 1917*. Joel Carmichael, ed., 2 vols. New York, 1962.

Glossary of Russian Terms

diak(i) secretary(ies)

Duma parliament

dvor(y) court, quarters

Ezhegodnik Yearbook

iarlyk patent of authority

kaznachei treasurer

kollegiia administrative college

mir village community

Nemetskaia Sloboda German, or Foreign, Settlement

Oprichnina separate domain

orda (ordy pl.) horde

pechatnik chancellor

podiachyi sub-secretary

Porte Ottoman government

posolskii dvor Ambassadors' Court

Posolskii Prikaz Ambassadorial Board

Rus territory of later Russia, c. 850–1300

sovet council

streltsy musketeers

tovarishch-ministr assistant minister

ukraina(y) borderland

Varangian Viking, Northman

zemskii sobor assembly of the lands

zemstvo(a) local assembly 1864–1917

APPENDIX A

Muscovite Grand Princes

Ivan I, "Kalita"	1328–1340
Simeon	1340–1353
Ivan II	1353–1359
Dmitri Ivanovich "Donskoi"	1359–1389
Vasili I	1389–1425
Vasili II	1425–1462
Ivan III, "the Great"	1462–1505
Vasili III	1505–1533
Ivan IV, "the Terrible"	1533–1547

Russian Tsars and Emperors After 1721:

Ivan IV, "the Terrible"	1547–1584*
Fedor I	1584–1598
Boris Godunov	1598–1605
Dmitri I	1605–1606
Vasili IV	1606–1610
Mikhail I Romanov	1613–1645
Alexis I	1645–1676
Fedor II	1676–1682
Ivan V	1682–1696
Peter I, "the Great"	1682–1725 (Emperor from 1721)
Catherine I	1725–1727
Peter II	1727–1730
Anna Ivanovna	1730–1740
Ivan VI	1740–1741
Elizabeth I	1741–1762
Peter III	1762
Catherine II, "the Great"	1762–1796
Paul I	1796–1801

Russian Emperors

Alexander I	1801–1825
Nicholas I	1825–1855
Alexander II	1855–1881
Alexander III	1881–1894
Nicholas II	1894–1917

*Crowned tsar in 1547

APPENDIX B

Nikita P. Panin	1801
Victor P. Kochubei	1801–1802
Alexander R. Vorontsov	1802–1804
Adam J. Czartoryski	1804–1806
Andrei G. Budberg	1806–1807
Nicholas P. Rumiantsev	1807–1812
Karl R. Nesselrode	1812–1855
Ioannes Capodistrias	1812–1822
Alexander M. Gorchakov	1856–1882
Nicholas K. Giers	1882–1895
A. B. Lobanov-Rostovskii	1895–1896
M. N. Muraviov	1897–1900
V. N. Lamzdorf	1900–1906
Alexander P. Izvolskii	1906–1910
Sergei D. Sazonov	1910–1916
Boris V. Stürmer	July–November 1916
N. N. Pokrovskii	November 1916–March 1917
Paul N. Miliukov	March–May 1917
Mikhail I. Tereshchenko	May–November 1917

APPENDIX C

Some Foreign Language Works on Tsarist Foreign Policy, 1800–1917

Astafiev, A.I. *Russko–germanskie diplomaticheskie otnosheniia, 1905–1911 gg.* Moscow, 1972.

Bestuzhev, I.V. *Borba v Rossii vo voprosam vneshnei politiki, 1906–1910.* Moscow, 1961.

Bovykin, V.I. *Ocherki istorii vneshnei politiki Rossii. Konets XIX v.–1917 g.* Moscow, 1960.

_____. *Iz istorii vozniknoveniia pervoi mirovoi voiny. Otnosheniia Rossii i Frantsii v 1912–1914 gg.* Moscow, 1961.

Emets, V.A. *Ocherki vneshnei politiki Rossii v period pervoi mirovoi voiny.* Moscow, 1977.

Fainberg, E. Ia. *Russko-iaponskie otnosheniia 1697–1875 gg.* Moscow, 1960.

Fedosov, I.A., ed., *Rossiia i osvobozhdenie Bolgarii.* Moscow, 1982.

Feoktistov, E.M. *Vospominaniia. Za kulisami politiki i literatury, 1848–1896.* Leningrad, 1929; republished, Cambridge, England, 1975.

Galuzo, P.G. *Turkestan–koloniia. Ocherk istorii Turkestana ot zavoevanii russkimi do revoliutsii 1917 g.* Moscow, 1929.

Goriainov, S. *Le Bosphore et les Dardanelles.* Paris, 1910.

Hayit, B. *Turkestan zwischen Russland und China.* Amsterdam, 1971.

Hoetsch, O. *Russland in Asien. Geschichte einer Expansion.* Stuttgart, Germany, 1966.

Hüningen, G. *Nikolaj Pavlovic Ignatiev und die russische Balkanpolitik, 1875–1878.* Gottingen, Germany, 1968.

Ignatiev, A.I. *Russko–angliiskie otnosheniia nakanune pervoi mirovoi voiny.* Moscow, 1962.

Itogi i zadachi izucheniia vneshnei politiki Rossii. Sovetskaia istoriografiia. Moscow, 1981.

Khalfin, N.A. *Prisoedineniie Srednei Azii k Rossii (60–90e gody XIX v.).* Moscow, 1965.

_____. *Rossiia i khanstva Srednei Azii (pervaia polovina XIX v.).* Moscow, 1974.

Kiniapina, N.S. *Vneshniaia Politika Rossii vtoroi poloviny XIX veka.* Moscow, 1974.

_____, ed., *Vostochnyi vopros vo vneshnei politike Rossii. Konets XVIII–nachalo XX v.* Moscow, 1978.

Lamzdorf, V.N. *Dnevnik V.N. Lamzdorfa, 1891–1892.* F.A. Rotshtein, ed., Moscow–Leningrad, 1934.

Linke, H.G. *Das zarische Russland und der Erste Weltkrieg. Diplomatie und Kriegsziele, 1914–1917.* Munich, 1982.

Materialy po istorii franko–russkikh otsoshenii za 1910–1914 gg. Moscow, 1922.

Miliutin, D.A. *Dnevnik, D.A. Miliutina.* 4 vols. P.A. Zaionchkovskii, ed., Moscow, 1947–1950.

Ministry of Foreign Affairs, Soviet Union. *Vneshniaia politika Rossii XIX i nachalo XX veka, 1801–.* vols. I–XIV, Moscow, 1960–.

Narochnitskaia, L.I. *Rossiia i otmena neitralizatsii Chernogo moria, 1856–1871 gg.* Moscow, 1989.

Narochnitskii, A.I. *Kolonialnaia politika kapitalisticheskikh derzhav na Dalnem Vostoke, 1860–1895*. Moscow, 1956.

Nikitin, S.A. *Slavianskie komitety v Rossii 1858–1876 gg*. Moscow, 1960.

Nikitin, S.A., et al., eds., *Osvobozhdenie Bolgarii ot turetskogo iga*. 3 vols. Moscow, 1961–1967.

Ocherk istorii Ministerstva Inostrannykh Del, 1802–1902. St. Petersburg, 1902.

Oldenburg, S.S. *Tsarstvovanie Imperatora Nikolaia II*. 2 vols. Munich, 1949.

Opisanie russko–turetskoi voiny 1877–1878 gg. na Balkanskom poluostrove. 9 vols. and 6 supplementary vols. St. Petersburg, 1901–1913.

Polovtsov, A.A. *Dnevnik gosudarstvennogo sekretaria A.A. Polovtsova*. 2 vols. P.A. Zaionchkovskii, ed., Moscow, 1966.

Potemkin, V.P., ed., *Istoriia diplomatii*. 3 vols. Moscow, 1941–1945.

Rostunov, I.I., ed., *Russko–Turestskaia voina 1877–1878*. Moscow, 1977.

Russko–iaponskaia voina 1904–1905 gg. Rabota Voeeno-istoricheskoi kommissii po opisaniiu russko–iaponskoi voiny. 9 vols. St. Petersburg, 1910.

Russko-kitaiskie otnosheniia, 1689–1916. Ofitsialnye dokumenty. Moscow, 1958.

Sbornik materialov po russko–turetskoi voine 1877–1878 gg. na Balkanskom poluostrove. 97 vols. St. Petersburg, 1898–1911.

Schweinitz, H.L. von. *Denkwürdigkeiten des Botschafters General von Schweinitz*. Berlin, 1927.

Shatsillo, K.F. *Rossiia pered pervoi mirovoi voiny. Vooruzhenye sily tsarizma v 1905–1914 gg*. Moscow, 1974.

Skazkin, S.D. *Konets avstro–russko–germanskogo soiuza. Issledovanie po istorii russko–germanskikh i russko-avstriiskikh otnoshenii v sviazi s vostochnim voprosom v 80-e gody XIX stoletiia*. Moscow, 1928, 1974.

Slavianskii sbornik. Slavianskii vopros i russkoe obshchestvo v 1867–1878. Moscow, 1948.

Tarle, E.V. *Krymskaia voina*. 3 vols. Moscow–Leningrad, 1950.

Tatishchev, S.S. *Imperator Aleksandr II. Ego zhizn i tsarstvovanie*. 2 vols. St. Petersburg, 1903.

Zaionchkovskii, A.M. *Vostochnaia voina*. 4 vols. St. Petersburg, 1908–1912.

INDEX

Abaza, Admiral A. M. 144
Aberdeen, Lord 45
Adrianople, Armistice of (1878) 81
Adrianople, Treaty of (1829) 88
Aehrenthal, Alois von 161, 162
Afghanistan 98, 128, 158
  and Pendjeh Crisis (1885) 124, 130
Aigun, Treaty of (1858) 103
Akkerman, Convention of (1826) 45
Ak-mechet 93
Aksakov, Ivan S. 70, 78, 79, 85, 117, 125
Aland Congress (1718) 31
Alaska (Russian America) 42, 99, 104–106
Albania 164
Alekseev, Admiral E. I. 144, 145, 147
Aleksei Mikhailovich (ruled 1645-1676) 30
Aleutian Islands 104, 106
Alexander I (ruled 1801–1825) 22–25, 27,
  32–36, 38, 40–43, 46, 105
Alexander II (ruled 1855–1881) 52–69,
  73, 74, 76, 78, 80, 81, 83, 85, 86,
  89, 92, 93, 95–98, 102, 108, 110, 114,
  166
Alexander III (ruled 1881–1894) 57,
  110–121, 124–128, 130, 137, 139
Alexander of Battenberg (prince of
  Bulgaria) 125, 126
Alexandra (empress of Russia) 114, 176,
  179
Algeciras Conference (1906) 157
Ali, Mehemet 45, 46
Alma, Battle of (1854) 52
Alvensleben Convention (1863) 64
Ambassadorial Board (see also College of
  Foreign Affairs) 29, 31
Ambassadorial Court 29
Amur Valley 135, 136
Andrássy, Count Gyula (foreign minister of
  Austria-Hungary) 65, 66, 75
Andrássy Plan (1875) 75, 76
Anglo-Japanese Alliance (1902) 144
Anglo-Russian Alliance (1805) 22
Anglo-Russian Convention (1907) 160
Annuaire de l'empire de Russie 34
April Uprising (Bulgaria 1876) 76
Arakcheev, Count Aleksei 40
Armenia 44, 122
Armenians 88
Artamonov, Colonel Viktor 169
Asiatic Department (of the Russian Foreign
  Ministry) 33, 34, 59, 60, 108, 132

Astrakhan Khanate 7
Austria (also Austria-Hungary) 18, 19,
  38–42, 46, 47, 52, 53, 62, 70, 71, 73,
  75, 78, 80–83, 85, 86, 108, 116–121, 124,
  126–128, 157, 161–162, 164, 167, 168,
  173, 175, 177, 181
Austrian Succession, War of
  (1740–1748) 16
Austro–German Alliance (1879) 118
Austro–Russian agreement (May 1897) 122
Azov 14, 30

Badmaev, P. A. 139
Bagration, General P. I. 24
Balkan Crisis (1875–1878) 66, 73–85, 98
Balkan League 71–73, 76, 164
Balkans 3, 14, 20, 38, 41, 44, 47, 53, 57,
  67–69, 72, 73, 80, 85, 86, 99, 108,
  116–119, 124, 125, 137, 155, 158, 161,
  164, 166, 175
Balkan Slavs 68, 70, 73, 80, 82, 163, 169
Baltic Germans 112
Barclay de Tolly, Mikhail 24
Bariatinskii, Prince A. I. 88, 89, 93
Batu Khan 3
Beijing, Treaty of (1860) 71, 103, 104, 135
Bekovich–Cherkasskii, Prince Alexander 89
Belgrade 70, 71, 73–78, 81, 126, 167–170
Belorussia 5, 19
Bennigsen, General Leon 23
Berchtold, Count Leopold 168
Bering, Vitus 104
Berlin, Congress of (1878) 67, 83, 85, 108,
  116, 117, 119, 124, 125, 166
Berlin Treaty (1878) 85, 124, 126, 162
Bessarabia 35, 38, 49, 52, 72, 86
Bestuzhev–Riumin, A. P. 16
Bezborodko, Prince A. A. 18
Bezobrazov, A. N. 143–144
Bichurin, Father N. Ia. 101
Bismarck, Otto von 62, 64–67, 116–120,
  127, 157
Björkö, Treaty of (1905) 156–157
Black Sea clauses (of Paris Treaty) 64–65
Bobrikov, G. I. 82, 83
Boer War 130, 133, 144
Bolshevik Party 181–182
Borodino, Battle of (1812) 24
Bosnia (also Bosnia–Hercegovina) 66, 71,
  73, 76, 80, 81, 83, 86, 116, 162, 167
Bosnian Crisis (1908–1909) 153

Boxer Rebellion (1900) 142–143
Brandenburg, Erich 170
Brusilov, General A. A. 177
Bucharest, Treaty of (1812) 38, 45
Buchlau meeting (1908) 162
Budapest Convention (1877) 66, 81
Budberg, A. 36
Bukhara, Emirate of 90, 93, 95, 97, 98, 128, 131
Bulgaria 69, 71–73, 76, 79–82, 85, 114, 121, 124–127, 164
Bulgarian Crisis (1885–1887) 117–119
Bulgarian Exarchate 73
Bülow, Chancellor Bernhard von 155
Butakov, A. I. 93
Byzantine Empire (*also* Byzantium) 2, 3, 5, 20, 27, 30

Canning, Lord Stratford 48–50
Capodistrias, Ioannes 33, 35, 41, 42
Caprivi, Leo von 119
Castlereagh, Lord 40–41
Catherine II (ruled 1762–1796) 16–21, 27, 32, 40, 46, 107, 172
Caucasus 22, 44, 52, 53, 69, 88, 89, 93, 167, 176, 181
Cavour, Count Camillo di 62
Central Asian Railroad 131
Central Powers 176, 177
Chancellor, Captain Richard 7, 28
Charles X (king of France) 46
Charles XII (king of Sweden) 14
Charykov, N. V. 164
Cherniaev, General M. G. 74–80, 93, 95, 96, 102, 128, 131
Chernyshevskii, N. G. 72
Chimkent 93, 95
China 3, 100–105, 135–145, 150
Chinese Eastern Railroad 140–143, 145, 148, 149
Chingis–khan (of the Mongol Empire) 3, 91
Circassians 89
College of Foreign Affairs (1718, formerly the Ambassadorial Board) 31–33
Concert of Europe (1815–1821) 40, 42, 47, 50
Congress System 40
Constantine, Grand Prince 20
Constantinople 2–5, 19, 45, 46, 49, 60, 68, 71–73, 80, 81, 116, 117, 122, 124, 129, 164, 165, 175, 181
Constantinople Conference (1877) 80
Continental System (1806) 24
Corfu 41

Cossack Brigade 132
Cossacks 9, 11, 22, 29, 44, 88, 93, 100, 179
Crimea 92
    incorporation by Russia of (1783) 21
Crimean Khanate 7
Crimean Tatars 9, 19, 28
Crimean War (1853–1856) 43, 45, 47–55, 58, 62–64, 68, 69, 88, 89, 91, 93, 101, 104, 105, 116, 147, 150, 155, 167, 181
Curzon, Lord George 131, 133
Cuza, Prince Alexander 69
Czartoryski, Prince Adam 35, 62

Dacia, Kingdom of 20
Daghestan 89, 90
Danilevskii, N. Ia. 79
Danilov, General G. A. 168
Danubian Principalities 38, 45, 49, 50, 52, 63
Decembrist Revolt (1825) 42–43
Denmark 14, 18, 158
diaki 28
Diderot, Denis 32
Dimitrijević–Apis, Colonel Dragutin 161, 169
Diplomatic Chancellery (of Russian Foreign Ministry) 58, 60
Diplomatic Revolution (1763) 16
Djordjević, Dr. Vladan 71
Djunis, Battle of (1876) 79
Dogger Bank incident (1905) 155–157
Dreikaiserbund; *see* League of Three Emperors
Dual Monarchy 161, 162
Dubasov, Admiral F. V. 149
Duchy of Warsaw 24
Dungans 137

Eastern Question 41, 44, 71, 78–81, 98
Eastern Rumelia 124, 126
Egypt 46
Elizabeth I (ruled 1741–1762) 16, 17, 32
Engels, Friedrich 68
Entente Cordiale (1904) 157
Erzerum 45
Estonia 14
Evdokimov, General N. I. 89

Fay, Sidney 170
Ferdinand (prince of Saxe–Coburg) 127
Ferdinand, Archduke Franz 167
Ferdinand (king of Bulgaria) 164
Fergana 98
Finance Ministry (Russia) 91, 97, 112, 138
Finland 24, 35, 38, 40, 112

Fischer, Fritz 170
Fish, Hamilton 108
Fon–Kaufman, General K. P. 96–99, 102, 128
Foreign Affairs, Ministry of (Russia, 1802–1917) 32–36, 58, 60, 69, 71, 74, 79, 80, 82, 86, 95–97, 101, 114, 116, 125, 129, 130, 135, 140, 143, 145, 163
Fourth Duma 179
Four Years Diet (1787–1791) 21
France 19, 21, 24, 29, 38, 40, 41, 44–49, 58, 66, 69, 70, 95, 101, 103, 116, 118–120, 122, 140, 142, 145, 150, 151, 155–158, 167
Franco–Russian Alliance (1893) 114, 119–122, 147, 150, 155, 156, 166
Frederick II (king of Prussia) 16, 18, 19
French Revolution (1789) 21, 22, 46

Gagemeister, I. A. 91
Galicia 4
Garašanin, Ilija 63, 69–71
Geiss, Imanuel 170
Geok–Tepe 98, 117, 128
Georgians 88
Germany (*also* German Empire) 38, 52, 58, 65, 66, 79, 86, 114, 116, 118–122, 140, 141, 145, 150, 153, 155–157, 160, 166, 169, 170, 181
Geyer, Dietrich 135
Giers, N. K. 60, 69, 114–117, 120, 121, 126, 128, 129
Gladstone, Prime Minister W. E. 64, 65, 130
Golden Horde 3–5, 7, 27
Golovnin, V. M. 107
Goluchowsky, Agenor 122
Gorchakov, Alexander M. 58–70, 72–83, 85, 92, 93, 95, 105, 106, 108, 114, 116, 117, 137
Gorchakov, Prince M. D. 52
Gordon, General Charles G. 130
Great Britain (*also* England and Britain) 7, 22, 24, 28–31, 42, 44, 45, 47, 49, 62, 76, 80, 81, 83, 85, 88, 92, 95, 101–106, 119, 124, 128, 129, 132, 133, 136, 142, 145, 150–153, 155, 157, 158
Greater Serbian policies 63, 76, 78, 79, 82, 161
"Great Game," The 131
Great Northern War 14, 30, 31
"Great Reforms" (1885–1874) 54–57, 60, 110
Greece 69, 71, 73, 164
Greek Project 20–21
Greek Revolt (1821) 41

Greeks 28, 41, 42, 44, 45
Grey, Lord Edward 157, 159, 176
Grigorevich, Admiral I. K. 153
Grimm, Baron Friedrich 32

Hamburger, A. F. 58
Hangö, Battle of (1714) 14
Hanseatic League 5
Harbin 140, 142, 148
Harriman, Edward 150
Hartvig, N. G. 163, 164, 170
Hawaii 42
Herbert, Sidney 50
Hercegovina; *see* Bosnia–Hercegovina
Hindu Kush Mountains 91, 124, 130
Holstein 18
Holy Alliance (1815) 40–42
Holy Places (Jerusalem) 48–50
Holy Roman Empire 5, 27, 28
Hötzendorf, General Conrad von 168
Hungary 47

Ianushkevich, General N. N. 168
Iarkand 104
Ignatiev, Count N. P. 60, 68, 71–75, 80–82, 93, 103, 104, 108, 117, 163
India 91, 92, 98, 128, 129, 133, 158
Ingria 14
Inkerman Heights, Battle of (1854) 52
Islam 81, 90
Issyk–Kul 90, 93
Italy 28, 41, 121, 158, 176
Italo–Turkish War (1911–1912) 164
Ito, Viscount Hirobumi 144
Ivan III (ruled 1462–1505) 5–7, 25, 27, 28
Ivan IV, "the Terrible" (ruled 1533–1584) 6, 7, 28
Izvolskii, Alexander P. 150, 157–159, 161, 162, 170

Japan 107, 108, 133, 135, 137, 139–144, 148–153, 155, 157
Jassy, Treaty of (1792) 21
Jefferson, President Thomas 42
Jelavich, Charles 114, 115
Jesuits 100
Jews 111, 112
Jomini, Baron A. G. 58, 69, 74, 75, 80, 86
Joseph II (emperor of Austria) 20, 21

Kalmuks 90
Kamchatka 107
Kanlidze, Conference of (1862) 71
Karadjordjević, Alexander (prince of Serbia) 70

Karadjordjević, Peter (king of Serbia) 161
Karakorum 3
Karelia 14
Kars 53
Kartsov, A. N. 74–76
Kashgar 104
Kasimov, Khanate of 91
Katkov, M. N. 83, 117–118
Kaulbars, Baron A. V. 127
Kazakhs 89–91, 101, 166
Kazan, Khanate of 7, 29
kaznachei 28
Kenesary Kasimov, Khan 90
Kennan, George F. 121
Kerenskii, Alexander F. 181
Khabarov, Erofei 100
Khabarovsk 102
Khalfin, N. A. 91
Khiva, Khanate of 15, 16, 90, 91, 93, 98,
    131
Khmelnitsky, Bogdan 9
Khomiakov, A. S. 70
Khorezm 91
Kiakhta 102
Kiakhta, Treaty of (1727) 101
Kiev 72
Kliuchevskii, V. O. 4, 16, 18
Knox, Philander 150
Kokand, Khanate of 90, 91, 93, 95, 98
Kokovtsov, V. N. 153, 162
Korea 135, 139–145, 148
Kosciuszko, General Thaddeus 21
Kossuth, Lajos 47
Kostenko, L. F. 98
Kronstadt 120
Küchük–Kainarji, Treaty of (1774) 19
Kuldja 104
Kurile Islands 107, 108
Kurino, Shinichiro 145
Kuropatkin, General A. N. 131, 142, 143,
    145, 148
Kutuzov, General M. I. 22, 35
Kwangtung 145

Laibach Conference 41
Lamzdorf, Count V. N. 34, 115, 120, 121,
    132, 143–145, 156
Land Captain Law (1889) 112
Lansdowne, Lord 133
League of Three Emperors (*Dreikaiserbund*)
    (1873) 65, 72, 75, 76, 78, 82, 116–118
Lee, Francis 31
Lenin, V. I. 181
Lhuys, Drouyn de 48
Liaoyang 148

Li Hung–chang 135, 140, 141
Li–Lobanov Agreement (1896) 140–141
Lithuania 4–7, 28
Livadia 73, 80
Livonia 14, 28
Livonian Order 28
Livonian War (1551–1581) 7, 28
Lobanov–Rostovskii, A. B. 115, 140
Lombardy 63
London, Treaty of (1915) 176
Louis XI (king of France) 5
Louis XIV (king of France) 12, 29
Louis Philippe (king of France) 46

Macedonia 87, 124, 127, 164
Malakhov bastion 52
Manchu dynasty 104, 140
Manchuria 136, 137, 140–150, 153
Manstein, General C. H. von 32
March Revolution of 1917 151, 179
Marinović, Jovan 75
Maritime Province 101
Marković, Svetozar 73
Martens, F. F. 137
Marvin, Charles 128
Marx, Karl 68
Matveev, A. A. 30
May Constitution (1791) 21
Mediterranean Agreement, First (1887)
    118
Menshikov, A. S. 14, 48, 49, 52
Metternich, Prince Klemens von 25, 40–42,
    47
Milan Obrenović (king of Serbia); *see*
    Obrenović, Milan
Miletić, Svetozar 73
Miliukov, Paul N. 175, 181
Miliutin, Dmitrii A. 56, 57, 60, 78, 79, 81,
    83, 85, 88, 89, 92, 93, 95, 96, 110
Moldavia 41, 49, 69
Mongols (*also* Mongolia) 3–5, 89, 101, 104,
    136, 137, 142
Monroe Doctrine 42, 105
Montenegro 69–76, 80–82, 85
Montgelas, Max von 170
Moroccan Crisis, First (1906) 157
Moscow 4–6, 9, 25, 28, 29, 32, 44, 52
Moscow Benevolent Committee 70, 72
Moscow Slav Committee 78, 117
Moscow Slav Congress (1867) 70
Motono, Ichiro 150
Mukden, Battle of (1905) 148
Mullah, Kazi 44, 88
Münchengrätz, Treaty of (1833) 46
Muraviov, M. N. 115, 133, 141

Muraviov, Count N. N. 102, 103, 105–108, 138
Muridism 44
Mürzsteg Agreement (1903) 122
Muscovy 4, 5, 7, 12, 27–30, 34, 40
Muscovy Company 7
Muslims 90, 91

Nanking, Treaty of (1842) 101
Napoleon Bonaparte (emperor of France) 22–25, 34, 35, 38, 40
Napoleon III (emperor of France) 47, 48, 62–64
Napoleonic Wars 22–25
Navarino Bay 45
Nazi–Soviet Pact (1939) 24
Near Eastern Crisis
    (1839) 46
    (1896) 122
Nekliudov, A. 163, 164
Nelidov, A. I. 117, 122, 124
Neratov, A. A. 162–164
Nerchinsk, Treaty of (1689) 9, 100
Nesselrode, Count Karl V. 36, 41, 44–46, 49, 50, 57, 58, 102
Nevesinje 73
Nicholas I (ruled 1825–1855) 38, 42–57, 69, 88, 93, 102, 110, 173–175
Nicholas II (ruled 1894–1917) 35, 112–115, 124, 130, 132, 133, 135, 137, 139–141, 143, 145, 148–152, 155, 156, 162, 163, 169, 172, 176–179
Nicolson, Sir Arthur 157
Nikola (prince of Montenegro) 73
Nikolaevich, Grand Prince Konstantin 56, 105, 106
Nikolaevich, Grand Prince Nikolai 81, 173, 177
Nikolaevsk 102
Nolde, Boris 61, 114
Novgorod 2, 4, 5, 27
Northern System 18
Novikov, E. P. 58, 80
Novi Pazar 162
Novosiltsev, Nicholas 22
Nystadt, Treaty of (1721) 14, 31, 32

Obrenović, Alexander (king of Serbia) 127, 128
Obrenović, Mihailo (prince of Serbia) 63, 70–72, 76
Obrenović, Milan (king of Serbia) 73–76, 79, 86, 125–127
Obrenović, Miloš (prince of Serbia) 70
Obruchev, N. N. 80, 121, 126

October Manifesto 152
Odessa 21, 72
Okhotsk 100
Opium War, First (1838–1842) 101
Oprichnina 7
Ordyn-Nashchokin, Afanasii L. 29, 30
Orenburg 90, 91, 93, 95, 96
Orenburg–Tashkent Railway 131
Organic Statute of 1832 46
Orlov, Alexis 58
Orthodox 48–50, 53, 68, 70, 87, 111, 114
Orthodox Church and faith 3, 5, 7, 9, 12, 18, 19, 41, 48, 49, 85, 110
Orthodox mission (Beijing) 101
Osterman Andrei I. 16, 31, 32
Osten–Sacken, Baron Theodor 58, 106
Othon (king of Greece) 63
Ottoman Empire 18, 20, 29, 41, 44–50, 63, 68, 70, 75, 116, 161, 164, 167, 175, 176

Paléologue, Maurice 172, 173, 175, 176
Paleologus, Zoe 5
Palestine 48
Palitsyn, F. F. 158
Palmerston, Lord 48, 65
Pamir Agreement (1895) 130
Panin, Nikita 18
Panslavism 68, 70–74, 79, 80, 83, 86, 110, 116, 125, 127, 130, 137, 163, 166
Paris 29, 35
Paris Congress (1856) 62
Paris Treaty (1856) 52–53, 54, 56, 63–65, 69, 72, 108, 166
Pašić, Nikola 161, 169
Paskevich, General I. F. 44–46
Paul I (ruled 1796–1801) 21, 22, 33, 104
People's Will 67, 110
Perovsk, Fort 93
Perovskii, Count V. A. 91, 93
Perry, Commodore Matthew 107
Persia 15, 44, 88, 98, 124, 128, 130–132, 153, 157, 158
Pestel, Paul T. 42
Peter I (ruled 1682–1725) 12–18, 27, 30, 31, 40, 68, 89, 100
Peter II (ruled 1727–1730) 32
Peter III (ruled 1762) 16–18, 32
Petrograd (*see also* St. Petersburg) 172, 177–179
Petrograd Soviet 179, 181
Piedmont–Sardinia 47
Pishpek 93
Pleve, V. K. 144, 151
Plevna, Battles of (1877) 81

Ploesti 80
Pobedonostsev, K. P. 78, 110, 111
Poincaré, Raymond 168
Poland 4, 5, 7, 9, 13, 14, 17–19, 21, 28, 30, 35, 38, 40, 46, 47, 52, 62, 69, 121, 172
 partitions of (1772–1795) 18–24
Poliakov, S. S. 125
Polish Insurrection of 1863 63
Polovtsy (Polovtsians) 3
Poltava, Battle of (1709) 14
Poniatowski, Stanislas 19
Ponsonby, Lord 46
Poppel, Nicholas 27
Porte; *see* Ottoman Empire
Portsmouth, Treaty of (1905) 149, 150, 156
Posen 173
Posolskii prikaz 29–31
Potiomkin, Grigorii 18, 20
Potiomkin, V. P. 18
Princip, Gavrilo 167
Provisional Government (of Russia, 1917) 179, 181
Prussia (*see also* Germany) 16, 24, 32, 38, 40, 46, 52, 62
 and German unification 63–65
Przhevalskii, Nicholas M. 136, 137
Putiatin, E. V. 103, 107, 108

Quadruple Alliance (1814) 40

Radovanović, Pavle 72
Rasputin 176, 178
Rediger, A. F. 153
Reichstadt Agreement (1876) 78
Reinsurance Treaty (1887) 118, 119
Reitern, Mikhail 92, 106
Reshid Pasha 49
Revolution of 1905 151
Revolutions of 1830 46
Revolutions of 1848 38, 46, 47, 151
Rich, Norman 47
Ristić, Jovan 71, 73–75, 78, 125, 127
Riurik 2
Romania 80–82
Romanov dynasty 9, 39, 53, 92, 99
Romanovskii, General D. I. 96
Romanticism 46
Roosevelt, President Theodore 149
Rosen, Baron R. R. 127
Ross, Fort 42
Rozhdestvenskii, Z. P. 148
Rumiantsev, N. P. 36
Rus 1–6
Russian–American Company 102–107
Russkii mir (*The Russian World*) 74, 75

Russo–American Agreement (1824) 105, 106
Russo–Chinese Bank 140
Russo–Japanese Treaty (1910) 150
Russo–Japanese War (1904–1905) 116, 124, 139, 145, 147, 149, 151, 153, 155, 167, 172, 182
Russophobia 46
Russo–Turkish War (1877–1878) 78–81, 82, 86, 108, 124, 167
Rybakov, Boris 2

Saburov, P. A. 58, 117
St. Petersburg 12, 14, 31, 32, 35, 42, 64, 68, 70–76, 79, 82, 83, 93, 95–97, 100, 102, 105, 107–109, 117, 119, 120, 122, 124, 125, 127–129, 133, 136, 145–151, 156, 158, 162, 166, 167–169
St. Petersburg, Treaty of (1881) 104, 108, 135
Sakhalin Island 108, 135, 136, 149
Salisbury, Marquis of 83
Samarkand 131
Samsonov, General A. V. 177
Sanders, Liman von 165, 166
San Francisco 105
San Stefano, Treaty of (March 1878) 67, 82–86, 124, 126
Sarai 3, 4
Sarajevo assassination (June 1914) 167–169
Sardinia 62, 63
Sazonov, Sergei D. 162–168, 172–176
Schlieffen Plan 170
Schuyler, Eugene 97
Semenov, P. P. 91
Serbia 69–83, 86, 124, 127, 128, 161, 163–169
Serbo–Bulgarian War (1885) 118
Serbo–Turkish War (1876) 78
Serbs 41, 45, 73, 76, 78, 79, 125, 166, 167, 172
Sevastopol 21, 52, 53
Seven Years War (1756–1763) 16, 18, 32
Seward, William 106
Shamil 44, 50, 52, 88, 89
Shchelkalov, Andrei 29
Shchelkalov, Vasilii 29
Shimoda, Treaty of (1855) 107
Shimonoseki, Treaty of (1895) 139, 140
Shuvalov, Paul A. 80, 83, 85, 118
Shuvalov, Peter 118
Siberia 7, 9, 29, 42, 93, 100, 101, 104, 107, 113, 135, 137, 139
Silesia 173
Sinkiang 137

Sino–Japanese War (1894–1895) 139, 145
Sinope 50
Sino–Russian Convention (1792) 100, 101
Skerskii, Captain 130
Skobelev, General M. D. 98, 117, 128, 131
Slav Committees (*see also* Moscow and
    St. Petersburg Committees) 74, 75,
    78, 79
Slavs 2, 3, 71, 81, 85, 87, 117, 128, 161,
    166, 167
Smolensk 24, 29
Sobolev, General L. N. 128, 129
Soloviev, Vladimir 137
South Manchurian Railroad 142, 148,
    149
Spain 30
Stackelberg, Count Ernst 62
Stalin, Joseph 7, 16
State Duma 152, 153, 172, 175
Stoeckl, Baron Edvard 106
Stolypin, Peter A. 152, 153, 158, 162
Straits Convention (1841) 46, 50
Stremoukhov, P. N. 60
Stürmer, Boris V. 176
Suez Canal 138
Sukhanov, N. N. 179
Sukhomlinov, General V. A. 153, 168, 177
Šumatovac, Battle of (1876)   79
Suvorov, General A. S. 19, 21, 22
Sweden 5, 7, 13–14, 24, 29–32
Syr–Daria Line 93

Taiping Rebellion 103
Taiwan 140
Talienwan 141
Talleyrand, Charles 24
Tashkent 90, 91, 96, 98, 125, 128, 131
Taylor, A. J. P. 157
Temperley, Harold 47
Terentiev, M. A. 128
Third Section (1826) 78
Tientsin, Treaty of (1858) 103
Tilsit, Treaty of (1807) 24
Time of Troubles (1598–1613) 29
Todleben, Colonel E. I. 52
Togo, Admiral Heichahiro 148
Trakhaniot, Iurii 28
Transcaspian Railroad 93, 98, 131
Trans–Siberian Railroad 113, 137–140,
    148
Triple Alliance (1882) 119–122
Triple Treaty (1856) 65
Troppau Conference (1820) 40
Troppau Protocol (1820) 41
Trotskii, L. N. 181

Trubetskoi, G. N. 175
Tsushima Strait, Battle of (1905) 149, 150
Turcomans 117
Turkestan 88, 92–99, 102, 109, 128–131,
    166
Turkey; *see* Ottoman Empire
Turkmanchai, Treaty of (1828) 44, 88
Turkmenia 98, 128, 131
Turks 28–30, 42, 45, 48, 53, 65, 71–76, 80,
    85, 88, 166
Tver 5, 27
Tyrnovo Constitution (1879) 125

Ukhtomskii, E. E. 137
Ukraine 9–12, 29, 30, 54, 172
Union of Pereiaslavl (1654) 11
United States 1, 42, 95, 103–107, 150
Unkiar–Skelessi, Treaty of (1833) 45–47
Unofficial Committee (1801) 22
Urquhart, David 46
Ussuri region 103, 135
Uzbeks 91, 96, 99

Vannovskii, P. S. 139, 140
Varangian (Viking) influence 2
Vasili II (ruled 1425–1462) 5
Vasili III (ruled 1505–1533) 5, 6, 28
Vasiliev, V. P. 137
Verevkin, Colonel N. A. 93
Vernadsky, George 4
Vernoe, Fort 93
Versailles 65
Victoria (queen of Great Britain) 130
Vienna 73, 82, 161, 169
Vienna, Congress of (1814–1815)
    25, 27, 33, 35, 38, 40, 64, 166, 167,
    181
Vienna Note (1853) 50
Vienna Settlement (*see also* Vienna, Con-
    gress of) 40, 46–48
Viskovatyi, Ivan M. 28
Vitovt 5
Vladimir I (prince of Kiev) 2
Vladivostok 103, 104, 108, 135, 139, 140,
    148
Vojvodina district 73
Volhynia 4
Voltaire 32
Volynskii, Artemii 15
Vonliarliarskii, V. M. 143
Vorontsov, A. R. 36
Vorontsov, Prince M. S. 88, 89
Vorontsov, S. R. 33
Vorontsov–Dashkov, Count 143
Vostochniki (Easterners) 136, 137, 139

Wallachia 49, 69
War Ministry (Russia) 60, 92, 96, 98, 102, 125, 128, 129, 131
Warsaw 19
Western Settlement (*Nemetskaia Sloboda* 12
William I (king of Prussia, later emperor of Germany) 57, 62, 67, 119
William II (emperor of Germany) 119, 120, 141–144, 149, 155, 156, 166
Witte, Sergei Iu. 112–115, 131, 138–145, 149, 152, 156, 175

Witte System 112, 121
World War I 66, 122, 153, 155, 167, 170, 172–176, 179–181

Yalu Concession (1897) 143
Ypsilanti, Alexander 41
Yugoslavia 176
Yugoslavs 73

Zhukovskii, V. A. 54
Zinoviev, I. A. 132